A STUPID BOY

A STUPID BOY

THE AUTOBIOGRAPHY OF THE CREATOR OF *DAD'S ARMY*

JIMMY PERRY

C

CENTURY

First published by Century in 2002

Copyright © Jimmy Perry 2002

The right of Jimmy Perry to be identified as the author of this work has been asserted by him in accordance with the Copyright, Designs and Patents Act, 1988

First published in the United Kingdom in 2002 by
Century, 20 Vauxhall Bridge Road, London, SW1V 2SA

Random House Australia (Pty) Limited
20 Alfred Street, Milsons Point, Sydney, New South Wales 2061, Australia

Random House New Zealand Limited
18 Poland Road, Glenfield
Auckland 10, New Zealand

Random House South Africa (Pty) Limited
Endulini, 5a Jubilee Road, Parktown, 2193, South Africa

The Random House Group Limited Reg. No. 954009
www.randomhouse.co.uk

A CIP catalogue record for this book is available from the British Library

Papers used by Random House are natural, recyclable products made from wood grown in sustainable forests. The manufacturing processes conform to the environmental regulations of the country of origin

Designed by Andrea Purdie
Typeset in 12/17pt Bembo
Printed and bound in the United Kingdom by Butler & Tanner

ISBN 0 7126 2338 8

Contents

PICTURE CREDITS

Acknowledgements

John Laurie once said to me, 'You know, James, you are semi-literate.'
Well, I didn't argue – I never do when people are banging on about
writing. I create characters and write words for them to say, I create
situations and stories. However, I really enjoyed writing this story
because it has brought back so many memeories and people that
were dear to me.

I have to thank Anna Cherrett at Random House for persuading me
to do this book in the first place. I never use a typewriter or word-
processor, I always write by hand, and I must thank Gary Adams for
putting it into print for me.

Other thanks to:
Frances Topp for her picture research; my brother Charles for
searching out old family photographs; Mark Lineham (Bean
Processed, Northants) for restoring some very old photographs; Don
Smith for taking new photographs and hunting out old ones.

Finally, to all ex-members of the Royal Artillery Concert Party,
Deolali (Including John Stevenson – 'Steve' – and Ron Sluys who
unfortunately are in none of the photographs. Steve had a wonderful
comic flair; he was years ahead of his time.), and members of the
CSE (Combined Services Entertainments), New Delhi, wherever
you may be – thank you for all those amazing memories.

PART ONE

GROWING UP

I was born just a few doors down at No. 20, but because my father was of restless spirit, we moved to No. 38 in 1929

38 NASSAU ROAD, BARNES, LONDON SW13 – 1936

The Perry family was just finishing breakfast. At the head of the table, my father was opening the morning post. He wore a high starched collar with tissue paper tucked around the top to protect it until he left for his antique shop in South

2

Kensington. My sister Mary (fifteen) and my brother Charlie (eighteen) got up from the table; Mary to go to school and Charlie to open Dad's shop. My brother and sister were very goodlooking and my father used to say, 'You know, I hate ugly people, there's too many of them about. Thank goodness there's none of them in our family.' Now, this wasn't strictly true because whenever there was a family occasion it used to puzzle me that the house was simply *filled* with weird-looking uncles and aunts.

My mother picked up a small silver bell in the shape of a lady in a crinoline. No sooner had the tinkle died away than Minnie, the Welsh parlourmaid, entered and did a little bob.

'You can clear in five minutes, Minnie,' my mother said. Minnie bobbed again and made a swift exit.

I was left alone with my mother and father. Alarm bells rang in my head, I got that feeling of panic that I was no stranger to – dry throat and a cold sweat. 'I'd better get going; I'll be late for school,' I said. My father wiped his General Kitchener moustache and his lips below formed the words: 'Your mother and I want to talk to you.'

The cold sweat got worse.

'It's your school report. Listen to this: "*So in conclusion, we regret to say your son shows very little ability for anything. He's wasting our time and your money – we fear for his future.*" What are we going to do with you?' the lips shaped. 'You must have some qualifications.'

I decided to make a stand. 'I don't need any qualifications,' I said. 'I'm going to be a famous film star or a great comedian.'

Me, on the beach, showing off as usual. The stones I am standing on were arranged in such a way that I thought made me look tough – it was agony!

3

A sad look came over my old dad's face and he uttered three simple words: 'You stupid boy!'

I grabbed my school satchel and got out of the house as quickly as possible, and ran down Nassau Road to the bus stop outside the Sun Inn. Now, there were two types of bus that, for a penny, would carry me to my dreaded destination: a red one – London Transport – or a chocolate-and-cream pirate bus. 'Don't go on a pirate bus,' my mother used to warn me, 'the conductors are all Bolsheviks!'

A pirate bus! My mother used to warn me against travelling on them, saying the conductors were all Bolsheviks.

It didn't bother me. I thought the pirate bus conductors were great; they wore their caps at a rakish angle and their uniforms had a sort of *foreign* look. The dreary old London Transport conductors, with their dull uniforms, never stood a chance, but to the middle-class people of Barnes they were (to quote my mother) 'respectable and reliable'.

I was in luck. A pirate bus came round the corner and as I was the only passenger waiting, it didn't stop, just slowed down, the conductor leaned out from the platform and, with the words 'Come on, son, don't want to be late for that posh school of yours', scooped me up. The bus crawled up Castelnau Road, crossed Hammersmith Bridge and approached Hammersmith Broadway. My mother always shopped there at Palmer's Stores – advertised as the cheapest store in London. She refused to shop in Barnes. According to her, they rooked you and had ideas above themselves. We passed West London Hospital and arrived at my destination, my prep school, Colet Court.

As I got off the bus I could smell cakes baking at Cadby Hall, the huge Lyons cake factory next door. The smell of those cakes and buns hung over the whole area and wafted into the classrooms during the entire morning. As I went through the arch into the main building, the sheer terror in the pit of my stomach, made worse by the smell of the cakes, increased. How I survived those years of trying to avoid losing my reason escapes me. Every day I would lie, cheat, hide in order to survive.

In recent years, several of my so-called 'intellectual' friends, when I tell them about that dreaded school, are amazed. 'You went to one of the best schools in the country and you threw it all away!' No one seems to understand that I just couldn't cope, just couldn't keep up.

I often wanted to say to my parents, 'Why can't you send me to a school for comedians? There must be one somewhere. A place where I could learn to be funny and muck about – I love mucking about, pulling faces and making people laugh and showing off.' But I didn't have the courage to ask. They would never have understood anyway. They thought they were doing the right thing by sending me to one of the best and most expensive schools in the country.

I think only two things made my life bearable: a warm, loving

The Ranelagh Cinema, Barnes – my palace of dreams.

family and the Ranelagh Cinema in Barnes. The love my dear mother gave me and her memories have sustained me through some very bad times throughout my life. And, ah, the Ranelagh Cinema, where I spent so many magic hours gazing up at that screen, loving the dream world those people inhabited. The men, wearing immaculate, smart clothes, always white tie and tails or dinner jackets, and beautiful, beautiful women in amazing dresses. Alas, all dead and gone so many years ago. I call them my 'Silver Ghosts' but, thanks to TV, they will never be forgotten. I just wanted to get up into that screen and join them in their magic world.

One afternoon, I'd been to the Ranelagh Cinema with my stepsister, Cissie, to see *The Sacred Flame*, a hoary old tear-jerker by Somerset Maugham. I was on cloud nine. Later, alone in my bedroom, I started to act a scene from the film in front of the mirror. I played all the parts: 'Please don't leave me,' I begged my reflection. 'I just can't live without you.' The tears streamed down my face. I was really giving it stick when my mother walked in.

Later I heard her telling Dad. His reply was, 'If you ask me, he's not all there, the stupid boy.'

That mirror in my bedroom became my own screen; I played so

many wonderful film parts into it. My great hero was Ronald Colman, especially in *A Tale of Two Cities*. I'd practise his accent and imitate a sort of whimsical smile he had, which only affected half his face. Unfortunately it made *me* look as if I was mental, but I didn't care. With Ronald's wonderful accent and the half-smile, I would mount the steps of the guillotine and do the final scene: 'It is a far, far better thing that I do, than I have ever done. It is a far, far better rest I go to than I have ever known.' A tear – just one tear perhaps, if I could manage it. Oh, that beautiful dream world.

My dad was not the only one to question my sanity. My grandmother was always telling her daughter, 'You really should have that boy looked at, Dolly, he's not normal.' That, of course, was another stock middle-class word: 'normal'. It was used all the time: 'Most *normal* people . . . It's not *normal* behaviour, etc. etc.' Looking through the family photo album one day my father remarked, 'In every one of these photos Jimmy is pulling faces; he's not *normal* in any of them.'

I didn't care – who wants to be normal? If I became a famous film star I would be like Ronald Colman and if I became a great comedian I would be like Max Miller, quite a normal ambition for a boy of ten. (Now I've got myself doing the 'normal'!)

Over the years I've so often heard young actors and comedians say, 'Well, I could never decide what I wanted to do for a career, but

Grandma Govett. 'You really should have that boy looked at, Dolly. He's not normal!'

7

when I was up at university I was asked to take part in a drama production; after that I rather got the taste for performing. One thing led to another and, by the time I was into my twenties, I knew what I really wanted to do.'

It didn't take me until I was in my twenties; by the time I could stand up without falling over I knew what I wanted to do – get up on that stage and show off. No doubts at all, total certainty. Be an actor, be a comedian, be *anything* so long as I was in that limelight. The sad side of all this is that there are quite a few clever sods who didn't realise, until they got to university, that they wanted to be actors and have turned out to be brilliantly clever. Whereas I know so many people who love being actors – eat, drink and sleep it, buy *The Stage* every week, read it from beginning to end, discuss Shakespeare endlessly, queue up for cheap theatre seats and sit up all night discussing the show – but when they act, they're awful. Which of these two categories I fall into I'll never know – anyhow, it's a bit late for me to find out now.

Being a sensitive child in the 1930s was not easy and was inclined to provoke a very hostile reaction. 'I hope he's not going to turn into a damned nancy-boy etc.' If ever you pass a school playground and see a boy or girl standing away from the others and not joining in any of the games, dawdling, dreaming, in a world of their own, you can be sure that child is creative. Thank God, nowadays children are allowed to be different and are mostly, I repeat *mostly*, treated with respect.

Now, to quote a song I can't stand, from the musical *The Sound of Music*, 'Let's start at the very beginning'.

Place: 20 Nassau Road, Barnes
Time: Two o'clock in the morning, 20 September 1923
Present: Doctor, maids, midwife, my mother and me

I make my first appearance. I was born with an erection, ready for action (which, by the way, was also the name of the show I toured the Far East with, twenty-two years later). How do I know I was born with an erection? Well, my mother told me she said to the doctor, 'Is he all right?' and he replied, 'Well, there's *one* thing that's all right, I can tell you that for a start, Mrs Perry.' She only revealed this to me a year or two before she died; never a drinker, she was foolish enough to down a second glass of sherry one Christmas. When I asked her what *was* the one thing that was all right, she blushed and said, 'Well, you know…' Whenever my mother mentioned anything of a sexual nature, she'd always blush and say, 'Well, you know.'

20 Nassau Road. I was born in the front room upstairs. When we moved along the road to No. 38, it was decided that we would economise by not hiring a van, moving everything by hand instead.

A Stupid Boy

Before I go on, a few news headlines from 1923:

FLASH: LONDON. LADY ELIZABETH BOWES-LYON MARRIES THE
DUKE OF YORK
They subsequently became King George VI and Elizabeth, the
Queen Mother.

FLASH: MUNICH. AN OBSCURE EX-CORPORAL, ADOLF HITLER,
TRIED TO SEIZE POWER IN MUNICH TONIGHT, HE WAS ARRESTED
THE INSTANT HE EXPOSED HIMSELF

FLASH: LONDON. THE BBC [the British Broadcasting Company as
it was known then] OPENS UP NEW WIRELESS STUDIOS AT THE
SAVOY HILL IN LONDON. IT PROMISES BETTER SOUND AND, IN
RESPONSE TO CRITICS ABOUT DULL PROGRAMMES, ANNOUNCES
TWO NEW ONES: *Woman's Hour* AND *In and Out of the Shops with
Miss Fusspot*. (Nothing ever changes.)

I was born into a middle-class London suburban family. We were so
middle-class our housemaid was not allowed to put the dustbins out
until after dark. One of the first words I learned, after 'Daddy' and
'Mummy', was 'common'. 'Don't speak with your mouth full, dear,
common children do that.' 'Don't shout in public, make a noise when
you drink, butt in when grown-ups are talking, that's what common
children do.' Then there were 'common' girls: 'Like one of those girls
who work in Woolworths – long fingernails and too much lipstick.'
Well, I must confess I always liked so-called common girls, with bold
eyes that didn't look down, but straight into your face, who laughed
loudly and were fun, fun, fun. Well brought-up young men didn't
have anything to do with girls of that sort. What those young

middle-class men missed! I didn't, they did. There's an old saying: 'Nice girls get nice presents, naughty girls get *great big* presents!'

And then, of course, there was – 'Did you see that nasty common man? Holds his table knife like a pen.' Now, to hold your table knife like a pen was a cardinal sin. Even today I always look to see how people hold their knife and fork – completely absurd, but I just can't help it. A few years ago I watched a documentary on TV about recruiting Gurkhas from Nepal into the British Army. The standard is so high that, for every one accepted, ninety-nine are turned down. Johnny Gurkha, as he was patronisingly referred to when I was serving in the Far East, is a wonderful soldier, amazingly brave and someone definitely to have on your side. Towards the end of the documentary, after they'd completed their training, the Gurkhas were shown how to eat Western style with a knife and fork. Their natural way of eating was, of course, with their fingers and a chapatti (a sort of pancake which you wrap round your food and put in your mouth) – much, much better – but they were being shown how to use a knife and fork by a British Army NCO, and – wait for it – *he was holding his knife like a pen*. Oh, the humiliation! Through no fault of their own, those great warriors, who were never defeated in battle, from then on held their table knives like a certain Tory politician.

There were so many other things that gave away a person's background:

He wears suede shoes – must be a nancy-boy.

Has his hair plastered with brilliantine – I bet he's Jewish.

Dirty fingernails – obviously working-class.

A grammar school boy – licks his lips when he's eating, calls lunchtime dinner time, cuts his roll with a knife instead of breaking it. You can see he never went to a public school; he wears a striped shirt with a striped suit!

During the first week's rehearsal of Dad's Army, *Arthur Lowe was all at sea. 'I hope we haven't made a big mistake casting him,' David Croft said to me. 'So do I,' I thought.*

For over twenty-five years I worked in the middle-class, rather snobbish environment of the BBC. I'm ashamed to admit it, but it suited me down to the ground. As a creative person (I won't go as far as to say artist) I flourished in the environment. When David Croft and I started working on *Dad's Army*, in 1967, all sorts of people were suggested for the part of Captain Mainwaring. Michael Mills was then Head of Comedy. He'd been a lieutenant-commander in the Navy during the war and was inclined to shout at you as though he was on the ship's bridge in a force 10 gale. He started every sentence with 'Now, look here'.

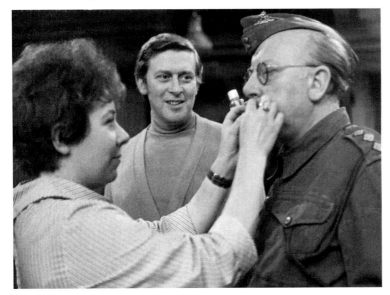

I kept suggesting Arthur Lowe to him and his reply was 'Now look here, we don't know him at the BBC, we just don't use him. He does that thing up North, *Coronation Street*.' He didn't actually say it, but I could see he was thinking, 'North? *Coronation Street*? All rather common.'

In the end we got Arthur Lowe thanks to the back-up that David Croft gave me. Arthur was the only member of the *Dad's Army* team that I cast. I had no power whatsoever in those days, but for some reason I was convinced he was the right person. I kept repeating his name to David like some idiot; I even took him to the Windsor Theatre to see Arthur in a play called *Baked Beans and Caviar*. It was a disaster! The play was Italian and done in English. It just didn't seem to work, and dear Arthur was hopelessly miscast and quite awful. In spite of this I still persisted and, in the end, Arthur was cast in the part of Captain Mainwaring. The rehearsals for the first episode were very difficult. Arthur just didn't seem to be able to get it together. On the last day of rehearsals, before we went into the studio to record the show, David turned to me and said, 'I hope *we* haven't made a big mistake.'

My legs turned to water when, the next day, we recorded the show in front of a live audience. And it worked! It will always be a puzzle to me why David Croft backed me so strongly over Arthur Lowe. Michael Mills also backed me in the end. To my mind he was the best Head of Comedy the BBC ever had – a bit of a fanatic and slightly potty, he had the knack of making things work and was a tremendous enthusiast, always looking for new ideas. He was responsible for so many hit comedy shows. In one in particular, *Some Mothers Do Have 'Em*, he brought together a young inexperienced writer, Ray Allen, and Michael Crawford. In the stage play, *No Sex Please, We're British*, Michael had developed a character that was the original template for Frank Spencer. When I first saw him in the play I thought he was quite amazing; he could get huge laughs with just a pause or look. *Some Mothers* was a tremendous success and the character, Frank, must have been 'done' by every impressionist in show business. Michael Mills was married to perhaps one of the most beautiful women I ever met. Her name is Valerie Leon and every time I see her she takes my breath away. Michael had tremendous faith in David Croft and me, and was the one that thought up the title *Dad's Army* – a slight improvement on my awful original, 'The Fighting Tigers'!

Valerie Leon. Every time I see her she takes my breath away.

In later years, when I gave Michael a new script to read, he'd let me have it back with dozens of notes written in the margin, 'Now look here,' he'd say, 'rewrite it and follow these suggestions. I think it will help.' He was always constructive.

Some years after he had left the BBC, I took a new idea to the then Head of Comedy. He handed the script back to me across the desk with the words, 'I'm sorry, Jimmy, I just don't think it's funny.' No other comment.

But to get back to being born into a middle-class family, and the word 'common' — still used so much by people of my generation today, including the late and great Noël Coward, who was, of course, considerably older than I but came from a similar, suburban middle-class background (Teddington, actually, which is just a stone's throw from Barnes).

In the late 1980s I organised the Writers' Guild Awards at the Dorchester every year. My main problem was getting people of note, or stars, to present them. I contacted a famous film producer/director/gourmet to ask him to present the Best British Film Script Award. To my surprise, he was very affable and charming, and told me to get in touch with his business partner with all the details. I subsequently contacted the partner . . . and then it started; he told me the great man wanted a list of all the people attending the function, so that he could let us know exactly who he wanted to sit with, and so it went on, phone call after phone call. He wanted to make sure he wasn't pestered. Finally, 'How about the security?' the partner said. 'If you organised the Awards properly we wouldn't have all this trouble.'

That did it. I prided myself on my organisation and I'd had enough.

Livid with rage, I used the only weapon with which I could hit the mark: 'Why are all you film people so rude and bad-mannered' – and then the big one – 'and, and – *common?*'

There was an explosion at the other end and the phone went dead. Somehow the word 'common' always seems to hit the mark. From the security of the cosy BBC I frequently referred to 'those rude, common film people'. But it was only because – to use the words of my dad – I was fiendishly jealous. Above everything in the world, I wanted to become a film star and I couldn't. (I tell you this because, as the book goes on, you'll realise at times that I can really be a bit of a nerd.) Above all, you can't be a film star with a finger missing – well, not in those days. (How I had the misfortune to lose the finger, I will explain later.) In films today no one cares what you look like, which is either wonderful or awful, depending on whether you've got a finger or some other bit of your body missing and you want to be a film star.

The one time the word 'common' really upset me was when I was about eight or nine. The River Thames flowed past the bottom of Nassau Road and every year we used to watch the Oxford and Cambridge Boat Race go by. I loved it and wore a huge Cambridge favour. (I supported Cambridge only because my Uncle Willie had a heraldic shop there on King's Parade.) When the tide was high all sorts of flotsam swept past on the river, including the occasional body. Our daily woman, Mabel (upon whom I based the character of the char in *You Rang, M'Lord?*), seemed to see one every week. When she arrived she'd say, 'I saw another corpse go by as I came here this mornin', Mrs Perry.'

'What was it like?' I'd ask.

''Orrible, 'orrible, Master Jim,' she'd say, 'all swolled an' bloated.'

I'd often go down to the bottom of the road in the hope that I'd see a body float past. One day, as I was standing on the towpath, the tide was out and a young boy, about my age, came up the steps staggering under the weight of a wet sack full of driftwood he'd collected. Even after all these years I can still see him. Thin-faced, with bright, hungry eyes, his legs red and chapped, no socks, just a pair of broken shoes with no laces. 'Excuse me, mister,' he said. 'Can you help, please?'

So I picked up a corner of the sack and we dragged it round to Kitson Road where he lived. In those days Kitson Road, with its row of terraced workman's cottages, was considered a bit of a slum. Today those same properties are sought by the Luvvies who live in Barnes as being 'most desirable' and the dinky little terraced houses change hands at a quarter of a million apiece.

When I got home I told my mother where I'd been. She was most upset.

'I said you were not to have anything to do with those common children. You might catch something!'

Suddenly, at the age of nine, I thought, 'That's not fair. He can't help being common and poor and hungry.' And I think from that moment I unconsciously became a closet Socialist.

My father at school, 1873. Oh my poor little dad and those other poor boys. Note the bearded thug on the right, holding a cane – he looks as if he just can't wait to lash out.

My father, Arthur Edward Perry, was born in, believe it or not, 1869, at No. 2 Belgrave Square, London. In those days so little had been invented; no motorcars, no radios, no films, no aeroplanes, no TV – people must have been bored out of their minds! In America Alexander Graham Bell was in the process of inventing the telephone. The Yanks always say that the phone was an American invention, but in actual fact Graham Bell was a Scot who was living in America at that time. It seems to me that most modern inventions were by those clever sods, Scotsmen: penicillin, television and goodness knows what else. What also amazes me is that most of the inventions I've just mentioned were thought of during the course of about forty years. What the hell was the human race doing over the hundreds of years before the 1870s? I can only come to conclusion that they were either stupid, or just bone idle.

Above: My dad was convinced that once television got going, it would ruin the cinemas and theatres.

Below: The Albert Memorial. 'What an ugly brute! Pull it down!'

During his lifetime my father witnessed all these wonderful inventions and took them completely for granted! He never said, 'Isn't it amazing!' or 'It's a miracle!' and, in his eighties, he used to sit in front of the telly and grumble about the rotten programmes. 'It's about time they got some new stuff on,' he'd say.

In spite of the fact that he was a Victorian, he hated so many Victorian things. The Albert Memorial, for example, to him was an eyesore. In the Thirties there was a very popular movement to demolish it, which he heartily endorsed. 'Ugly brute!' he'd say. 'Ugly brute', or 'brutes' was one of his favourite sayings.

In 1944, on my first home leave from the army, I was going up to London from Watford with my mother and father in the car. Dad never drove – that was my mother's job. At the age of seventy-five he was doing war work. A fact that no one seems to know is that all the ships that brought men and munitions across the sea from America had to return across the Atlantic empty, so the British filled them with luxury goods that were made to earn much needed dollars. We also exported antiques and my father's job was to vet them, on behalf of the British Antique Dealers Association, to confirm that they were genuine. For this important war work he was granted a minuscule ration of petrol. Anyhow, we were driving through Bushey on the way to London when a policeman stopped the car. Out of a side turning marched a large column of German prisoners, guarded by British soldiers with fixed bayonets and, as they passed, they looked into the car and saw me in uniform and my dear dad who, let's face it, looked rather Jewish. Their eyes were filled with such burning hate. Since then I've only seen hate like that twice, the first time in 1947 in the bloody riots during the division of India and Pakistan, and the second when, quite recently, I told a Catholic priest that I liked the TV series *Father Ted*. As the Germans went by, my dad dismissed the whole thing with the words 'ugly brutes'. And how right he was. I also remember thinking at the time, 'Those thickheads must know by now that they're losing the war. How dare they stare at us like that?'

You may wonder how my dear old dad came to be born in a magnificent house in Belgrave Square. His father, who was born in 1830, was the butler in this grand establishment. He had served on HMS *Victory*. It had been taken out of service in 1812 and become the flagship of the Admiral of the Fleet, Sir Thomas Cochrane, who was C-in-C Portsmouth. As a domestic rating my grandfather was butler to the admiral who, shortly

My dad's father, the perfect butler. He was born in 1830, fifteen years after the Battle of Waterloo.

afterwards, was transferred to the Admiralty, and so in 1855 my dad's father was discharged from the Royal Navy and took up the post of butler at number 2 Belgrave Square. It seemed he had so many uncles who were sailors; one, William Perry, served on many ships, including HMS *Ganges*, with the rank of ship's corporal; he administered the rope's end. Ridiculous as it may seem today, flogging was not abolished in the Royal Navy until 1879.

My dad told me so many stories of his father, when he was the butler in Belgrave Square, which were the foundation for the TV series that David Croft and I made, *You Rang, M'Lord?*.

One of the great yarns always started with the words, 'Did you know your grandfather saw the last man hanged in public?'

My mother would protest, 'Oh, not again, Arthur, please!'

But I was enthralled and, egged on by me, he'd say, 'It was 26 May 1868. Lord, what a day it was; you never saw so many people in all your life. Everybody wanted to be there – after all, it was going to be the last hanging in public. I can't think why they abolished it, but there you are. Anyhow, this fellow was an Irishman, Michael Barrett, a Fenian [what would now be called an IRA terrorist]. He'd blown up something or other and killed a woman. The gallows were set up in front of the old Newgate Prison – where the

Dad's father used to say: 'Pity they stopped public executions. It was a great day out – the only trouble was that it was so difficult to get home afterwards!'

Old Bailey is today – then they brought this Irish fellow in a cart from Clerkenwell. Now, there was a pub, the Baptist's Head, and they'd stopped there for the prisoner to have a drink; then he got back into the cart and it certainly was the last drink that he ever had. Believe it or not, that's where the expression "On the wagon" comes from. I've told you that before, haven't I, Dolly?' My mum nodded her head in despair. 'Anyhow,' Dad continued, getting into his stride, 'this fellow was pushed up on to the scaffold and they put a sack over his head. Then the crowd shouted, "Hat's off!" and, when everyone was bareheaded, the crowd went dead silent – not a whisper – even the birds stopped singing. The hangman drew the bolt and the drop fell with a loud boom. A huge cry went up from the vast crowd and that was the end of him. My father used to say his dad told him there was only one snag with those huge crowds; you had a terrible job getting home after the execution.'

My mum hated hearing my dad's long, gruesome tales, but I felt privileged to hear about a first-hand account of something that happened over 60 years before.

It was Charles Dickens, along with Sir Robert Peel, who strongly campaigned against public executions. Interesting to note that, when the abolition of public hangings threatened to become law, a large deputation of publicans presented a petition to No. 10 Downing Street protesting that it would ruin their business as, on the day of an execution, they opened at three o'clock in the morning to cater for the vast crowds.

When Dad's first wife died she left him with three young children, Eddie, Arthur and Cissie. He was on his own with a young family to bring up but not for long; a pretty young girl of twenty-four came into his life. Her name was Dorothy Millicent Govett. It was my dear mother, Dolly. She worked in her father's antique shop just around the corner from Dad's. It seems that everyone in our family had an antique shop at some time or another. Her father would send Mum round to dad's shop with the instructions, 'Go and see if old Perry's got anything worthwhile.' 'Old Perry' was twenty-three years older than her, but love blossomed and they married. She had to endure bitchy remarks from her sisters: 'You're going to marry that old man with a ready-made family?' But she knew what she was doing and, with thousands of young men being slaughtered every day in the trenches, she had no intention of being left on the shelf like them. In spite of this it really was a love match, full of warmth and affection.

When Dad was about eighty-four, Mum said, 'I'm taking your father to see a specialist, he's ruptured himself.'

'Don't be absurd, Mum, how can he possibly do that?' I said. 'He never does anything strenuous, just walks about all day and talks.'

My dear Dolly blushed and said, in her usual way when *sex* loomed up, 'Well, er – *you* know.'

Dear old Dad, game to the last, finally had to draw stumps at the age of eighty-four.

Arthur Edward Perry, Fine Art Dealer and Talker, died in 1961 at the age of ninety-two and, within a year, my dear mother followed him. It seems she didn't want to go on alone. One of the last things

Grandpa Govett and my mother, Dolly. My mum worked for Grandpa in his antique business, and he'd often say, 'Go round to old Perry's shop and see if he's got anything worthwhile.' One day he had – my father asked Dolly to marry him.

21

she said to me was, 'He always appreciated everything I did. He didn't know one end of a paintbrush from the other and never lifted a finger, but if I was doing some decorating, he'd come in and say, "That looks very nice, Dolly, you're so clever." He was bone idle, but I do miss him so.'

My mother was an amazing woman, who fought for her family tooth and nail. Whenever I hear the song 'My Yiddisher Momma' I just can't hold back the tears; it describes her perfectly, although she had no Jewish blood. On the other hand, as regards my father, the jury's still out.

My mother seemed to have an endless stream of sisters – one, Auntie Madge, was married to Uncle Jack, who had a draper's shop in Eastry, a small village in Kent. I thought it was a magical place; it sold everything including cheap penknives on a card. My father was rather derisive and referred to the place as 'having old workman's trousers hanging up outside'.

I later used this in *Dad's Army*, when Captain Mainwaring was talking about his father being a member of the Master Tailors Guild, who had a shop in the very best part of Eastbourne. Corporal Jones whispers, 'I knew that shop. He had pairs of old workman's trousers hanging up outside!'

The Perry family. Sandwich Bay, the 1920s.

During the summer holidays we quite often stayed at Eastry, which was a lovely little village not far from Sandwich Bay, but my dad really had it in for Uncle Jack and constantly told the story about how, one morning, Jack had taken a bottle of beer out of the cupboard, poured himself a glass and then, with the words 'I usually have one at this time', had put it back in the cupboard.

Auntie Madge and Uncle Jack had no children of their own and adopted a sweet little girl, Margaret. I always called her Peggy and have so many happy memories of her when we were kids. Later she went into local politics and eventually became the Mayor of Basingstoke.

Auntie Carrie, married to a successful surveyor, lived in a large house in Chiswick, with servants and a tennis court in the grounds. In the 1930s to have a tennis court was a sign that you'd really arrived. I thought it all rather boring. Auntie Carrie was inclined to give herself airs.

Then there were two brothers, Uncles Reg and Ted as well as Auntie Winnie, spinster; Auntie Isabel, spinster; Auntie Irene, spinster. Lovely women cruelly deprived of partners and children by the 1914–18 war.

Auntie Madge, Little Peggy and Grandma Govett. I never did find out if the camel was real!

Grandfather Govett died long before I was born, but I remember Grandma. She was a complete autocrat, very snobbish. In 1929, when the talkies came in, the British people heard American accents for the very first time. Grandma used to come to lunch occasionally. One day she arrived in a terrible state. 'You've never heard anything like it in all your life, Dolly,' she said. 'I was coming out of the station and I heard a dreadful common man say to an awful woman, "Okay, Toots"! Okay Toots? What sort of language is that to use in public? No business to be allowed! It was all I could do not to hit him with my umbrella!'

The dreaded Uncle Tom. He bored for England.

My mother's Uncle Tom was perhaps the most boring person I have ever known. He kept a tatty old antique shop at the bottom of Watford High Street. My father, who referred to himself as an 'Art Dealer', was rather disdainful of this establishment because Uncle Tom mostly sold Victorian chests of drawers and wardrobes. In the 1930s, to be antique things had to be at least a hundred years old. In fact Dad used to say, 'I never have anything in my shop later than Regency.'

Uncle Tom had been a remittance man. A remittance man was usually the black sheep of the family who, perhaps, had got a servant girl into trouble or committed some other unmentionable crime. Uncle Tom had been packed off to Australia and was sent a regular sum of money provided he did not return to England. He spent many years as a drover of cattle and sheep, going up and down that massive continent, and also as a gold prospector, with no luck. He only returned many years later, when the money dried up. It was rumoured he had a relationship with Marie Lloyd.

My family, plus Uncle Tom, on the beach at Margate. Note the lack of seaside clothes – no one had them in those days.

Now, there was a magazine called *The Wide World* and it was full of stirring adventure stories of the British Empire, and all these stories, at one time or another, Uncle Tom would recount as his own experiences. The pattern was always the same: he would turn up for

Sunday lunch about 12.30, settle in the most comfortable armchair in the room and fill his foul pipe with black plug tobacco, which he rubbed in his hands. Then he'd light up and clouds of smoke would curl up to the white ceiling, much to my mother's annoyance – she was a great DIY expert and did all the decorating in the house and, because of Uncle Tom, had to repaint that ceiling every three months – then he'd look inside his oilskin tobacco pouch and the following dialogue would ensue:

'What a nuisance, very little makings [tobacco] left. The paper shop will be closed in half an hour. Can the boy go round and get me some?' Then old Tom would thrust his hand into his pocket. 'Damn. Right out of small change. Can you let me have a shilling, Arthur?' My dad would obediently hand over the coin and Tom would hand it to me.

The particular brand of tobacco that Tom smoked was advertised as 'The Shilling Tobacco with The Halfpenny Change' and as usual, he'd say, 'The boy can keep the halfpenny, right, Arthur?'

Dad would nod, and so I'd run round to Fox's the newsagent for an ounce of 'Afrikaner Flake'.

At that time everybody smoked – continually. In the cinema a huge swirl of tobacco smoke would revolve in the beam of the projector – it was a wonder we could see the film. People smoked in theatres, in trains, in buses, everywhere. I smoked a pipe from the age of fifteen; I did so in the first place to look grown-up and then I got to love it and I smoked pipe and cigars for the next fifty years. Suddenly, in 1990, I contracted bowel cancer, almost at the same time as Audrey Hepburn. That lovely girl died; I survived. I'm convinced it was a brilliant surgeon called Peter Hawley who saved my life. He sat on my bed after the operation and in his own words described how he'd '. . . just cut out about *that* much' – he indicated about eight inches – 'and sewed the ends together.' What a wonderful understatement!

Travelling on the London Underground in the early morning, the smell of BO plus tobacco smoke would knock you over – even worse when it was raining. Thousands of fag ends on the floor of the train and millions on the line. Take it from me: they were definitely *not* the good old days.

By the time I got home from the newsagent, Mum would be 'dishing up', Minnie, the maid, would be carrying in the vegetables and the joint, Mabel would be lurking in the kitchen, and we'd sit round the table for our Sunday dinner (not 'lunch', dinner). Mum always carved and served Uncle Tom first. Quite often Tom, without waiting for anybody else, would cut off a large piece of meat, thrust it into his mouth, then promptly let it drop out again on to the plate. He'd take a gulp of water and shout at Mum, 'It's scalding hot, Dolly!'

She'd quickly reply, 'Things that come out of the oven usually are.'

Tom then ate very fast and would soon clear his plate, his eyes darting everywhere, then – back to the dialogue: 'Are those sprouts going spare, Dolly? Anybody want that crispy bit of meat?' By the time he'd finish, he'd end up with another dinner. My mother would ring a little silver bell and Minnie would come in and clear the dishes. Mabel lingered in the hall looking through the crack in the door to see how much food was left for her. She never went short in our house, but Sunday dinner was special; she never had roast beef except with us. The pudding would be served; fig pudding, date pudding, treacle pudding – one or the other – with plenty of custard. Then, when everything was cleared, Uncle Tom would settle back once more in his chair and regale us with his stories. If Mum nodded off, he would shout,

'Are you listening to me, Dolly?'

His favourite yarn was the time when an Aborigine had attacked him with a spear. It always started the same way:

'You can never trust those blacks!' (In those days nobody had ever heard about genocide or the disgraceful treatment of the Australian Aborigines.)

'Listen,' he'd go on. 'This great ugly brute tried to pull me off my horse. I hit him with my whip but he managed to stick his spear into my leg. You never saw so much blood! Are you listening to me, Dolly? There was blood everywhere. I pulled out my revolver and let him have it between the eyes. Well, it was either him or me. Are you listening, Dolly? You're not falling asleep, are you? No, you can never trust those blacks. I've still got the scar today!' Then he would pull up his trouser leg and long johns. Underneath there was a thin white scar, which didn't look like very much to me.

Then he would get on to his favourite topic: 'Salties', which were huge, salt-water crocodiles, and 'Freshies', sharks that were in the river. 'Listen, Dolly,' he'd shout, 'you're not falling asleep are you? Those Salties could sometimes be nearly twenty foot long.' Then he'd get up and mark the distance with two chairs, at the same time breaking wind. Can you imagine? I'll never forget it. 'I was in Fort Darwin and was walking along the jetty. This Saltie was waiting underneath, almost human intelligence; he knew those boards were rotten, you can take it from me. Then it happened – listen, Dolly – the boards gave way and I went through up to my waist. Quick as a flash, the

'Are you listening to me, Dolly? That croc knew those boards were rotten.'

27

One of Uncle Tom's collection of naughty photos.

huge croc leapt out of the water and I just managed to pull my legs up when I heard those huge jaws snap together. Another six inches and the brute would have had my legs off. It was so close he got the heels of my boots. What do you think of that, Dolly?' he asked, poking her again. Poor Mum, what she went through. Now that I'm rather old I realise it must have been terrible for her – denying someone sleep is the very worst torture; the Gestapo used it to great effect during the war.

Why did everyone put up with this terrible old bore? The only explanation being, they all thought he had money. My mother just did it from the kindness of her heart.

When he died, in 1940, some members of the family went to his solicitor's office. On the desk was a black deed box. The solicitor told the assembled vultures. 'This deed box is the only effect Mr Govett left. I want your permission to break it open.' The vultures licked their lips and eagerly agreed. He prised open the lid. It was empty, except for a bundle of Victorian photographs of scantily clad ladies.

The shadow of the First World War hung heavily over everything when I was young. Most people were connected with it in some way or another. I remember John Laurie, who had served, saying, 'You know, laddie, I still have nightmares about that time.' Even after all these years. In the 1970s I did a TV series called *The Old Boy Network* (terrible title, but who am I to talk – I once wrote a TV series called 'Lollipop Loves Mr Mole'!). I featured John Laurie in one of the episodes and we told the story of his life. In the section about the War I threw up a huge picture of the Battle of the Somme behind him. A single tear trickled down his granite face and he whispered,

'Take it off, I just can't bear to look.'

Arnold Ridley also served in that war and was wounded twice. He had a huge scar from a bayonet wound that went right up his forearm. The wound had left his arm with very little strength in it.

How it must have brutalised those young men. My Uncle Reg told me this terrible story (these were his words). It's not politically correct so, if you're sensitive, don't read the next bit.

'In the last few months of the war, in the autumn of 1918, after years of stalemate the Allies broke out of the trenches and started to advance. We fell in with these Yanks. You should have seen their

Uncle Reg.

29

equipment; they had everything of the very best and as for food, they even had ice cream and tins of apple pie. Anyhow, a column of Germans were going along the road led by a band with a great big fat bandmaster in front – fat as a pig he was. We were lying in wait and opened fire; killed the lot of 'em. We ran forward to make sure they were all dead and I was with this Yank, a great big nigger – huge, you never saw anything like it. He started to take the watch off the dead bandmaster's wrist and I said, "What are you doing?" He held the bayonet under my nose and said, "I'm having this watch, boss, you got any objections?" Well, I wasn't going to argue with a big nigger like that!' After telling me that dreadful story Uncle Reg laughed. Dear Uncle Reg, who was such a lovely, kind man, laughed his head off.

Oh, that terrible war, the flower of British manhood butchered, a million dead and another million crippled, not to mention the French and the Germans. Everywhere after the war, men with an arm or leg missing, suffering from shell-shock or the effects of poison gas. I don't think our dear old country ever recovered from it.

Most of the houses in Nassau Road, Barnes, had a parlour maid. Impossible to believe it now, but there were thousands of poor girls from all over the country who worked their socks off for a pound a week, plus food and keep. They usually had a dingy room at the top of the house, with an iron bedstead and a minimum of furniture. As a rule my mother tried to avoid employing Irish girls. Nothing wrong with the Irish, of course, how could there be with the name Murphy in the family? ('On your father's side,' my mother reminded me.) But if they were Irish it might lead to all sorts of things – perhaps a *priest* coming round to the house to check up on them!

My parents had a horror of priests and hinted at all sorts of strange, dark things. They messed about with choirboys, young girls (or both) and then, of course, Catholic servant girls would have to be given time off to go to Mass and come back stinking of incense – ugh! Nasty, foreign religion! Of course they added the word 'common'. Far better to stick to Welsh girls.

One Christmas night the whole family (and there were a lot of 'em – they came from near and far – the house was packed) was in the drawing room playing games and having a marvellous time. I went into the kitchen for a glass of water and Minnie, the maid, was sitting at the table. The stark bare light shone down on the white enamel top, and on it were a banana, two toffees, some nuts and a cracker. She gave me a little smile and got me a glass of water. I offered to pull her cracker with her but she just shook her head. I opened the door and looked back; she was slowly unwrapping a toffee. She gave me another little smile. I have never forgotten it, it all seemed so wrong. I went back to the drawing room. 'Minnie's all alone, Mummy,' I said. 'Can't she come in here and join in the fun with us?'

'Don't be silly, dear, whatever next?' She sniffed my breath. 'You haven't been drinking that sweet Martini again, have you?' I shook my head. 'Remember last year,' she shouted. 'Jimmy helped himself to the Martini and fell over.' Everyone roared with laughter. She gave me a great big kiss and said, 'Don't look so sad, darling, it's Christmas.' How could anyone as kind as Mum not understand about Minnie being alone in the kitchen?

During a general election we were having tea with another great load of relatives, when the maid popped her head round the door and said, 'I'm off now, Mrs Perry.' We heard the front door bang, and Auntie Carrie said, 'Where's the maid going at this time of day?'

'She's off to vote,' said Mum.

'Huh!' Carrie sniffed. 'I expect she'll vote Labour – no business to be allowed.'

Looking at the paper recently, the headlines read: 'IS THE COUNTRY HEADING FOR RECESSION? People are putting off changing their cars this year, and quite a lot are taking only one holiday abroad. Restaurants report that there has been a drop in bookings, Summer Sales takings are down 10%.' *This* is a recession? Let me tell you about a recession, or slump, as it was called when I was a young kid. Over three million out of work, no Social Security, no Housing Benefits, no Family Allowances, just the dole – a pittance, subject to a means test. Welsh miners shuffling along in the gutter of Hammersmith Broadway, singing beautifully, the leader with a collection box. Thin-faced desperate men, wearing World War One medals, offering to keep an eye on your car for a penny, children with no socks and worn-out shoes (if they were lucky). Those who were fortunate enough to be in work, constantly scared in case they should do something to upset their employers and be 'given their cards', as it was called – in other words, sacked. This was 1932, the year before Hitler came to power. Europe was in turmoil: riots and constant civil unrest. The dreaded word on British middle-class lips was 'Bolsheviks'.

A few years before I'd stood in Hammersmith Broadway with my mother and watched truckloads of soldiers in steel helmets and with fixed bayonets go by. 'What are they going to do, Mummy?' I asked.

'Don't be afraid, dear,' she said. 'Those brave men are going to protect us from the wicked Bolsheviks.'

In the *Daily Mirror*, there was a strip cartoon for children called 'Pip, Squeak and Wilfred'. One of the characters wore a black, broad-brimmed hat. He was a sort of anarchist-cum-Bolshevik, who carried a large, round, black bomb with a sparkling fuse in the top and was always trying to blow things up. My father of course always read the *Daily Telegraph*, which he went through very carefully at breakfast. The *Mirror*, in his opinion, was read by 'shop girls and bank clerks'. Dear Arnold Ridley (Private Godfrey) and I used to have long talks about the Twenties and Thirties. I remembered the 1930s so well, but only had vague memories of the Twenties. 'You don't realise, James,' he said, 'how terrified the middle classes were.'

During the General Strike, in 1926, the Soviets had only been in power in Russia for nine years, and everyone talked constantly about revolution. In 1924 most of the media took every opportunity to discredit Britain's first Labour government. When Prime Minister Ramsay MacDonald decided to go to the country to support Labour policies, a week before the election the Zinoviev Letter, as it became known, mysteriously came to light. It was a message, signed by Grigori Zinoviev, the president of the Communist International, to the Communist Party of Great Britain – four days before the polls; the *Daily Mail* published the letter in full. Headlines read, in good old *Daily Mail* style: MOSCOW – ORDERS TO OUR REDS, GREAT PLOT DISCLOSED YESTERDAY TO PARALYSE THE ARMY AND NAVY. It was certainly a fiery document, which whipped up the *Daily Mail* readers to fever pitch. The letter went on, 'In the event of the danger of war, it is possible to paralyse all military operations of the bourgeois and make a start in turning an Imperial War into a Class War.' Heavy stuff. Ramsay MacDonald and his Labour supporters protested that they had nothing to do with the Bolsheviks. No matter, the cry went up, they were all Reds; no smoke without fire, they all took their orders from Moscow. It did the trick. The Conservatives, lead by honest Stan Baldwin, swept back into power with a huge majority. Later it turned out that the *Daily Mail* had been duped – the letter was exposed as a clumsy forgery.

Nothing changes. (I keep saying that all the time, but it's a fact.) During the Harold Wilson government, a very nice member of my family – terrible old Tory – with all sincerity, looked me straight in the eye and said, 'You realise, don't you, that Harold Wilson goes round to the Russian embassy once a week to get his orders?'

When Clive Dunn got his OBE, Arthur Lowe remarked, 'What did he get that for, delivering half a dozen eggs to Harold Wilson at No. 10 Downing Street once a week?'

The Ghost Train. *Clockwise: Bob Grant, me (mugging as usual), John Newbury, John Clegg, and Jill Hyem, who became a well-known writer.*

Arnold told me it was the Bolshevik scare that gave him the idea for his classic play, *The Ghost Train*. This play revolves around a group of people stranded on a wayside station on the South Cornwall Joint Railway, who are warned by Saul, the stationmaster, about the 'Ghost Train' that rushes through during the night. One of the passengers, Teddy, posing as a silly ass, is a member of the Secret Service, and it is he who uncovers the plot: the so-called Ghost Train is carrying machine guns for a Bolshevik uprising.

After the General Strike in 1926, when eventually the miners were forced back to work at reduced wages, it was revealed that there were no 'Reds under the beds', no groups of heavily armed Bolsheviks ready to take to the streets and man barricades. The good old British compromise had won the day. As King George V remarked, 'What a rotten way to run a revolution, I could have done it better myself.'

Bluff 'Sailor George' was a man who liked life without frills. When he came to the throne, the first thing he did was to sack the fancy French chefs at Buckingham Palace (much favoured by his playboy father, Edward VII). One can almost hear him saying, 'I've had enough of those Frog chefs downstairs. Let's have some good hot dinners!' Many years later it was suggested that there should be a Royal Command Show of a famous ballet. His comment was, 'I don't want to see a lot of nancy boys poncing about on the stage. Let's have some turns; I like a good turn. Put George Robey on, old George always makes me laugh!'

A year or so before he died, we all lined the road outside Colet Court as he passed in a coach with Queen Mary. We boys had been instructed that if we didn't cheer loud enough there would be dire results. Any excuse to get that old cane into action by those sadists. As the coach passed the King was so heavily made-up he looked like a wax dummy. 'Perhaps he's dead,' I thought, 'and somebody's under the seat working his arm up and down.'

Reds under the bed have always been the scare. When the last war broke out there were posters everywhere: 'Careless Talk Costs Lives'. But this time it was the Nazis not the Reds – after all *they* were on our side this time, weren't they? I wrote a line for Captain Mainwaring in *Dad's Army* where he said, 'The Russians *are* on our side. In times of war one cannot be too fussy about one's bedfellows.'

There was constant talk of Fifth Columnists and spies; in fact, there were no Fifth Columnists, except a small section of right-wing people who thought we should make peace with Hitler, but they kept their opinions to themselves after a number of their fellow-travellers, including Mosley, ended up in prison. As for spies, the few who were landed were so hopelessly incompetent that they were very quickly captured.

There were lots of things we didn't talk about – sex, for instance. One day I picked up a copy of a woman's magazine, which my mother read; I flicked through it and there were two ladies with no clothes on or, to be more explicit, bare tops! I goggled. Before I could recover myself Mum snatched it out of my hands with a shrill cry of, 'You can't look at that!'

'Why not?' I asked.

'You know it's not right for boys of your age to look at that sort of thing.'

It seemed all right to me; two ladies, if rather matronly, with bare er . . . breasts. It certainly turned *me* on – but in those days *any* bare lady turned me on, even an old photograph of Venus de Milo with no arms! 'I only wanted to read it,' I lied.

'Wait a minute,' she said and then, taking a pencil out of a drawer, she proceeded to cover up the boobs with a heavy scribbled bra.

On one of our annual holidays in Kent we went down to Sandwich Bay and the weather was, in the tradition of all those summers of our youth, wonderful. We drove the car to the end of the road that led to the beach and unloaded it to carry down deckchairs and picnic baskets. As we staggered through the sand dunes, dear old Dad suddenly went stark staring mad; he turned purple and shouted, 'Disgusting! Filthy, lewd people! Someone ought to send for the police! Come on, quick!' he said, leading the way through the dunes. I looked to see what the cause of his apoplexy was: a young couple was having a cuddle in the dunes, but believe it or not, the filthy swines were wearing *bathing costumes*!

One day, in the playground at school, I heard a boy reciting a poem:

The Venus de Milo.
When I was eleven, she
was the nearest I got to
naughty pictures!

'The boy stood on the burning deck
Drinking a pint of mild,
Someone touched him up the rear
It must have been Oscar Wilde!'

All the boys roared with laughter. I couldn't understand it at all. I certainly didn't know anything about homosexual, heterosexual, transsexual, or, if it comes to it, any other sort of sexual. I'd heard quite a few jokes about Oscar Wilde but they always involved people bending down and things like 'If the wind blows your hat off and Oscar Wilde's around, you'd better kick it down the street before you pick it up.' It was all Greek to me. When I asked my dad about Oscar Wilde, his face went purple, his eyes nearly popped out of his head: 'Oscar Wilde? Oscar Wilde? That disgusting sodomite! Filthy swine, they should have hanged him! Don't ever mention his name again! Filth! Filth!' He left the room, banging the door behind him, leaving me in a very puzzled state. What on earth was a sodomite? And why was Oscar Wilde the cause of so much humour and rage? I had to find out, so I asked one of the older boys at school.

In those days at an English prep or public school you could never, *never* reveal your first name, just your initial – at all roll-calls I was 'Perry, J'. If, heaven forbid, anybody found out your first name you were bullied mercilessly, so this led to boys having nicknames. I had two. One was particularly charming: 'Piss-Pot Perry'.

'Did you hear that?' shouted the miniature thug when I asked him. 'Piss-Pot Perry wants to know what a sodomite is. It's a *bum-bandit*, stupid!' With that he opened my school satchel, tipped the contents on the ground, kicked them, then walked away, jeering. I was still none the wiser.

When one looks back at the English middle-class attitude to sex, it's a wonder that any of us remained sane. Such sayings as 'Men! They're only after one thing!' – I could never understand what that one thing was.

My mother used to have long whispered conversations with my sister in her bedroom, and I'd creep up and listen outside the door. I could just hear snatches of 'Well brought-up young girls keep their virginity intact until their wedding night.' What was this virginity that you had to keep? Why did my mum keep saying to my sister, 'Once you've lost it, that's it'? I used to think, why couldn't you buy another one?… Whatever it was.

I heard vicars go on about the Virgin Mary and Immaculate Conception – total mystery! I didn't know what 'conception' was, nor 'virginity'. I knew what 'immaculate' was – Fred Astaire in the film *Top Hat* (I thought Fred wore white tie and tails all the time, even at breakfast). Listening outside the door, I could hear my mum hissing at my sister, 'Once a man gets what he wants, that's the finish of a girl! He'll never want her again.' What was this thing that a man wanted but, once he had it, didn't want any more? Had it anything to do with the talk the school chaplain gave us about self-abuse? With his eyes on the ground, the chaplain managed to blurt out, 'Boys, whatever you do, do not touch yourself *there*' – pointing to his crotch – 'you are in grave danger of ruining your lives.'

It seemed to me that this *one thing*, whatever it was, kept ruining everybody's life. The chaplain warmed to his subject: 'To drain your body of precious fluids is the path to Hell and Damnation. To touch yourself there, or even – and I have to say it, boys – to let another boy touch you, is beyond redemption. Once a boy has started to practise masturbation…' – now getting into his stride, he rolled the word round his tongue – '… *masturbation* it's the end. He becomes pale and sickly, with poor eyesight.'

Then it dawned on me – 'he's talking about wanking!' – something I'd thought very little about until then. I can still remember my first orgasm, which had blown the top of my head off, but after that it had become somewhat routine. Then I started to worry. I certainly didn't want to wear glasses! There was only one thing for it: I would restrict myself to one wank a week, preferably at the weekend so I could recover my strength. In the end I settled for two a week with an extra one at holiday time like Christmas, Easter or Bank Holidays.

When I was five I was sent to a small private kindergarten for posh middle-class kids, in Barnes. Nowadays it's called a nursery school. It was run by two Scottish spinster ladies called Wallace. I remember them with great affection; there was no mucking about with bits of plasticine and daubing paint all over the place; we sat upright on benches and used slates and slate pencils ('easy to rub out and *so* economical'). Most of the lessons were by rote:

A blazing hot day on the beach at Littlehampton. Clockwise: Auntie Winnie, Mum, Dad, my stepbrother, Arthur (who made no concession to the heat), and the three of us. In spite of the beautiful weather, the beach was empty – the simple reason being that very few people had cars.

'Now, children – what is the purpose of education?' and we'd chant, 'To-read-and-write-and-speak-correctly.'

And every day we'd start with our tables: 'Three-ones-are-*three*, three-twos-are-*six*, three-threes-are-*nine* . . . ' It had a rhythm that made it easy. I remember once having a very strong argument with a schoolteacher friend of mine. 'No, no, no,' she said, 'the children have got understand *why* three twos are six.'

'Well, I never forgot that three twos are six. I didn't need any explanations.'

The standard of education at that little school, kept by those two lovely Scottish ladies, gave me a wonderful grounding. No wonder the Scots are such clever sods. If one of us put a hand up and said, 'Please, Miss…', they'd say, 'I'm not a waitress in a Lyons tea shop, my *name* is Miss Wallace.'

Then, if we got impatient and put our hands up and said, 'Miss Wallace, Miss Wallace!' they would retort, 'Are you the King, that has to be attended to at once? Kindly await your turn and be quiet!'

Then they were constantly reminding us of the story of Robert the Bruce; he had just been defeated by the English and was lying in his cave feeling pretty miserable. He watched a spider climbing to the roof on a thin silken thread and it fell back. Time and time again this happened, until at last the spider reached the roof. 'And what does this teach us, boys and girls?' And then we'd chant, 'If-at-first-you-don't-succeed, try-and-try-and-try-again!'

'Robert the Bruce was determined to follow this example, so he and his men dug deep pits, which they covered over and, when the English knights charged, they fell into the pits. And that's how we Scots won the Battle of Bannockburn. Mind you, there are some who'd say it wasnae fair, but all's fair in love and war!'

Bless their hearts; I've never forgotten those two dear ladies.

But the day came when I reached eight years old and had to say goodbye to the Miss Wallaces and start at St Paul's Preparatory School, Colet Court. My whole world changed as I was thrust into a strong academic atmosphere, albeit in a very junior way. I used to think, 'Why, oh why, is everyone so serious and cross?' No one ever seemed to smile. Masters wore a cap and gown at all times. They would enter the classroom, cane in hand, hang it on the hook at the side of the desk and call the roll.

Colet Court.

So many of the masters – they were never called 'teachers' – were victims of the First World War. One, a Mr Percival, has stuck in my memory for over sixty years. He wore a large primitive deaf aid, his

40

right arm shook continually and he was subject to bad attacks of coughing caused by poison gas. The boys used to tease him with the words, 'Would you like me to run out and fetch you some cough mixture, sir? Should I get you some water, sir?' There is no one so cruel as twelve-year-old boys. Sometimes he would shout, 'Take cover!' and hurl books at us from behind the desk. The boys then joined in with great gusto.

When I saw John Mortimer's play, *A Voyage Round My Father*, this exact scene was in it. Recently I asked him if he was at Colet Court, but he was at another prep school. All of them must have had a quota of those poor wretches.

Another master, a Mr Downes, was a complete sadist. If we made a mistake he would get us to stand up on the desk and hold us up to ridicule, encouraging the rest of the class to jeer at us – which they did readily. One day we were asked to write an essay in our own words about the Pied Piper of Hamelin. I wrote, 'When the Mayor told the people he would hire a Piper to get rid of the rats, they shouted, "The Mayor's gone barmy!"' This was meat and drink to Mr Downes.

'Listen to this,' he said and read it out to the boys. 'Barmy. Barmy? What's that mean?' At the same time he brought the cane down on the desk, then grabbed me by the ear and pulled me into the centre of the classroom. He circled round me, demanding to know what the word 'barmy' meant. Unfortunately I hadn't spelt it 'barmy', but 'balmy'.

'Well, you said, sir, to write the story in my own words!' I protested.

How long the torture continued I can't remember, but it always ended with 'Bend over' – and down came that cane.

Apart from 'Piss-Pot Perry', which the boys called me, my other nickname was 'Mouse' because I would always blush and couldn't

Clockwise: Charlie showing off his pecs, me, Mum, Mary, and dear little Peggy. You may be wondering why this potty family spent so much time on the beach? Simple really – we only took photos when we were at the seaside.

speak up. The young master who christened me that was an Oxford Rowing Blue who was too young to have been in the war. Another was an amateur boxing champion, a complete thug. His favourite punishment was to make two boys stand back to back, then bend down with their behinds pressed against each other, he would then whack between their two bottoms with his cane.

I never liked the idea of caning. The only thing it does is to fill the victim with hate and I certainly learnt to hate at Colet Court. My mind was constantly filled with thoughts of revenge: I was a boy detective who exposed one of the masters as a Nazi spy; I was a member of the Secret Service – junior branch of course – intent on exposing a Fascist spy ring among the masters. I wasn't far wrong, most of them were appallingly right-wing. In fact, the one who insisted on calling me 'Mouse' volunteered to fight for Franco in the Spanish Civil War; unfortunately he survived. Another plan was to blow up the entire school. I would set the bomb off and run outside, pressing myself against the wall. It would mean, of course, most of the boys would be killed as well as the masters, but it couldn't be helped. In any case, I hated them all.

Every morning, in the Main Hall, there would be a morning service before Assembly – Church of England of course. All the boys who were Jewish, Muslim, Catholic or other religions, filed into the gym during the service. When it was over they would file out again. In charge of them was the PT instructor. No PE in those days (Physical *Education*) but PT (Physical *Training*). An ex-soldier who was only referred to as 'sergeant', his vocabulary was limited to 'sir' or 'move yourselves!' with various inflections. Absolutely immaculate, he wore white slacks, white top and shoes to match, and his red hair was cropped almost to the bone.

As the last notes of the final hymn died away, the door of the gym would swing open and, encouraged by the sergeant with the words 'Come on, boys, move yourselves!', out would file the other religions. One thing you could say about Colet Court, there was never a hint of racism; all races were welcome, Jewish, Hindu, Sikh, Muslim, there was no prejudice…provided, of course, your father was a maharaja, wealthy Jewish businessman, African king, prince, or Chinese warlord. Apart from the fees, these wealthy parents were inclined to make very generous donations, so any hints of anti-Semitism, colour prejudice, or any other racial prejudice were nipped in the bud with a sound thrashing. The school chaplain constantly reminded us that all men are equal, no matter what race, creed, or colour, as long as they are rich.

Two of my classmates were the sons of Haile Selassie, the Emperor of Abyssinia (or Ethiopia, as it became). They were great fun, but rather given to arrogance, which is understandable considering their dad was the Lion of Judah, or the 'Main Man' as my Rasta friends in Barbados refer to him. I would never admit to them that I'd actually been in the presence, day after day, of two of his progeny. Haile Selassie was then in exile in the UK, Benito Mussolini having pinched his country. Benito was the Fascist dictator in charge of Italy at the time – played in the film, *The Great Dictator* by Jack Oakie, what a funny man. To my mind he stole the picture from the great Chaplin. It was not released in the UK until the war, for fear of upsetting the Axis. It had some great moments, in particular the dance that Chaplin did with a balloon shaped like the world. I thought *The Great Dictator* was unfortunately rather spoiled by a sentimental, maudlin ending. I always think

The main man – the Lion of Judah, Haile Selassie.

43

Chaplin's work was inclined to get a bit too schmaltzy. Having said that, the final scene in *City Lights* never fails to get the old waterworks going (upstairs, not down) so maybe Chaplin was a genius after all.

Anyhow, to get back to Benito Mussolini, having decided that he would follow the example of his friend, Hitler, who was proud of the Third Reich, which he said would last a thousand years, Benito was going to build the Roman Empire Mark II. So he looked around, but all the best seats in Africa had already been booked by the other Empires, British, French, Spanish etc. – the only bit left that had never been colonised was Abyssinia. It had an air force of twelve very old planes, but very few modern weapons of war. However, in spite of this, Benito, using dive-bombers, tanks and poison gas, attacked and, though it took nearly two years, managed to subdue those poor, ragged-arsed tribesmen. Unfortunately for Benito, the Roman Empire Mark II only lasted four or five years; the country was liberated by the British quite early in the war. They were lead by General Wingate, a remarkable man who created the Chindits in Burma later in the war; sadly, he was killed in a plane crash and never lived to see the result of his ideas.

The King of Kings, the Emperor Haile Selassie, returned to Abyssinia in 1942 and ruled for many years. He was not exactly a democrat, more of a despot. There were several attempts to overthrow him and one of them was lead by his eldest son, Crown Prince Asfa Wassan, who was actually below me in the class at Colet Court. Even though he was descended from King Solomon and the Queen of Sheba, he was still pretty thick! Anyhow, he lead a *coup d'état* against his dad, promising the people their freedom, but the Lion of Judah had him arrested and he was going to be shot. At the trial, his dad changed his mind and pleaded for Wassan's life, saying his son had been duped (in fact, as I've already told you, his son was an idiot). His dad quoted his school reports – my name must have been mentioned, because I was at the bottom of the class with him – and thus saved him from being stuck up against a wall, under the African sun, and shot. Being a *stupid boy* has its compensations.

The son of a very famous British champion boxer, Len Harvey, was also in my class and it was decided to hold a boxing tournament in the Main Hall. Most of the boys were eager to see their classmates knocking the stuffing out of each other – they loved it. Our master, who was the amateur boxing champion, the one who liked to hit two boys on the bum at the same time, decided to put on an exhibition bout with the great Len Harvey. After a few rounds of pussyfooting, something went wrong and Len landed a punch on our tormentor. The blood flowed and poor Len Harvey rushed over to console his victim – definitely one of the great moments of my early life: accidental revenge, how sweet!

Another, rather weird-looking, boy in my class was the son of a famous actor, Henry Oscar. He was always bragging about the times he had played a schoolboy in one of his father's films and, needless to say, I hated that boy. Only two masters showed me any understanding or kindness; one was the art master. Art was the one subject I was good at. On reflecting over the years, he was obviously gay. Poor man. If he was, he had to keep well in the closet at a boys' prep school in 1936. The other was a Monsieur Manise, the French master, a charming elderly man, with the front of his black gown covered in food or snuff stains. He liked me because, whenever we read in French, I did an impression of Charles Boyer or Maurice Chevalier. He'd get very excited and shout, '*Extraordinaire*! You must have French blood in you somewhere.'

I'd just shrug my shoulders and say, '*Mais oui*.' I loved that old Frog.

When it comes to speaking languages, it's amazing what you can get away with. Some years ago on holiday in Malta, a charming Italian couple was staying in the hotel with their sweet little girl of about three. One day I threw my hands in the air and, with my best cod Chico Marx accent (Get your-a tutti-a-frutti ice-a-cream!) I exclaimed, '*Bella bambino, molto elegante!*'

That did it. From then on nothing could dissuade them from the illusion that I spoke perfect Italian and they prattled away to me for the rest of the holiday. I just shrugged my shoulders and said, '*Bene, bene.*'

A few years ago I was interviewed by a woman journalist from one of the Sundays. When I told her about the school and the terrible time I had, she was appalled, especially when I said I would rather have gone through the war again (well, 90 per cent of it, that is, leaving out the nasty bits!) than my days at Colet Court – at least in the army I had a rifle to protect myself. She listened, snapped shut her notebook and beat a hasty retreat.

I only found out a few years ago that Nicholas Parsons was at Colet Court at exactly the same time as me and he never stops singing its praises. He remembers the names of all the masters and the wonderful times he had there. In the end I was forced to say, 'Nicholas, is there any *insanity* in your family?'

The secure middle-class world I lived in was, to me, not always as safe as it seemed. To a ten-year-old boy, a constant worrier, there was always a threat out there. It was brought home to me one day, with a vengeance, when I woke up one morning feeling sick and ill. My mother put her hand on my forehead and pronounced the magic words, 'You can't possibly go to school, you're far too ill.'

'Hooray!' I thought. 'A reprieve from that redbrick hell Colet Court. A day in bed reading and being fussed over by my mum.' In spite of feeling rotten it was worth it. Three days later, however, things changed dramatically. I was much worse. Dr Heeks, our family GP, was sent for. He arrived quickly, dressed in black jacket, striped trousers and spats. Of course, he also wore the obligatory watch-chain with his gold Hunter on the end, which he looked at as he felt my pulse, then 'Tut-tutted' as he shook his head (as seen in so many 'our-hero-is-ill' scenes in those good old black-and-white movies). This time, however, he played it very low-key. After snapping his watch shut he rose and said, 'Can I have a moment of your time, Mrs Perry?' They went outside the bedroom door and I heard mutterings. The doctor was saying, 'I'm afraid there is no alternative, Mrs Perry, he must go. Please have the prescription made up at once.'

Go where, I thought? Where was there to go? Well, I couldn't possibly go back to school. My mother came back in shortly afterwards and told me that another doctor would be coming to see me. He arrived later that day: not at all like our own polite GP. As he examined me this one shouted questions and called me 'son', a thing I loathed. Alarm bells began to ring in my head. He made copious notes and was very brusque to my mum; I could see she was almost in tears. I'd never had any dealings with a brusque doctor before, I thought they were all like Doctor Heeks, with his smooth bedside manner, and went riding in Richmond Park on Saturday mornings. Events moved very swiftly after that and I was soon in an ambulance on my way to Mortlake Isolation Hospital. I had the dreaded scarlet fever.

Like diphtheria, it is a disease which, thanks to antibiotics, has largely disappeared. As I was very contagious, the only treatment was to isolate the patient until I got better…or not, as the case might be. The isolation hospital itself was a grim Victorian building run by the local authorities. I was quickly put to bed in a single room, then in came the 'Welcome Committee'. To my mind they seemed to fill the whole place, it was almost Dickensian: a very large matron, rather like Hattie Jacques in the *Carry On* films, stood beside the doctor in charge, who examined me. The matron was starched all over: cuffs, frills, apron, cap, any part of her that stuck out was rigid. She was surrounded by subservient nurses who kept bobbing all the time. One of them set up a sort of lectern with a huge leather-bound tome for the matron's notes, the other held a tray containing an inkwell with a pen. The doctor kept shouting at me, 'Are you deaf, boy? Can't you answer simple questions?'

I was frightened and confused, but I had the solution: I quickly slipped into the film *Hell's Angels*. I was a young World War One air ace – the doctor and his staff faded away, and were replaced by my fellow flyers.

The squadron leader (played by Basil Rathbone) took my hand. 'Well done, old man,' he said. 'You got the Red Baron, he went down in flames, but I'm afraid the doc's got some bad news.'

The doc (played by Nigel Bruce), wearing a white coat over his uniform, pushed his way forward. In his bluff, hearty voice, he told me the bad news: ''Fraid that leg will have to come off, old chap.'

'Can't you save it, doc?'

''Fraid not, old man, it's only hanging on by a thread as it is.'

Basil Rathbone leaned over. 'There's a French chappie here to see you, Jimmy.'

And there he was – Monsieur Manise, the French master from Colet Court. He was covered in gold braid and leaned over me. '*Courage, mon brave*, I award *vous* the Croix de Guerre.'

He kissed me on both cheeks and pinned the medal on my chest.

Unfortunately I was only wearing my pyjamas and it stuck into me. 'Ow!' I shouted and my comrades all disappeared in a flash. It wasn't the pin and the medal sticking into me, it was the doctor's finger. 'Wake up, boy,' he shouted. 'What's the matter with you?'

I just stared at him.

'I'll see him again in three days, matron,' he said and, with those few words, they all trooped out. At first I felt a huge relief that I wasn't going to lose my leg, but this was quickly replaced by a feeling of loneliness and despair; this was the first time I'd ever been away from home on my own.

Over the next five weeks I learnt to adapt to the strange world of an old-fashioned isolation hospital. The only way my parents could visit me was to stand in the open, outside the window of my room and talk to me through the glass. Rain or shine they came to see me and I was spoilt to death with a continuous flow of comics, books and Cadbury's Dairy Milk chocolate. I was constantly reminded by the staff that other children in the hospital, who came from poor families, didn't get any comics and chocs but, when I offered to give the poor kids some of mine, they reminded me that everything was covered in my germs, but it would be all right for the *staff* to have some of the chocolates because they were immune to the infection. Even at the age of ten I couldn't quite work this out, but I gave them the Cadbury's Dairy Milk.

Incidentally, what a great choccy! I've been a fan of it all my life. It's best kept in the fridge – but don't let it get *too* cold – then break off a chunk, not a neat square, a big chunk, pop it in your mouth…hmmm, hmmm, hmmm – ecstasy! Not quite as good as sex, but why not have sex after the choccy? Two for the price of one!

At last the time came for me to go home, where I was rapturously received by the family and, as it was a Saturday night, I was allowed, as a special treat, to stay up late and listen to *In Town Tonight* on the wireless. During the programme the announcer said, 'And now, ladies and gentlemen, we are taking you over to Elstree Studios for an interview with the famous American actor, Mr Douglas Fairbanks, who is in England to make *The Private Life of Don Juan*.' Then I heard his voice: 'It's just great to be here in little old England, folks.'

Ah, I was *safe* in my warm middle-class home, away from those creatures who staffed the Mortlake Isolation Hospital. Safe. Able to slip into my dream world with no one to stop me. But the whole thing taught me one very valuable lesson and I've never forgotten it: *do not take things for granted*. When you're doing well, be on your guard, you never know when something's going to come round the corner and hit you right up the backside.

A few months ago *The Private Life of Don Juan* was on TV; it was dated, according to the details in the *Radio Times*, 1933. It had Arthur Lowe's great friend in it – Bernard Shine.

With hindsight, I realise that the poor 'creatures' that staffed the isolation hospital were only unpleasant because they were on pitiful wages and worked to death; the harsh attitude from the top down reflected on them and those under them. One word out of place and they could be sacked on the spot. The young ward maid, who cleaned my room, asked me if I would speak to my parents about giving her a job. She said she would work for two shillings a week less than our present maid, just so that she could live in a warm comfortable home instead of the hospital. 'What a good idea!' I thought. 'We could have two maids!' The next day, when I shouted this to my mum and dad through the window they did not take to it too kindly, especially when I told them I'd sort of promised her the job. My father rolled his eyes to heaven and his lips formed the words, 'Stupid boy!'

What terrible times they were, when a young girl of seventeen had to ask a boy of ten to use his influence to get her a job.

Despite the social unrest of the so-called Roaring Twenties, the Perry family was riding high, the 'upper classes' were still buying antiques and there were a lot of people about with money. But after the 1929 Wall Street Crash the 'Slump' spread slowly to Britain. Within two to three years things were terrible, nobody wanted to buy antiques; in fact nobody wanted to buy

Let the good times roll. Dad and Mum in their new standard car – it actually had crocodile-skin seats! This was 1928, and the following year saw the Wall Street Crash.

anything. I often heard my father saying, 'What *are* we going to do, Dolly?' My dear mother was always optimistic and reassured him that things would be all right. But how? Shops were closing; thousands of businesses were going bankrupt. I was too young to realise how serious things were. There was still plenty of food on the table and I was still going to Colet Court (worse luck!). Family treats, however, were few and far between.

Then one day, it happened, it was almost a miracle that came out of the blue: one afternoon my father was in the shop with a regular customer, Lady Tollemarche, when the phone bell rang and the voice on the other end was in a panic, could he speak to Lady Tollemarche? It was her butler. She took the receiver and he informed Her Ladyship that the cook had been taken ill and what was going to happen about the food she was going to prepare for the dinner party that evening? Lady Tollemarche flew into a panic: some very important business associates of her husband were due – it was then three o'clock and dinner was at eight – where could she get a cook at that time of day? When the frantic butler on the other end had finished and hung up, my dad calmed Her Ladyship down, picked up the phone and spoke to my mum. After a short while, he hung up and said, 'Don't worry, Lady Tollemarche, my wife will cook for your dinner party tonight.'

And that was that. My mum went to the house, took instant charge of the kitchen staff and prepared a magnificent meal for eight persons. The dinner party was a great success and, a few days later, a cheque arrived for five pounds – five pounds, when the average wage was four pounds a week! In her letter of thanks Lady Tollemarche asked Mum if she would consider giving her cookery lessons. And so, once a week, she was driven down to Nassau Road and that was the start of it all.

At that time very few people thought anything about cooking; there was no TV, of course, and the standard of cookery in the average British home was not high. My mother, although a wonderful natural cook, had had no formal training, but then, neither had anybody else. The bookcase was full of cookery books. Cooking was her passion. Lady Tollemarche's visits were the start of the 'Barnes School of Cookery'.

Mum placed an advert in *The Lady*, which read as follows:

> Lady Chef will accept a limited number of pupils for private cookery lessons in her own personal kitchen.

Amazingly it took off. Society ladies would come down to Nassau Road, Barnes, and, while their chauffeur-driven cars waited outside, they would be shown into the drawing room by Minnie the maid, dressed in her best uniform with highly starched cuffs. My mother would then make her entrance attired in a smart white, highly starched overall with a badge on the pocket. On it were the letters 'B.S.C.' (Barnes School of Cookery) and the whole effect was crowned by an also highly starched half-sized chef's hat. Then my mother would politely interview them as if she were doing them a favour and she'd mention, in an offhand way, that the fee was one guinea per lesson (in present day money, £1.05, but in those days a fortune). This certainly rocked them back on their heels but they'd look round the room at the magnificent antiques (that no one wanted to buy) and write out the cheque on the spot.

This has taught me one lesson in life: if a show is expensive and difficult to get into, everyone wants a seat, but if it's nothing special and anyone can buy tickets, you just can't give them away.

Mrs Perry's private lessons in 'her own personal kitchen' became the 'in thing' in Café Society; she even got a mention in *The Tatler*.

One of her great wheezes was her pastry lessons (pastry played such an important part in cookery at that time). Some time before the pupil arrived she would make up a piece of pastry and place it on a marble slab in the dark depths of the larder; then, when the lesson had got under way and the pupil had made her own pastry, my mum would say, 'Now we put it on a marble slab in the dark for half an hour.' Which she did. When the time was up, Mum would take the pastry *she'd* made out of the larder and they'd cook it. Result? The pupil was delighted. Not quite a con trick because Mum had literally hundreds of letters of thanks over the next five years, several of which said her cookery lessons had saved their marriage.

One day one of her pupils asked her if she would make a special cake for her father-in-law, an old retired general, and, if she was willing, he would come down and see her personally. A few days later he arrived in a chauffeur-driven Rolls and was shown into the drawing room by Minnie. Mum made her usual entrance and, after a quick introduction, he started, 'Got to be quite frank with you, ma'am, I'm passionately fond of cake but can never get the right sort. Tried Fortnum's. Tried Harrods. They just can't get the damn thing right. Now, what I want is this – a rich dark fruit cake with no raisins, plenty of chopped brazil nuts…' and so he went on. Mum made careful notes as he warmed to his subject: 'Now, the marzipan, ma'am, one inch thick on the top, no more than one inch, no less, no icing. Does your marzipan shrink, ma'am? Can't abide shrinking marzipan.' Mum assured him it didn't, providing he kept it in an airtight tin. He left and, three days later, returned to collect his cake. Once again he was shown into the drawing room and Mum presented him with the cake. He asked for a slice, which she gave him with a glass of sherry. That did it! He was over the moon.

'At last, at last, a cake that's right! Haven't tasted one like that since thirty years ago – the Chinese cook at Raffles Hotel in Singapore made it for me. Mind you, took him years to get it right, and then he up and died! So now, ma'am,' he said. 'I want you to make me a cake like this every two weeks. Congratulations. Never thought I'd live to see the day, eh, what?'

And that was the family story of the General's Cake.

Living opposite us in Nassau Road, Barnes was a famous American comedian, Fred Duprez. Fred was a big star in England during the 1930s. He wrote a play called *My Wife's Family* which, many years later, I quite often appeared in. Fred was on the radio a lot, and starred in variety theatres and British films. His stock-in-trade act was something that is now taboo – wife and mother-in-law jokes: 'My wife's so fat, when she got on a Speak-Your-Weight machine, it said, "One at a time, please." She's got so many chins, her face looks as if it's on top of a pile of pancakes. I took my mother-in-law to the waxworks; the attendant said, "Would you mind keeping the lady on the move, sir, we're stocktaking."' Golden, golden material. I used it for so many years.

When we were having Sunday lunch, which was in the front room, looking directly across the road, Fred would invariably return from playing golf. He drove a smart white Jaguar coupé and dressed in large plus-fours with check, multicoloured stockings. The whole effect was topped off with a huge cigar, which he never seemed to light, sticking out of the corner of his mouth. My father's comment was always the same. 'Just look at that low comedian,' he'd say, putting down his knife and fork in disgust. 'No taste whatsoever. I bet the entire house is furnished with modern stuff from Maples.'

But I worshipped Fred and one day, when I saw his white Jag outside, I plucked up courage and knocked on his door. Fred opened it wearing an amazing dressing gown covered in gold dragons. Taking his unlit cigar from his mouth and pulling a bit of leaf off his lower lip, he machine-gunned me with, 'You're the kid from across the street, hey, what's the matter? Have your mom and dad left home? Or is the house on fire? Or have you come to sell me insurance?' He rattled gags at me until finally I managed to blurt out, 'Please, sir, how can I become a comedian?' Then he started all over again: 'Lemme tell you about show business, son…' Then he did a fifteen-minute spot, gave me half a crown and pushed me out of the house. I learned my first lesson about comics that day: never talk to them about anybody else but themselves.

Fred had a daughter, June, who went to school with my sister. She was a very beautiful girl, with dark looks and

'Darling June' in The Four Feathers*, with John Clements as Harry Faversham. Mum was always convinced that her Mary was much better looking than June!*

almond eyes; sometimes she would come and have tea with us and, after she'd left, my mother would dismiss her beauty with, 'Huh! Looks like a hula-hula girl!' (What a hula-hula girl was, or where my mother might have seen one, I could never make out.) 'My Mary is much better looking.' And she'd bang on, 'A beautiful English Rose, not foreign like *her*.'

Dear Mum had only just got over a rather unfortunate incident with the Barnes Dancing School that Mary went to. They had presented their annual show at the Richmond Theatre and at one point a lot of the girls rushed on stage dressed as clowns with Mary in the middle. Mary's face was covered in a very heavy traditional clown make-up – impossible to recognise her. Driving home in the car, Mum kept on, 'I'm taking her away from that dancing school. How dare they cover my beautiful daughter's face with all that grotesque make-up! They're only jealous of her because she's the prettiest one of the lot.'

Much later, in 1938, Alexander Korda made a brilliant film, which has obsessed and haunted me for the whole of my life. I must have seen it dozens of times, know every frame. It stars Ralph Richardson, John Clements, C. Aubrey Smith, John Laurie and it was, of course, *The Four Feathers*, and whom did they cast in the female lead? June Duprez. Little June, from across the way, had become a film star. A couple of years later she starred in *The Thief of Baghdad*, but the war broke out and they had to finish it in America. In 1944 she played opposite Cary Grant in *None But the Lonely Heart*, a very unusual film for him. Cary played Ernie Mott, a cockney drifter – the first and last time he played a down-at-heel loser. The public stayed away in droves. The film was dark and moody; the setting was Hollywood's idea of the East End of London, with plenty of fog and lines such as 'Cor blimey, guv'nor, you're a toff!'

With reservations, the critics, on the whole, liked it, but Cary was bitterly disappointed; the whole thing had been his idea in the first place, returning to his cockney roots, but audiences wanted the suave, sophisticated Grant. The strange thing was he was nominated for an Oscar for his performance, but was pipped to the post by Bing Crosby in *Going My Way*.

Poor June Duprez. Although quite beautiful she had a simpering voice and always seemed on the verge of tears. My dear old mum thought she was awful, not a patch on her lovely daughter.

'But Mary's not an actress, Mum,' I kept saying.

'No, but if she was, she'd be much better than June Duprez!'

So, let me tell you about the antique business.

The House of Perry, as I jokingly call it, has been connected with antiques for well over a hundred years. Dad was one of the founder members of the British Antique Dealers Association and apart from his shop, my brother Charles later had his own shop, his son Christopher has a shop and, long before

Dad's shop in South Kensington. So many members of our family were in the antiques business, but show business was the only business for me.

that, my step-brother Eddy, his sister and goodness knows who else all had antique shops. I was the only one who never went into the antique business; after all, I was going to be a star, wasn't I? Show business was the only business for me. Now, the one topic of conversation round the family table was always antiques. When we were kids we were bored stiff as it droned on, even worse when boring old Uncle Tom came to Sunday lunch, because he told us all about *his* shop (to remind you – the tatty one at the bottom of Watford High Street). In vain I would try to bring the conversation round to films, to radio programmes, or whatever else, but I was quickly smothered. In an almost subliminal way, by listening to all this dull stuff, I learnt quite a lot about antiques.

My dad would say, 'I went to see a bow-front Queen Anne chest of drawers. Thought it was right (pro talk for 'genuine'). One of the drawers had been badly repaired, found two small screws in it – what does that tell you?' (Blank look from me.) 'Screws were not invented in Queen Anne's time; that repair must have been done well over a hundred years later.'

Today I enjoy antiques very much and, in a sort of instinctive way, can usually tell if a piece is 'right' or not.

Most Saturdays Mum would drive Dad and me down to Brighton to look in the antique shops. There were dozens of them, as there are today, and as Dad knew all the dealers they would put things on one side for him. I've always loved Brighton, with its smell of beer, fish and chips and, of course, the wonderful ozone of the sea. On the

For some years Dad worked for the great Charles Davies in Bond Street. Just imagine what that chair would be worth today!

journey down I would sit in the back of the car with, perhaps, one of my favourite adventure books by G.A. Henty: *Stirring Tales of the British Empire*, yarns like *With Buller to Natal* (the Boer War), *Frontier Days* (the North-West Frontier of India) – ridiculous! Only ten or so years later I would actually be standing on the Khyber Pass looking at those grim mountains where, for 200 years, the British fought the Pathans and Afridis…but more about all that later.

One Saturday, Mum and I were parked outside a particular antique shop waiting for my dad, both getting hungry for our obligatory fish and chips. 'Oh, dear,' Mum said, 'your father's got talking.' She always used to say to him before he went into the shop,

'If they've got nothing, come out; don't get talking.' He'd nod, and take no notice – something I'm afraid I've inherited from him. Never phone me up if you're in a hurry, I do go on a bit: new shows, new films, scandal, gossip, will add quite a bit to your phone bill. Always ask me to ring you back. Anyhow, as we were getting more and more impatient for our fish and chips, two women passed the antique shop and looked in, 'These antique dealers are all crooks, you know,' said one, pointing to my dad. 'Look at that old Jew poking about in there.'

The antique business is so strange. After a lifetime of being loosely connected with it, I've never stopped puzzling how they can make a living. If you take a bus in London down the Pimlico Road, Fulham Road, King's Road, you will pass about a hundred antique shops. No one seems to go in; no one seems to come out; are they a front for something sinister? It seems to me the only people antique dealers sell to are each other.

When I was twelve, I was playing with a toy pistol and cut the index finger on my right hand. Within a short time it started to swell up; it was the dreaded septicaemia, or blood poisoning, as it was more generally known in those days. I became seriously ill and languished in bed for weeks. This was the 1930s and there were no antibiotics – you either recovered naturally or you died. I had several operations on my hand, which were done at home under somewhat primitive conditions. I ran a constantly high temperature. I remember waking up in the middle of the night to find my dear mother beside me, praying, 'Oh, God, please don't let my little boy die.'

I've never forgotten those words The effect on me was very traumatic; I couldn't quite understand, I was mystified. I didn't for one moment think I was dying, but then children never do. I could have lost my hand but I slowly started to pull round and ended up with just the loss of my finger. Just a finger? Having a finger missing has coloured my whole life, I've been so self-conscious about it. I remember my mother saying, 'Well, there's one thing – they won't have you for a soldier.' How wrong she was – they had me all right, I just used the second finger to fire the rifle.

'How can you become an actor with a finger missing?' was the question asked not only by myself, but many other people with their tactlessness. Eventually I managed to work out a technique but this was only on the stage. When it came to film work I always shied away from going to see casting directors. Even working in the theatre I lived in fear and dread that a director would ask me to do something that would expose my hand.

Reading this today, a lot of people will say, 'Fancy making such a fuss over a finger.' No problem if you're a bank manager, or most other professions. Today it doesn't bother me at all, but to a young actor, when I first started out, it was a huge hurdle. Then, actors were expected to be perfect. It amazes me how insensitive some people are; when I shake hands they sometimes look down at my hand, some even keep hold and examine it, which, even today, gives me a cold feeling down my spine.

When I was working at Butlin's I used to organise the Fancy Dress Competition and there was a young girl with a big red mark, which covered half her face. She turned up for the parade dressed in a costume made of newspapers and she'd covered her face in red make-up, which completely blotted out the mark. She had a note on the front of her costume with the words 'All Read'. She told me she did the same costume every holiday, 'You see, dressing like this sort of sets me free,' was her comment.

Once a week, in the Perry house, it was 'Hoover Day' – impossible to imagine how a big household in the 1930s was run without machines, but it was. No fridge – in the summer milk was constantly going off and the bottles were kept in large earthenware jars – not that it helped much, I hated those little bits of milk floating on top of my tea. No washing machines, Monday was 'wash day' when Minnie and the daily woman carried out a vast wash by hand – sheets, shirts, socks, everything – and by the time they'd finished at least two clothes lines were full. There was always washing being hung up or taken in. If you refer to the photo of me when small, you will notice some washing hanging in the background, out of sight of the neighbours, of course – in the winter, with no leaves on the trees, it was a constant battle to conceal it.

On Hoover Day a man arrived dressed in bowler hat, dark suit and bicycle clips. Behind his bike was a sort of home-made trailer with several vacuum-cleaning machines. He'd arrive about nine and leave a Hoover or a Goblin and the daily woman, supervised by Minnie, would spring into action and start to vacuum every bit of carpet in sight as it was so absurdly expensive (a shilling an hour). There was not a moment to lose. The noise was thunderous; it almost used to shake the house. After three hours the man would return, collect his three shillings, his machine and depart.

I used to worry a lot. 'No one will see the washing will they, Mummy?'

There were so many wonderful variety theatres within a stone's throw of Hammersmith: the Chiswick Empire, the Shepherd's Bush Empire, the Hammersmith Palace (not to be confused with the famous dance hall, the Hammersmith Palais!). My dad loved variety and occasionally he'd take me with him. 'I love a good turn,' he used

Give my regards to Hammersmith Broadway. This was a magical place, with five theatres and six cinemas within a stone's throw. The huge illuminated sign advertising Sandeman's Port used to flash into the window of a Lyon's tea shop where I would have a meal with Mum and Dad before a visit to the theatre. It is a wonderful memory, and one which has sustained me during some of the black times in life.

to say. Strangely enough, many years later, John Betjeman said exactly the same thing on a television programme.

I have a love/hate relationship with comedians; many of them can be a pain in the backside, but how can I knock them – after all, I was going to be one. Most stand-up comedians are so insecure and who can blame them? To be on stage facing an audience alone, you live or die every time you go out there, with no one to help you.

To me, going to a variety theatre – or any other kind of theatre, for that matter – was magic. We'd go on a number 9 bus from Barnes and, as we came over Hammersmith Bridge and saw the lights of the Broadway in the distance, my blood would start to race. We'd have a meal at Lyons, which always included chips, and then on to the theatre. The shows were generally twice nightly, 6.30 and 8.15; we always went to the second house. This was because my mum could never rely on dad coming home from his shop on time. As you entered the theatre you were greeted with a wonderful smell; a mixture of orange peel, cigarettes smoke and size (that's the stuff they put in scene paint to stop it flaking) and the whole thing was mixed with the odour of Jeyes Fluid, a disinfectant with which they used to spray the theatre, to keep down 'the germs'! The band would file into the orchestra pit and play the overture.

At the end of the show, in order to get the audience out as quickly as possible, they would then play very fast. Once when we sat in the front row I jumped up and looked down into the pit, and found that the members of the band were only wearing half a dinner suit – a black jacket with a bow tie – and their trousers were all sorts of odd colours, the bottom of the pit was full of empty beer bottles and the conductor was wearing bedroom slippers! He hissed at me, out of the corner of his mouth, 'Piss off, son!'

When we got outside I complained about all of this to my mum. She said, rather sharply, 'You shouldn't interfere in things that don't concern you, dear.'

One day, when my dear Auntie Madge was staying with us, it was decided that we would go for a night out at the Hammersmith Palace. As I've said, my dad loved turns, but there's always the exception to the rule, and the one turn he didn't like was Max Miller. He considered him a filthy, low, vulgar, crude comedian. In spite of this, Dad was overruled and off we all went. In those days Max was at the height of his fame; to my mind he was the greatest stand-up comedian ever. He made his entrance. A tall, good-looking man with flashing eyes, dressed in a suit of plus-fours made of flowered curtain material, the whole thing topped off with a white homburg hat. He had a special ramp built out across the orchestra pit so that he could get close to the audience. Then he'd launch into his act.

The great Max Miller. There will never be another like him.

'I went home the other night – now, there *is* a funny thing – a man was standing in the hall stark naked. – How's your memory, lady?? – I said to the wife, "What's going on?" She said, "Keep your hair on, Miller, he's a nudist come in to use the phone!"'

That did it. My Auntie Madge started laughing in a high-pitched tone and Max picked her out. He addressed most of his act to her, much to the embarrassment of my father who went very hot round the collar. On the way home he went into a deep sulk. (Sometimes dear old Dad could be a miserable old thing!) 'Filthy brute!' he said. 'That's the last time we go and see him.'

I thought Maxy was wonderful. In present-day parlance he was my role model – but I kept it all to myself.

During my fifty-odd years in show business I've met many comics, some good, some bad, some just awful. The first time I met Tommy Trinder I was overwhelmed, he was my hero. 'I remember seeing you at the London Palladium, Tommy,' I said, 'on my final night of embarkation leave. I went with my mum and dad, the next day I returned to my unit and went overseas, I didn't see them again for nearly three years.' By now I was really wallowing in the schmaltz. 'I'll always remember that last night together, Tommy.' I droned on. He just nodded. 'The show was called *Happy and Glorious*, you were great in it.'

Tommy, who had, up to then, shown very little interest, suddenly exploded: '*Happy and Glorious*? The trouble I had in that show!' and then he went on about his billing, his dressing room, the musical director, and all the problems. 'Mind you, Jim, I got rave reviews and we did sell-out business.'

My sob story had gone right over his head, the only thing he'd been really interested in was the fact that I'd seen him in *Happy and Glorious*.

In 1982 I became a member of the Grand Order of Water Rats and, in the past twenty years, my life has been full of comedians. I love being a member of the Order – a lot of people don't really understand what we do. The Order was founded in 1889 and, quite simply, we help members of our profession, men and women, who are down on their luck, and we do so without any fuss or bother. For many years now I've had the privilege to be the Curator of the Order and, in 1989, Bob Hope became a member; it was a beautifully hot summer's day and a few of us were waiting outside our headquarters in Gray's Inn Road for him to arrive. When the limo drew up and the great man got out, although he was well into his eighties, here he was, in the flesh, a living legend. When the Initiation Ceremony was over we all went on to the Hilton Hotel in Park Lane for lunch.

Now, at that time there was a comedian named Ken Roberts in the Order; Ken has been dead now for quite a few years but I have never forgotten him. He was a charming man, always cheerful and happy, he was what we call a 'Second Spot Comic' – in other words, although he was a good entertainer, and appeared in summer shows, revues and pantomimes, he was never a star – but Ken was quite content with his lot, he just loved being in show business and enjoyed life. One of Ken's 'stock bits' was to go down on one knee and sing, in a high voice, 'The Hills Are Alive with the Sound of Music!' – everyone laughed but I must confess, I just didn't get it. The Bob Hope lunch was going well when suddenly, in the middle of the sweet course (raspberry crumble), Ken Roberts crossed round to the front of Bob's table, went down on one knee and sang, 'The Hills Are Alive with the Sound of Music!'

There was a deadly silence in the room, followed by a long pause…then the great Bob Hope stood up, raised his spoon and solemnly pronounced, 'That guy's *funny*!' It was like a blessing from the Pope. The whole room exploded and Ken got to his feet with a look of rapture on his face. He turned round and, in a voice, which was almost inaudible, mouthed the words, 'Bob Hope said I was funny!'

Bud and Ches. As a boy they were my heroes. I never thought that one day I would know them.

The story of how I wrote the signature tune to *Dad's Army* has been told many times, so I won't go into it too deeply, but there was one side that has never been mentioned, and that was Chesney Allen's connection. A lot of people think that 'Who Do You Think You Are Kidding, Mr Hitler?' was an old wartime song and it always seems to come as a shock to them when I tell them that, in fact, I wrote it. It was never mentioned in the titles of the show. The afternoon I spent in the old Riverside Studios at Hammersmith was the most wonderful moment of my whole career. To think that my great music hall hero, Bud Flanagan, was recording a song that I had written. Sadly, that afternoon was the first and last time I met him. What no one knows is that I originally wrote the song for Flanagan *and* Allen. I slightly knew Chesney Allen, so I phoned him and asked if he'd like to record the number with Bud. 'Oh no,' he said, 'I've been ill, I'm far too weak. I just can't do it, Jim, sorry.'

So Bud recorded it on his own and that was the last thing he did; a few months later he died. That was in 1968, but Chesney Allen just went on and on. In 1975, when we were doing the stage show of *Dad's Army* at the Shaftesbury Theatre in London, one of the big numbers in the show was the entire cast, dressed as Flanagan and Allen, singing 'Home Town'. Some bright spark suggested that, just for the opening night, Ches would come on stage and join Arthur Lowe, who was playing Bud Flanagan in the number. So I phoned Ches and asked him if he'd like to do it.

'Oh no, I couldn't possibly, Jim,' he protested, 'I'm quite ill.'

'But you told me that seven years ago, Ches, when I asked you to record "Mr Hitler" with Bud!'

Eventually he was persuaded to appear just for the one night. But then came the problem: we'd arranged for Ches to sit in the front row of the stalls so he could easily get on to the stage.

'I couldn't do that,' he said. 'Sit in the front row during the entire show? Everyone will recognise me. It will take the attention away from the stage!' (Bear in mind that dear Ches was now in his mid-eighties and bore very little resemblance to the Chesney Allen that everyone remembered!) Ches sat all through the show and no one knew who he was. Came the Flanagan and Allen number, Ches went up the steps and joined Arthur Lowe. There was a short silence, and then the whole audience burst into applause and rose to its feet and cheered.

Roy Hudd told me that, when he played Bud Flanagan in *Underneath the Arches* in 1982 at the Prince of Wales Theatre, Ches used to make the odd appearance. He'd just phone and say he was coming up to London on the train and would it be okay if he went on? He always brought the house down. Chesney Allen died that same year at the age of 88.

In 1979 I was asked to do a show for BBC2 called *The Old Boy Network* – awful title, but then I'm a martyr to bad titles. The format of the show was simple; we just recorded the comedian's life story on stage at various theatres up and down the country. He, or she, stood in front of a live audience and, with the aid of a bit of archive film and photos, told their story. Now, it must be remembered that most of them were well in their seventies or eighties. I wrote the show and put it together, and, during the recording, crouched in the orchestra pit and held up 'Idiot Boards' (large white cards with the cues

The Old Boy Network. *Clockwise: Fred Emeny (sitting), John Laurie, Arthur Askey, me, Tommy Trinder, Don Sayer (the producer), Sandy Powell, Jack Warner.*

Front row, from left to right: Richard Murdoch, Doris Hare, Leslie Sarony, Nat Jackley. Back row: Chesney Allen, Percy Edwards, me, Don Sayer.

written on them in huge letters). If any of them forgot – which they did quite frequently – they'd shout down into the pit, 'Hold the card up, Jim!' or 'Can I borrow your glasses, Missus – Jim's not written it big enough!' When our director, Don Sayer, told them that viewers were not suppose to know that I was in the pit, they'd make the usual comic's reply: 'Just trying to get a laugh, guv'nor!'

Recording the shows was a nightmare, but, when they were put together they worked very well. Among the comics – Arthur Askey, Tommy Trinder, Sandy Powell, Jack Warner, etc. – I also persuaded Chesney Allen to make one. He was now eighty-six and, far from being reluctant, had got the bit between his teeth. On the night of the recording everything seemed to be going well, when suddenly Ches just stopped and stared blankly at the audience, he was completely lost. Crouched in the pit, my blood went cold and over the intercom, I heard Don Sayer say, 'He's gone! Do something, Jim!'

I climbed up on the stage and stood beside Ches. His eyes were blank. I nodded to the pianist and said, 'Let's do some of your old numbers, Ches.' I took him by the arm and lead him into 'Underneath the Arches'. His eyes lit up and he said, 'Nice to be back in front of an audience together again, eh, Bud?'

After that he was fine and we finished recording the show. The strange thing was that, when it was put together, it was one of the best we did.

So many people ask me who was the funniest comedian I ever saw. Without doubt, it wasn't a man, it was Hilda Baker, an amazingly funny artiste, but she fell out with nearly everyone and had a very sad life. In the end there were only six people at her funeral.

Apart from the variety theatres, there was also in Hammersmith the small Lyric Theatre and, of course, the grand King's Theatre, which presented tours of straight plays and a pantomime each year. The King's was very near Colet Court. One day, passing, I noticed that the great actor-manager, Matheson Lang, was to present a season from his repertoire, which included *The Chinese Bungalow*, *Othello* and *The Wandering Jew*. Now, for a shilling you could get a place right up in the gallery, but there were two problems: how to get hold of a shilling and how to get off school? By walking to school every day instead of taking the bus, and wheedling the odd copper out of my mum, I managed to overcome the financial problem. I would never have been allowed out in the evening to go to the theatre, so the only time I could go was, of course, the matinée. I took a chance: to use a favourite term of that time, I 'cut' school, and found myself sitting on the hard wooden benches up in the gallery, looking down on that magic world.

The great Matheson Lang. I just wanted to cross the footlights and join his world.

I had managed to see the first two shows in the repertoire without being rumbled, but this afternoon was my favourite, *The Wandering Jew*. The play was based on a rather creaky old book by Temple Thurston, which today I find extraordinary. Mattheus, the Jew – played, of course, by the great Matheson Lang – is an adulterer living with another man's wife. She's dying and in desperation he rushes out and intercepts Christ, who is on his way to Calvary, and asks him to cure her. Christ replies, 'Return the woman to her husband and she will be healed.' At this, Mattheus spits on him. Christ responds, 'You will not come to me until I come for you!' Meaning the Jew is condemned to wander the face of the earth for ever.

And so we follow him through the first Crusade, the thirteenth century in Palermo and so on. Many times he tries to kill himself, but the blade of the dagger always breaks. Finally, in the Middle Ages in Spain, he's brought before the Inquisition. Either he renounces his faith – which, of course, he refuses to do – or faces death. The last scene is the burning; Mattheus is tied to the stake and the fire is lit. As the flames leap up there is a clap of thunder and rain starts to pour down. Then comes the wonderful speech from Mattheus: 'O, Lord, let me die! Please, Lord, let me come to you!' The rain stops and the flames roar up…the curtain comes slowly down. The audience applauded and the cast took their bows, then the great man, Matheson Lang, took a solo bow, tossing his head back – as was the custom in those days – and bowing deep.

I hardly clapped, I was cast in a spell and I just sat there. The theatre emptied, being a matinée there were only a few people in the gallery and, as they quickly made for the exit, I trailed behind, not wanting to leave my magic place. I looked down, the house tabs were being slowly raised, and a man was sweeping the stage.

I revel in corn.

Then I heard a voice say, 'Haven't you got a home to go to, son?' It was one of the attendants. I slowly walked down the stone stairs, with my footsteps making a sharp echo, and reached the street still enchanted by the great man's final words: 'O, Lord, let me die! Please, Lord, let me come to you!'

Suddenly, I felt a searing pain in my right ear – it was the assistant headmaster. 'Where have you been, Perry?' he hissed.

'I was just going home from school, like you, sir.'

'Liar! Liar!' he said, giving my ear an extra twist. 'School finished over an hour ago. I saw you coming out of the theatre – you've been playing truant! See me in my office in the morning!' and, giving my poor ear a final twist, the

71

short-arsed little runt disappeared into the crowd. Strangely enough, I wasn't frightened, I was blazing with anger – how *dare* he intrude into my dream world like that? One day I'd get away from people like him, and be behind the footlights where I'd be safe with those wonderful people I'd just left!

The next morning I presented myself at his study for the obligatory six strokes of the cane. I waited outside with three other boys. They were pale and frightened, but I was determined that no trace of fear would appear on my face. I was Ronald Colman going up the steps to the guillotine in *A Tale of Two Cities*. I heard my name shouted from inside. There was no question of 'Piss-Pot Perry' now as one of the boys whispered, 'Good luck, Perry.'

'You, Perry, are a liar and a cheat!'

I went in. The assistant headmaster just pointed to the chair and I bent over it. It's difficult to describe the searing pain of the first stroke and you think you cannot possibly stand another five, but not a sound came out of me, though my whole being wanted to scream and plead for him to stop. When it was over I could hardly straighten up for a searing, red-hot pain that racked me from head to toe. At twelve I was quite tall, almost the same height as the master, and above everything I wanted to put my hands round his throat and squeeze and squeeze but, not being allowed to do that, I just stared at him. I stared him in the face with what was commonly referred to as 'dumb insolence'.

His twisted red face growled, 'You, Perry, are a liar and a cheat. I'm only allowed to give you six strokes, but if I had my way I'd thrash you until you couldn't stand!' His eyes blazed with hatred, which was only matched with the hate in mine. 'I'm giving you a note to take to your parents, and don't entertain any thoughts of destroying it. I've said I want an acknowledgement.'

I came out of the office and looked at the waiting boys. One of them whispered, 'You're jolly brave, Perry!'

Trying to straighten up, I replied, 'Do not despair, comrades, one day we shall all be free from this tyranny!' Because of the pain, I waddled off down the corridor, looking as if I'd done it in my trousers.

In the 1980s my agent, Richard Stone, rang me up, and asked if I had any scripts that could be adapted as a feature film. He'd been to Los Angeles and met an American producer who desperately wanted ideas and who, for some reason, was obsessed with British writers.

I said, 'I'll think it over, Richard.' And a few days later, it hit me – what about *The Wandering Jew*? I dug out Temple Thurston's original book and my first reaction was, 'What a load of melodramatic, sentimental old rubbish!' I rang Richard back and told him no.

He said, 'It's a bit late now, he'll be in London next week and I've arranged a meet. Don't let me down.'

'Oh, why not?' I thought. 'Film people will buy any old rubbish!'

A few days later I arrived at the Savoy to meet Mr Goldfish. It occurred to me he might be Jewish (!) and, therefore, sympathetic to the theme. I was shown up to his suite and ushered into the presence of the great man. There were brief introductions – he seemed totally uninterested.

'OK, shoot!' he said, 'Whatcha got?' (I love that. So many people, during my career, have said to me, 'Whatcha got?')

Then I went for it; I gave it everything! 'Mattheus is living in Jerusalem with a woman who is not his wife and she's dying. He hears that Jesus is on his way to Calvary, runs out into the street and there he is, carrying his cross. 'Heal my woman!' Mattheus shouts. 'Return her to her husband,' Jesus says, 'and all will be well.' Mattheus is furious and spits at Christ…'

'Hold it,' interrupts Mr Goldfish. 'Hold it right there. Jesus Christ! Are you crazy? You can't have Jesus Christ in it – make him some other guy!'

And so it went on; he didn't like the adultery or the spitting, and in any case Jesus Christ was *out*.

'Make him God – roaring down, "You are cursed to roam the world for ever, until you apologise!" God's easy to do, you just have a great big booming voice.'

'But, Mr Goldfish…'

'Mel! Call me Mel!'

'But, Mel, if he's not going to spit on Jesus, why should God get so angry?'

'How do I know?' said Mel. 'You're the writer, you fix it!'

And so, within five minutes, the Great Producer had completely destroyed the whole reason of the story. (A thing that I came across many times with film producers.)

'What's the title, Jimmy?' asked Mel.

'It's called *The Wandering Jew.*'

'Jew? Jew? You gotta be out of your mind! Jew in the title? I can't handle that – you'll have to make him a Gentile!'

Needless to say, I left very quickly after that and, as I came out of the hotel, I passed the Savoy Theatre. The show that was playing there was *Noises Off*!

There was a film made of *The Wandering Jew* in the 1930s, starring Conrad Veidt, and Frances L. Sullivan. I remember seeing it with my mum and dad, and I'd loved it. Now so many old films have gone for ever as they were made on nitrate stock, which disintegrates, but about ten years ago I got hold of a video with about half of the film that had survived. After looking at it and thinking very carefully, I realised that Mel Goldfish had been quite right in wanting to change it.

Going to the zoo was a wonderful treat – I loved it. In those days the 'big cats' – the lions and tigers – were in large cages, either asleep or constantly pacing up and down. Very few people understood animal welfare back then. What did they know, or care, about animals when they were busy trying to get enough to eat just for themselves? After the big cats, another favourite of mine was the reptile house. Entering the darkened cavern and looking at the brightly lit tanks, a shiver of excitement would run through me – supposing, just supposing, one of the smaller snakes had, unbeknown to anybody, escaped and was lurking in the gloom waiting to encircle my legs? So many of the snakes were asleep; in fact, they didn't look real. Then the thrill of looking down into the crocodile enclosure – they never moved either and their backs were covered in pennies and halfpennies that were thrown down to try to get some sort of reaction. Visiting the reptile house about fifty years later, nothing seemed to have changed. The huge crocodile was still there – was it the same one? Then I realised that its back was not covered in copper coins, but silver ones, so things have improved, no matter what people say!

On one beautifully sunny day we all piled into the car and made for Regent's Park. My mother had prepared the usual cold lamb sandwiches with Military Pickle (it was a great pickle – whatever happened to it?) and, of course, rock cakes – what we didn't eat, we could always feed to the elephants. No notices reading 'Do Not Feed the Elephants' then and besides, Mum's rock cakes could not possibly harm anybody; she used only the purest ingredients. She used to say, 'I always use butter. The day I have to put margarine into my cakes, it'll be time for me to hang up my apron.'

We wended our way to Regent's Park doing a steady 25 miles per hour. As we passed the Albert Memorial I said, 'It's still there, Dad, they haven't pulled it down yet.'

Dad retorted with, 'Hold your tongue.'

I crouched in the bottom of the car and gripped my tongue with my fingers, making a face; sister Mary giggled and brother Charlie looked, disdainfully, out of the window.

Dad's flapping hand reached out over the back of the seat in the hope of connecting with one of us. He gave up with the words, 'Can't you keep the children quiet, Dolly?'

Suddenly, out of the park gates, a runaway horse with a young woman on its back reared up and threw her into the road. All the traffic stopped. She lay motionless. People rushed forward, a policeman stopped a taxi and they picked her up. I can still see her now; dressed in black riding habit with a bowler hat, she looked like a broken doll; there was no mark on her. They put her in the taxi and the policeman stood on the running board furiously blowing his whistle as it sped off to hospital. We all knew she was dead but no one said a word. It was the first time I'd seen a dead person – sadly, it was by no means the last.

So the 1930s dragged on; then one day, at the breakfast table, my father lowered the *Daily Telegraph* and said, 'Do you know, Dolly, I think things are beginning to look up.'

Business was certainly improving all round and my mum could finally close down the Barnes School of Cookery, and would no longer have to give cookery lessons to spoilt society women and organise Lady Tollemarsh's dinner parties. I hated my dear mother having to put up with them patronising her. Whenever Lady Tollemarsh spoke in French so that Mum would not be able to understand their comments, my blood boiled with resentment. I later learnt it was of course another English 'class' thing but, although it was started by the English, it soon became international – in Russia the upper classes always spoke in French and so did all of the other aristocracies all over the world – *'pas devant les domestiques'* (not in front of the servants). How the French aristocracy managed I'll never know because surely their servants, being French, would be able to understand every word they said? Anyway, most of their aristocrats had had their heads cut off, and jolly well serve them right – forcing people to eat all that cake! The good times started to roll again – Dad gave up his shop in Exhibition Road, Kensington and moved up-market to Brompton Road, just opposite Harrods (which, by the way, my grandfather remembered when it started as a modest grocers shop in 1849).

I was not having a good time. In despair my parents took me away from school and sent me – wait for it – horror upon horror, to Clark's College to learn shorthand, typing and, the final degradation, *bookkeeping*! I will gloss over those nasty dark rooms full of typewriters and huge blackboards. The people who taught us were a bit different from Colet Court and St Paul's – they didn't wear caps and gowns, just dreary suits with black covers over their sleeves so that they'd not get the cuffs shiny. Of course there were no canes, all of us were about fourteen – dropouts to a man (or woman) – so any sort of violence on their part would bring swift retaliation. I struggled with Pitman's Shorthand for a few months, then gave it up. The smattering I had acquired I found jolly useful for copying comedian's jokes from the radio, but apart from that I'd had enough of Clark's College.

Then I discovered Edgar Rice Burroughs. It so happened that it was a wonderful summer and as Clark's College was at Putney, which is only a twenty-minute walk from Barnes, I stopped short of going right on to Putney and stayed on Barnes Common reading and reading and reading. I read all the 'Tarzan' books, followed by his science fiction ones. My mother used to pack me up a sandwich lunch and the days just flew by. I'd leave at 8.30 in the morning and return at 4. If it rained, I sat in the shelter by the Bowling Green with all the old men while they reminisced about the Boer War. When Clark's College sent letters enquiring as to my whereabouts, I'd quickly intercept and destroy them. I then read, on the back cover of one of the books, that Edgar Rice Burroughs, like me, had come from a middle-class family and had dropped out of school. In his youth he'd tried many jobs but nothing seemed to work. He finally ended up running an agency selling pencil sharpeners. Sitting alone in a dingy office day after day, he started writing. His first book was called *Princess of Mars*. Then he hit upon the idea for Tarzan.

In his books, he referred to tigers in Africa and the fact that Tarzan was an English lord. He'd never been to Africa *or* England, but it didn't matter to his readers. Millions read his books and he became the most famous writer of popular fiction in the English language. 'Not bad for an educational dropout!' I thought, 'Maybe I should become a writer? I'm sure I could think up as good a character as Tarzan.' It didn't matter if you were rotten at school, if you had ideas, that was all you needed to be a writer. But I quickly dismissed this idea because – after all – I was going to be a famous film star or a great comedian, wasn't I? So all my ideas piled up in my brain for nearly thirty years until I set them free.

An interesting fact about the first Tarzan film is that the screenplay was written by the King of Musical Comedy, Ivor Novello. Ivor was working in Hollywood under contract to MGM as a screenwriter. One day the head of the studio, Irving Thalberg, called him into his office and said, 'I've got something big for you, Ivor, it's about an English Lord who's brought up in the jungle by the apes, and I think it'll be a cinch! This guy, Edgar Rice Burroughs, has created a character called Tarzan. The books are selling by the million – it'll make a great picture.'

'But I don't know anything about Africa or apes!' Ivor protested.

'So what?' said Irving. 'How many people watching the movie will have been brought up in Africa by apes? Listen: you're English, you know all about earls and dukes and lords…'

'No I'm not, I'm Welsh!' said Ivor, starting to get annoyed. But Irving had got the bit between his teeth.

'You mean like that guy, D. W. Griffiths? He told me he was related to Welsh kings!'

'There haven't been any Welsh kings for a thousand years!' spluttered Ivor.

'I knew he was full of bullshit! Said he invented the movies. If he did, my cock's a bloater!' He pushed a book across the desk. 'There it is, *Tarzan the Ape Man* – get going.'

Ivor took it and left the office vowing to leave Hollywood as soon as his contract was up.

The resulting film, *Tarzan the Apeman*, starring the Olympic swimmer Johnny Weissmuller, Maureen O'Sullivan and, of course, C. Aubrey Smith, was a huge success. Watching it today, even though it's nearly seventy years old, and despite its cardboard sets and dear Johnny wrestling with a rubber crocodile, it still stands up. Whenever I see it on TV I'm always struck by one of the credits; 'Screenplay by Ivor Novello' – it looks so oddly out of place.

There is a strange postscript to this story: Ivor was returning across the United States by train to catch the boat home from New York when a porter told him about a fellow British writer who was on the same train.

'Oh? Ask him if he'd like to have a drink with me,' said Ivor.

'That's gonna be kinda difficult, boss,' replied the porter. 'He's in the box car in a coffin.' It was in fact the body of Edgar Wallace, who had died after finishing another popular classic, *King Kong*.

Of course the day eventually came when my mother discovered my absence from Clark's College. 'If your father found out you'd been sitting on Barnes Common reading all the summer, the shock would kill him.' So, as usual, she hushed it up.

Eventually a Family Council of War was held – 'What to do with the youngest son who had no desire whatsoever to go to school any more?' Finally, my father came up with the answer: 'The boy will have to go out to work.'

Waring and Gillow – furnishers to the best people.

At that time the school-leaving age was fourteen. All sorts of alternatives were suggested: an apprenticeship as a picture restorer? a cabinet maker? – no, that would involve getting my hands dirty and my mother rather drew the line at that. I became an apprentice at Messrs Waring & Gillow, a large, upmarket furniture shop in Oxford Street. I was to do a year in the carpet department, another year in soft furnishing and my final year in furniture. The salary was one pound a week. The carpet department at Waring & Gillow's was built in the shape of a mosque and took up two floors – magnificent carpets hung everywhere. The chief buyer had a little office that looked like an

Eastern tent, and there were lots of hidey-holes behind the mountains of carpets where one could sit and daydream. If an important customer arrived they were met downstairs by the floorwalker, a Mr Aldrich, resplendent in a tailcoat with a red carnation in his buttonhole. The customer would then be whisked up into the carpet mosque in the lift – operated by a page-boy in a pillbox hat – and the following routine, which never varied, would take place: Mr Aldrich would usher the customer into the mosque and – rather stating the obvious – boom, 'Forward, Mr Simpson! [He was the chief buyer, who would emerge from his eastern tent rubbing his hands.] This lady/gentleman desires to purchase some carpet.'

'Walk this way, sir/madam,' Mr Simpson would oil and, with an inclination of his head, boom, 'Thank you, Mr Aldrich.'

Who'd boom back, 'Thank you, Mr Simpson.'

Mr Aldrich would then get back into the lift – a sort of iron cage – and as it disappeared from sight you could just catch a glimpse of him clipping the cheeky page-boy round the head.

Having seated the customer, Mr Simpson would call, 'Forward, Mr Perry and Mr [whoever happened to be my partner-in-crime on that particular day].' We would emerge from the valley of carpets, remove our jackets and don white warehouse coats, take up our position each side of a pile and turn the carpets back one at a time for the customer to view. Quite often we would turn over fifty or sixty different carpets and, eventually, the customer would say, 'I'm sorry, I just can't see any of these in my house.'

Mr Simpson would then escort the customer to the lift and, as soon as it had disappeared, turn back, his face contorted with rage. 'Five thousand bloody carpets,' he'd hiss, 'and she can't see any of 'em in her bloody house! Bloody upper-class bastards, I hate 'em!' Then he'd make his way back to his office, kicking at the piles of carpets. 'Bastard carpets! Bastard upper-classes! I hate 'em! Their turn'll come one day!' Then he'd look back at us and shout, 'Get out of this place, or you'll end up like me!'

Every day I went up to Waring & Gillow, spent the day in that vast cavern of carpets and returned to Barnes. One day I wrote a sort of desperate note: 'Get me out of this hell. I can't stand it any longer. I shall die of carpet-itis. Someone save me, please. I'm going to end it all.' I suppose I was joking, or perhaps giving a cry for help for all the thousands of men and women who spent their lives in pointless, badly paid jobs, with little or no future. As I was writing I heard the cry, 'Forward Mr Perry!' and so I dropped the note and forgot all about it.

A day or so later Mr Simpson called me into his office; he had my note in his hand. 'Did you write this?' he said. I nodded. 'Why? Why? Why?' he persisted.

'I don't know,' I said. 'It was just a sort of joke.'

'Just a sort of joke?' he shouted. 'What's the matter with you? You! Writing suicide notes for *fun*? I've been watching you, I think you're barmy – playing the fool and larkin' about when you should be workin'. Well, one day, you'll get a big shock when you find out what life's all about. Take it from me, it's a *bastard*!'

PART TWO

THE HOME FRONT

And so, in the words of a proper novelist, 'the war clouds gathered'. A very large air raid shelter was built on Barnes Common, gas masks were issued and every post brought different leaflets — how to cover windows with sticky paper so that if the bombs fell they would not shatter the glass. How to deal with incendiary bombs — have a bucket of sand ready and always keep the bath full of water. How to cope with a gas attack. How to detect someone who might be a fifth columnist. An Anderson shelter was delivered. It was issued by the government (free) and consisted of a corrugated-iron frame, which we sank into the earth about four feet, and piled all the debris on top. It was a good design and could withstand just about anything except a direct hit. Or that's what we were told. We constructed it just outside the French windows, which involved digging up a great chunk of beautiful lawn. Everyone knew a war was coming but thought that somehow in the end, it could be avoided. A couple of years before we had all been constantly fed newsreel shots of bombing raids on cities in the Spanish Civil War and everyone had seen the film *Things to Come*, based on the H.G. Wells novel, starring Raymond Massey, Ralph Richardson and Margaretta Scott. At the start of the film there is a massive air raid on London by hundreds of enemy bombers and army trucks are going through the streets dishing out gas masks to a panic-stricken population. Within a few hours London is flattened. That's how everybody thought war would be, so we braced ourselves for the horror that was to come.

We young lads at Waring & Gillow were marshalled and driven out to Acton to fill hundreds of sandbags that were then stacked against the doors and windows of the huge depository the firm had. The inside of the warehouse was stuffed with vast amounts of furniture and carpets; the whole place would burn like tinder.

In spite of the film *Things to Come*, as regards Civil Defence, the whole country was remarkably well prepared – air raid wardens, heavy rescue, auxiliary fire service, ambulance drivers (driving vehicles converted from delivery vans or taxis), special constables, nurses, and many thousands of brave men and women fought for years under the most appalling conditions and saved London, Coventry, Liverpool and all the other cities that were heavily blitzed. After all this time why is it that there are so few monuments to them? Why can't we have some statues of Civil Defence heroes? Why not start by removing the one of General Haig from Whitehall, the man whose stupidity caused the deaths of so many hundreds of thousands of brave young men, and replacing it with a monument to members of the Civil Defence?

September the third 1939 was a normal Sunday breakfast in the Perry household. My father was reading the *Sunday Express*, the headline read: GERMANY INVADES POLAND – 'The Prime Minister will speak on the radio at 11 p.m.' My father's comment to all this was, 'It's rubbish! Of course there isn't going to be a war.' He never saw ahead very well.

When the fateful broadcast came my sister and I were alone in the house. My dad had gone on the bus to see one of his customers in Knightsbridge and my mother had gone off in hot pursuit in the car to bring him back. I can't remember where everybody else was, but no sooner had Neville Chamberlain uttered those immortal words, 'I have to tell you now that no such undertaking has been received, and consequently this country is at war with Germany' than the air raid sirens started. It was a false alarm but we were not to know that. There we were, two young teenagers, standing with our gas masks ready, waiting to be obliterated. It was the start of six years in which all of our lives changed beyond anything anyone could possibly have imagined.

The original 1931 films of Frankenstein *and* Dracula. *There have been so many versions over the past seventy years, but I do believe that Boris and Bela were the best.*

After the initial shock of the first air raid warning nothing happened. Cinemas and theatres closed, and there was a very strict blackout; everyone carried their gas masks everywhere. Shops started selling fancy gas mask cases for ladies. Everything was rationed: food, petrol, shoes, socks – the only thing that was off-ration was sex and, believe me, in that strict blackout there was plenty of it going on!

The weeks rolled into months – September, October, November, December, still nothing happened, no sign of the terrible air raids that were going to destroy all our cities. Theatres and cinemas opened up again, including my beloved Ranelagh, which, for some unknown reason, started showing very old films – don't forget that in 1939 the talkies had only been going for just over ten years. One week they showed a great double bill; two films, both made in 1931, *Frankenstein* and *Dracula*. They were the originals and of course in black and white, which was ideally suited for them. In *Frankenstein* the monster was played by Boris Karloff (whose real name was Bill Pratt), a very English actor who went to Hollywood early in his career. In *Dracula* the main character was played by Bela Lugosi – who can ever forget his opening lines – 'Count Tracular et your serveece!'?

Christmas 1939 was very cold with lots of snow and we were constantly being reminded on the newsreels of British Tommies and their French comrades manning the impregnable Maginot Line. Lots of shots of our brave boys giving the thumbs-up sign and, of course, George Formby and Tommy Trinder entertaining them. Little did I realise, as a boy of fifteen watching Tommy, that one day I would get to know and work with him.

The new year, 1940, started and there were still no air raids. People thought that perhaps the Germans would give in without a fight. More newsreels of British and French troops playing football and, as the weather improved, teaching the French soldiers how to play cricket. And all the time the French – as is their wont – boasting that the Maginot Line was impregnable. Then bang – it happened: on a beautiful spring day the Germans invaded the Low Countries; they didn't bother to attack the Maginot Line, they just went round the side. 'A typical shabby Nazi trick!' as Captain Mainwaring remarks in *Dad's Army*.

The air raids started and we went down to the Anderson shelter night after night. The only trouble was that it was cold and damp and had an earth floor. Every evening we crept down with our blankets and hot-water bottles, but after a week my mother decided that something had to be done and we moved back into the house under the stairs – which was not quite as safe but much more comfortable. Night after night the raids continued. People were saying, 'Why don't they do something?'

Then the heavens opened up as hundreds of anti-aircraft guns blazed away – not a single German plane was hit, but we felt better – something was being done. I was caught in an air raid in Oxford Street; a stick of bombs fell on John Lewis and Peter Robinson just behind me as I ran into Argyle Street. Next to the Palladium was a shelter down the area steps of a picture shop and I went down them two at a time. As far as I can remember I never felt a shred of fear, in fact, I was cracking jokes. Jokes! But then, what do boys of sixteen

know about death? But as the war went on I soon found out.

In the early 1990s I lived in Westminster almost next door to Jim Prior, who had been the Minister for Northern Ireland. A small bomb went off at the entrance to his flat. Now, a week or two before I had taken delivery of a new white BMW. It was parked in the street and I went out to see if it was damaged. Instantly several police officers surrounded me: 'Get back! Get back!'

'But I want to see if my car's all right,' I protested.

'Get inside at once!' they shouted. 'Don't you realise there could be other explosive devices about?'

I smiled.

'It's not funny!' they said. 'You have no idea what could happen. Get back inside!'

I didn't argue.

More recently I was in a taxi in Park Lane, suddenly the traffic came to an abrupt halt. A demented creature in a blue duffle coat stood right in front of our taxi in the middle of the road with his hand held up. He was glaring at us with his face contorted with rage. 'Don't move!' he shouted. 'This is an armed situation.' He tapped the bulge in his coat.

I couldn't help laughing.

He crossed over and hissed, 'It's not funny! You have no idea what's going on.'

He must have been Special Branch – I never found out what it was all about.

But what a change in attitudes! 'An explosive situation', 'an armed situation'. Well, my generation went through hundreds of those and they weren't 'situations', they were war. If we hadn't managed a few jokes, we would not have come through.

My mother, with her usual foresight, had, before the Blitz started, moved all the stock from my father's shop in Brompton Road down to Barnes, and now the house was ridiculously over-furnished. Not only that, most of the pieces still had their price tickets on. As the raids got worse she persuaded my Uncle Tom, who was then well in his eighties, to give up his shop at 237 High Street, Watford and she would take it over and we would all move in. I don't know how she managed it but she arranged for a large van to carry all the contents of our house as well as the large stock of antiques from the shop in Brompton Road. I think it took three trips.

At one time Uncle Tom's shop had been a magnificent Jacobean house, the downstairs being converted into two show rooms with oak panelling. The rest of the house consisted of a huge, old kitchen, and seven other rooms in which to live. Moving to Watford was only meant to be a temporary measure but, just a few days after we left, a bomb blew out all the windows of 38 Nassau Road making it uninhabitable. We were therefore trapped in Watford – a ghastly thought!

But I mustn't be too unfair to dear old Watford. It's played a big part in my life; it was there I did my service in the Home Guard and made my first appearance on any stage. In a strange way the two were connected to each other.

Suddenly my life had taken on a new meaning. I'd never have to return to Waring & Gillow and those rotten carpets! Then I heard that a bomb had fallen on Colet Court and, though it had been three years since I had left, my heart sang! The school had finally been blown up, just as I had planned all those years ago. That night, sleeping under the stairs with the rest of the family, during one of the lulls in the bombing I dreamt that I was in the playground when two ambulance men brought out of the ruins of the school a body on a stretcher. It was covered in a blanket but a lifeless arm was dangling over the side – it belonged to Mr Downes; the arm that had caned me so frequently – my plans for revenge had come true! I woke up in a cold sweat – horrified – and quickly said a silent prayer. I found out later that in fact Colet Court had suffered only superficial damage and no one had been killed.

The day before we left Barnes I went to say goodbye to the old Ranelagh Cinema. Like all other cinemas during the Blitz it was closed, and the posters outside were torn and flapping in the wind. So many wonderful memories of films I'd seen there, sitting impatiently waiting for the lights to go down, and then the thrill of excitement when the Certificate was shown on the screen – 'This is to certify that the following film has been passed for public exhibition' – it made my blood race. The Ranelagh Cinema had an amazing history. It was opened as the 'Byfield Hall' in 1906. Then, in 1925, it became the 'Barnes Theatre', at that time presenting rather highbrow plays, including a season of Chekhov, directed by the famous Russian director, Komisarjevsky, and featured many promising young actors including John Gielgud and Robert Newton. Charles Laughton made his professional debut there in *The Government Inspector* with a very young Claude Raines. In the end the theatre closed (it was a bit too 'arty-farty' for local tastes) and opened as a cinema in the late Twenties. In the 1960s it became a recording studio and many international artistes, such as the Rolling Stones and Tony Bennett, left their mark there. It's still a recording studio today, owned by Richard Branson's Virgin Group.

So many people ask me, 'What was the difference between the *real* Home Guard and *Dad's Army*?'

Strangely, not a lot. *Dad's Army* was based firmly on fact and the

The Watford Home Guard Commando Platoon. Rough, tough and armed to the teeth we were ready for anything Hitler could dish out. I am bottom right.

I took my helmet off for this photos, thinking it looked more heroic.

truth of the situation. In common with most other hit television situation comedies, like *Steptoe and Son*, *Till Death Us Do Part*, *Yes, Minister* and quite a few others, its foundations were real. Since the huge success of *Dad's Army* there have been many television documentaries about not only the Home Guard but the situation at the time – for instance, the Blitz. A number of programmes have been made recently trying to denigrate the spirit of the British people during the war – they have usually been by writers with no first-hand knowledge of the situation. Of course it wasn't a bed of roses; there were people in the Blitz who robbed dead bodies, looted ruined houses, took every advantage of the dreadful situation; there was a march in Liverpool with a crowd carrying banners which read, 'Stop the War', all of which was censored by the newspapers. But 90 per cent of the British public stood firm and came through. We were fighting for our very existence, fighting for our very lives.

I did not join the Home Guard until it had been formed about nine months, for the simple reason that my dear mum had pleaded with me not to go. What would happen if I were actually shot? Certainly the character of Private Pike was based on me, with my mother continuously fussing – she didn't go so far as making me wear a scarf, but she came pretty near.

By the time I signed on as a member of the Watford Company of the Home Guard of the Beds & Herts Regiment, it was fairly well armed with American Ross rifles that had been used by US troops in the First World War. They were very accurate and the magazine held five rounds. Thanks to the generosity of President Roosevelt, two boatloads of P14 and P17 rifles were sent to Britain; the only trouble was they were covered with thick grease, which was a hell of a job to remove. I'll never forget the day I was issued with my rifle – after all the muck had been removed it was mine, to be kept with me at all times – but no ammunition; we young boys were not allowed to take it home. If the church bells rang as a signal that the invasion had started, we had to jump on our bikes and pedal like hell to the headquarters to get our fifty rounds.

I shall never forget the lecture our commanding officer gave us about the responsibility of carrying arms. He was a major – unfortunately I can't remember his name – who was the manager of a Watford building society and was short and round, rather like Captain Mainwaring. He was always fussing and inspecting things. His famous expression to us, after we'd been on night patrol, was, 'You boys had better stop mucking about! I'm in no mood for jokes at six o'clock in the morning!' He'd served in France in the First World War but, I suspect, with a much more humble rank. He was delighted to be in charge and was always buying extra bits for his uniform – a dress forage cap, smart shirt and tie, and a brown leather Sam-Browne belt – all these items were, of course, for officers only. When he was told he couldn't wear the Sam-Browne belt with battledress, he was heartbroken: it was for wearing with a dress uniform and, unfortunately, he didn't have one. In spite of all this, if it had come to the push, he'd have been as brave as anyone else. 'Your rifle should be as vital to you as a third limb; keep it with you always, clean it and cherish it.' he told us. 'You could even take it to bed with you!' This was the only joke he ever made; sadly he had absolutely no sense of humour.

In common with most other young men at the time I was obsessed with guns, so I proudly took my gleaming rifle home with me for the first time.

When Mum opened the front door she nearly had a fit. 'You're not bringing that thing in the house!' she shouted.

'Sorry, Mum, it must be by my side at all times – there is a war on,

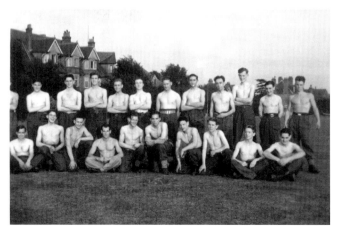

The Home Guard Commando Platoon, stripped for action and fighting fit. I'm second from the left on the bottom row.

you know' (a very irritating phrase that was used so much at that time).

When I first joined the Home Guard there were all age groups and they came from every walk of life. The comradeship was amazing. I know there were many jokes about the Home Guard using pubs as their headquarters, but who could blame them for getting together after a parade? Apart from their Home Guard duties, everyone worked during the day and they came from all professions – the plain battledress was a great leveller. Young boys like myself flocked to join – you must understand that there was no such thing as a 'teenager' then. You went straight from being a boy to a man and, from the age of fifteen, you dressed like a man, went into pubs and drank beer. You also smoked. I started smoking a pipe at the age of fifteen and no one said a word, everyone took it for granted – my father smoked a pipe and my mother cigarettes.

At the start of the Home Guard its ranks were filled with men in their sixties and seventies, veterans of the First World War and, in quite a lot of cases, the Boer War, but as time went by these older veterans were gradually weeded out. This included the original of Lance-Corporal Jones. I can't remember his real name but he wasn't a butcher, he worked as a French polisher for Goddard's, a furniture shop in Watford High Street. Yes, he had actually fought in the battle of Omdurman in 1898. He was an ex-regular soldier in the rifle brigade and had also served on the North-West Frontier in India. When I knew him he was in his late sixties and constantly regaled us with old soldiers' tales, including 'the Battle of Omdurman', which went something like this:

'As the dawn came up we took up our positions between two huge rocks. Now, in the Sudan, the dawn comes up very quickly, one minute it's dark, the next minute it's light, so you've gotta be on lookout, you've gotta be sharpish. We was armed with Martini-Henry rifles, when I say Martini I don't mean that posh drink that tarts are fond of imbibing in the saloon bar with a cherry in, but a very efficient rifle. The magazine held ten rounds and they were the latest invention, they'd only just been issued to the British Army. After a while the sun rose higher and higher 'til it was like a great burning ball in the sky.'

I would say, 'Did they issue you with sunglasses?'

'Sunglasses, lad?' he'd shout. 'Sunglasses? Certainly not. We were soldiers, not nancy-boys. We only had one water bottle, so we just used to take a little swallow a time. Then we heard the bugle and in the distance was a huge cloud of dust caused by thousands of dervishes. Nearer an' nearer they came, until we got the order to open fire. They kept coming on again and we kept firing until the bodies were piled ten-foot high. By now our rifles were well-nigh red 'ot, so we got the order, "Piss on your rifles, boys" but we couldn't as we hadn't had anything to drink, we hadn't got any wee-wee, so we had to pour the water from our bottles on the barrels. By the end of the day the Mahdi's army stopped charging and we'd won. Our tongues were all swolled an' black – 'cos, as I say, we hadn't had a drink – but we'd won. And there was General Kitchener, ridin' up and down on his 'orse, shouting, "Well, done, boys!"'

As I'd heard the story of the last public hanging from my dad, so I heard a first-hand account of a battle that took place over a hundred years ago. During the time I was with him the old soldier must have recounted that same story over a dozen times. Was it true? Well, he *was* at the battle of Omdurman because he had the medals to prove it. As regards the rest, he gave me a wonderful foundation for the character of Lance-Corporal Jones.

The real Battle of Omdurman was more of a massacre. As dawn came up on 2 September 1898, General Kitchener sat calmly on his horse, waiting for the dervishes to attack. A cold, ruthless, ambitious man, he had been preparing for a showdown with the Khalifa's forces for two years.

The dervish force numbered nearly 60,000 – the opposing British and Egyptian forces well under half that number – and, with a throb of drums, the dervishes attacked. None of them got nearer than 300 yards from the British lines; the murderous fire of machine guns, magazine rifles and howitzers firing lyddite shells cut them down. Again and again they attacked only to be scythed down. At midday they fled, leaving behind 11,000 dead and 20,000 wounded. Kitchener's losses were 119 dead, or wounded.

The Battle was declared a great victory for civilisation.

The original Corporal Jones's account of the battle was not quite accurate – the British troops did not use Martini-Henry rifles – these were used by the Egyptian troops. Instead, the British used the long Lee-Enfield rifle which, unlike the single-shot Martini-Henry, had a magazine of ten rounds.

The Charge of the 21st Lancers at Omdurman has gone down in history as the last charge of the British Cavalry. Taking part was a young second lieutenant, Winston Churchill. It was one of those historic blunders made by the British Cavalry during their distinguished history; they thought they were facing about 200 dervishes, so they charged, only to find they were up against 3,000. Too late to rein in their excited horses, they plunged on. Out of nearly 350 cavalrymen, 70 were killed or wounded. The heroism of the troopers was amazing, and three of them were awarded the Victoria Cross. One of the things that probably saved young Winston's life was that he had equipped himself with the very latest German automatic pistol that fired twenty rounds (instead of the usual, British Army, six-round revolver), and was therefore able to fight his way through the dervish masses without having to reload.

As Jones said, the dead dervishes were piled up ten feet high. 'They were real battles in them days.'

The film version of the Battle of Omdurman from A.E. Mason's famous adventure yarn, *The Four Feathers*, has been done many times, but the best, without a doubt, is Alexander Korda's 1938 version. He filmed the battle scenes in the Sudan which, at that time, was part of the British Empire, and he used the East Surrey Regiment, who were stationed out there, plus thousands of dervishes, some of whom had actually taken part in the original battle. When they were asked to fall over dead, they complained bitterly that it was most unfair, given they had survived the 'previous production'! Korda's amazing scenes of the charge have been used, time after time, as stock shots in many other films.

The *Dad's Army* version of *The Four Feathers* was done in a much more modest way, with a new title: 'The Two and a Half Feathers'. The plot was quite simple: a new recruit arrives to join the Walmington-on-Sea platoon and recognises Corporal Jones as someone he'd served with at the battle of Omdurman. He spreads a rumour that Jones was a coward and that he'd run away – which, of course, is a lie. Corporal Jones has to clear his name and return the white feathers, so we go back in time to when Jones was a young soldier and tells the story of what really happened. Arthur Lowe played the rough, brutal sergeant, John Le Mesurier the 'Toff' captain, James Beck was the cheerful cockney private, Ian Lavender the other officer, and Bill Pertwee and John Laurie the dervish hordes.

Our Battle of Omdurman was filmed in a sand quarry at King's Lynn.

We filmed our battle of Omdurman in the sand quarry at King's Lynn. It was quite a chilly day and we had to make it look hot. The actors were uncomfortable in the Victorian uniforms and the wind blew sand everywhere – it was not an easy day. We cut in the original film shots of the charge by thousands of dervishes with our brave *Dad's Army* heroes fighting them off. To cap everything, as a dervish, Bill Pertwee had to ride a horse – unfortunately he'd never been on one before. The rifles opened fire and the horse reared up, bolted and, with Bill on its back, disappeared among the sand dunes. It was not a very happy band of actors who filed on to the coach at the end of the day's filming.

When the time came that the older men had to leave the Home Guard – it applied to everyone over sixty – they were full of resentment. Our hero of Omdurman just couldn't believe it. I remember him saying, before he left, 'Don't you worry, lad, if those Jerries invade I'll be back, sharpish!'

Then our CO, the manager of a building society, was asked to stand down due to his age and we had a new one. He was much younger and had served in the International Brigade in the Spanish Civil War; he had no time for 'blimp tactics', as he called regular methods, he was a seasoned guerilla fighter and he hated Fascism. He was an amazing man, lean and very fit. I never found out what his daytime job was, but he lived and breathed the Home Guard. 'Don't take any prisoners, boys,' he'd say, 'shoot the bastards, or they'll get you.'

His name, appropriately enough, was Major Strong – he certainly lived up to it. He had a special revolver holster designed so that it strapped to his thigh. This gave him a 'quick-draw', which he'd demonstrate to us at the end of each parade. He would then wave his revolver in the air and shout, 'Kill Germans!' We would wave our rifles and shout, 'Kill, kill, kill!' and then dismiss.

Our enthusiasm verged on the fanatical. For the first time in my life I'd encountered real leadership.

'There's going to be a few changes after the war,' he'd say. 'We're going to build a fairer society, better – we'll do away with privilege and everyone will get a fair shake.'

He was an amazing man and we would have followed him to the death. An idealist. I wonder what happened to him?

He decided to form all of us teenaged boys into a commando unit and designed a special badge with a large 'C', which we wore on our shoulders. This was inclined to provoke ribald remarks from kids but we didn't care, we loved it and revelled in the special weapons we were issued with – a wire cheese cutter for creeping up behind Nazi sentries and decapitating them, sharpened bicycle chains for close combat, razor-sharp knives and knuckledusters. These were

Arthur was a bit grumpy that day – I didn't like the way he was pointing his rifle at me!

We couldn't afford 60,000 dervishes, so we had to make do with Bill Pertwee and John Laurie instead.

topped off with P17 rifles which we carried everywhere. The sight of us young men swaggering down the street, armed to the teeth, would have sent a modern-day social worker screaming into the bushes.

Our training never stopped and, quite often, took the form of competitions. A favourite was rather like *The Generation Game*. It involved two Lewis guns and two blindfolded contestants who would strip down the machine-guns and reassemble them. They were encouraged by cheers from the rest of the platoon, and by our CO with a stopwatch, shouting, 'Hurry up, the Nazis are coming!'

There was also the wonderful comradeship – booze-ups, dances etc.

Make no mistake, it was our finest hour. To be alive at that time was to experience the British people at their very best and at perhaps the greatest moment of their history. I'm proud to have lived through it.

Dad's Army was born out of desperation. In 1967 I was working, as an actor, with the legendary Joan Littlewood at Theatre Workshop. I'd been slogging away for seventeen years, singing in musicals, doing years of weekly rep, and I'd got precisely nowhere. I'd always earned a living, but lack of money was starting to get me down. I'd played small parts in sitcoms on television, but no one seemed impressed. There was only one answer – to sit down and write a sitcom myself, with a good part in it for me. So day after day on the train backwards and forwards to Stratford East, I racked my brains – then it came to me: the Home Guard! I only remembered it because I'd been in it as a boy. I made notes every day on the train; things like 'Vicar, Frank Williams; Spiv, me'. On the next Sunday, by sheer chance, I saw *Oh, Mr Porter*, the old Will Hay film, on television. 'That's it!' I thought. 'That's the combination – pompous man in charge, old man and young boy.' I started to write. The only writing I'd done up until then had been comedy sketches and bits and pieces. A fellow actor at Stratford East, Frank Coda, lent me an old TV script of *Z-Cars* so I could see how to set it out. At that time I was sharing a dressing room with Nigel Hawthorne, who was slightly younger than me, and had also been struggling for years. Every night, as we were getting ready for the show, I'd bore him with details of the script I was working on.

He was very polite. 'I hope it works for you, Jim,' he said, 'but I can't go on like this much longer. If I don't get a break soon I'm going back to South Africa.' I remember playing scenes with him, night after night, and looking across the stage and thinking, 'This man is a superb actor, why won't anybody take any notice of him? If it comes to that, why won't anybody take any notice of me?!' Five years later we met at a BBC party. I'd not seen him since the Stratford days and he'd just returned from India, where he'd been filming *Gandhi. Dad's Army* was getting 18 million viewers. I smiled at him and said, 'Well, Nige, we made it.'

'Yes, Jim,' he said, with a wry smile. 'We made it.'

I decided to do some research and found the Home Guard had almost been forgotten; the local library had nothing about it so I went to the Imperial War Museum, but all they had was a few training manuals and, strangely enough, a book of Home Guard cartoons. The *Daily Mirror* research library was much better and I spent weeks combing their vast collection of copies of the period. (No computers in 1967.) Gradually I started to build up a picture of the Home Guard, and my memories came flooding back. Day after day I went through the old, discoloured pages and became totally immersed in the period. So many people in the Sixties hated to be reminded of the war – my mother, who had died five years before, used to get very upset whenever it was mentioned. When I finished

Wilson: 'Would you mind awfully falling in please?'

Walker: 'I can get it for you.'

the first script I sat on it for quite a few weeks, wondering how to get it into the right hands. When Theatre Workshop closed for the summer, my agent at that time, who 'just happened' to be a lady named Anne Callender who 'just happened' to be David Croft's wife, sent me for a part in a situation comedy series that David was doing at that time. During rehearsals I showed him my script. He took an instant liking to it and we decided to work on it together. So that's how our partnership began – it was to last over twenty-six years.

So David and I started to work out the characters and locations of *Dad's Army*. We decided that the fictitious town, Walmington-on-Sea, should be a small one just across the Channel from France – right in the Front Line. Looking at the map, we found it could be any one of several along the coast from Eastbourne. We settled that our leading character, Mainwaring, should be a bank manager and after that all the others fell into place. Being shopkeepers, most of them had to come into the bank regularly so they would be constantly meeting each other.

Over the years there has been endless discussion as to why John Le Mesurier played the sergeant instead of the officer. This was based on the fact that so many people think of the cliché that a sergeant should be 'common' and an officer 'posh' – this was certainly not true in the Home Guard. Rank had nothing to do with class or background – in the Watford platoon one of my fellow privates was a doctor. A few years later, when I was a sergeant in India, an officer said to me, 'Why do you speak with a public school accent?'

'Well, I went to one,' was my reply.

'But you're only a sergeant!' he said. 'I don't understand. Why aren't you an officer?'

I won't go on. To try to explain the British class attitude is hopeless.

I wrote the part of Walker, the spiv, for myself, but that was quickly nipped in the bud: Michael Mills and David were dead against it. At first I deeply resented it, but looking back now, perhaps they were right; it would have been a constant source of irritation to the rest of

Godfrey: 'May I be excused, please?'

Frazer: 'We're doomed, doomed!'

Left: Pike – 'You wait 'til I tell my mum!'

Below: Vicar – 'May I remind you, Captain Mainwaring, that the church hall is mine?'

Right: Warden – 'Put that light out!'

Below: Corporal Jones – 'They don't like it up 'em!'

Left: Verger – 'His Reverence won't like this.'

the cast, rather like a cuckoo in the nest. As it was, James Beck played him brilliantly. Private Godfrey was purely David's creation and, as played by Arnold Ridley, he was delightful, his gentleness making such a wonderful contrast to Fraser's naked aggression. When we first thought up the part of Fraser he was simply 'A Scotsman'. Now, every southern English town has several Scots living in it, who are usually doctors, lawyers or chemists, and they form themselves into Caledonian Societies and do very well. What was it Dr Johnson said? 'The best sight a Scotsman ever sees is the English Border as he crosses it.' When Michael Mills told us he'd cast John Laurie in the part I couldn't believe it! I remembered all those wonderful characters he'd played in British films ever since I was a kid – the eagle face, with the mad, rolling eyes. Writing for him was a joy. I can still hear his voice saying, 'Can you no' hear the wind? It's the moans of sailors drowned at sea. Don't forget to lock your door tonight, and ignore any strange noises you may hear,' followed by, 'Doomed! Doomed!' And of course, the pale-faced, soppy-looking boy, beautifully played by Ian Lavender, the aggressive Warden Hodges (Bill Pertwee), the Vicar (Frank Williams – the very first name I wrote in my book on the train to Stratford East), his sidekick, the Verger (Edward Sinclair) and last, but not least, Clive Dunn, who brought Lance-Corporal Jones to life. The strange thing is, it's only in the last few years, watching the repeats, that I realise how funny he was. What a strange array of actors. David Croft and I had put in all these peculiar ingredients, mixed them carefully, and when the pudding came out of the oven it was beautifully cooked – in other words, it was perfect.

On the very first day of filming, April Fool's Day 1968, it was snowing. Swankpot David turned up in his old Rolls-Royce. Filming was delayed for some hours until the snow cleared, meanwhile the cast were sitting in the Rolls.

'Tell them we're ready for the first shot, Jim,' said David. I walked over to the car, the windows were all misted over, and I pulled open the door. 'Right, chaps,' I called, full of enthusiasm (in fact, bursting with it). 'We're ready to go!' They looked at me as if I'd just uttered some dreadful obscenity.

'Close the door,' said Arthur. 'We'll come when we're ready.'

I went back to David and said, 'David, we've got a right miserable lot of old sods here.'

When we'd finished making the first series of *Dad's Army* a few people at the BBC were very, very apprehensive, so they asked a market research company to carry out some test showings to get people's reactions. There was a separate showing of the first episode for three nights and I went through hell! What David thought I never knew – he's not a man to show his true feelings if he can help it – but he must have been going through hell like me. The market research company arranged for a hundred people per night from a cross-section of the public to view the episode at dear old Broadcasting House. Unfortunately, the person running it was a very attractive young Swedish woman who knew nothing whatsoever about the war.

They played the first episode, 'The Man and the Hour'. When it had finished there was a dead silence – nothing. The glamorous Swede addressed the audience: 'Ladies and gentlemen, I want you to give me your honest opinions as to the merits of the show you have just seen. Be perfectly frank and do not be afraid.'

'Shut up, you silly cow!' I thought, but her beautiful face, topped with golden hair, prattled on. 'Can't she see I'm dying on my arse? This is my lifeblood she's talking about, my soul, my everything, *my big chance*!'

'Now, come along, ladies and gentlemen, speak up,' said the

beautiful blonde. And they did; a large lady, in her middle fifties, proceeded to give it stick. She was what we call in show business a 'Mrs Woman' – let me explain what a 'Mrs Woman' is: usually a comic's delight, she sits in the audience and laughs very loudly and the delighted comic picks on her. (Rather like Max Miller and my Auntie Madge many years before.) The louder she laughs the more the audience follows her example. As she laughs she looks around for the approval of the rest of the audience, she's in her element, she's the centre of attention. Only *this* Mrs Woman wasn't laughing. 'Well, I think it's a rotten show,' she said. 'There's nothing to it. Haven't we had enough of this old wartime rubbish? And that bald-headed old idiot [Arthur] doesn't know his lines!'

David Croft and I cuddling Arthur Lowe, surrounded by the rest of the Dad's Army *cast. We had just won the Writers' Guild award for the Best TV Comedy Script for the third time running.*

The whole audience took up her mood and promptly tore the show to pieces, except for a small man who looked like a train-spotter. 'I think it's wonderful,' he said. 'It's going to be a hit.' I could have kissed him! I can never thank him enough…I wonder if he's still alive?

The three nights dragged on, with the majority of the research audiences hating it. I felt like Bizet after the opening night of *Carmen* when, the critics having torn his show to pieces, distraught, he went away and walked about in the rain, got soaked through, caught pneumonia and died. No one had invented antibiotics then – who knows what great operas he would have composed if they had. Was I going to suffer the same fate? One brief moment of glory and then nothing? Fortunately help was at hand in the shape of David Croft. He made arrangements for the report to come into his office, where he put it to the bottom of the pile in his in-tray and 'forgot' about it. Believe me, David Croft is a very, very clever man; but for him, perhaps *Dad's Army* would never have seen the light of day, not to mention all the shows that followed: *Hi Di Hi!*, *It Ain't Half Hot, Mum*, *You Rang, My Lord?* and, of course, *Are You Being Served?* and *'Allo, 'Allo* (which he wrote with Jeremy Lloyd) – sometimes fate hangs by a very thin thread.

As time went by, Arthur became Captain Mainwaring, and Captain Mainwaring became Arthur.

Before we leave the Home Guard and *Dad's Army*, just a little mention of Arthur Lowe. It's funny that, whenever the conversation gets round to food and cooking, as it seems to all the time nowadays, I always think of Arthur, who just loved his food. Many people have the idea that working in a hit comedy television show is a constant succession of laughs – far from it. We were a tough bunch of old pros and did not spend very much time socialising with each other; we had a job to do and we got on with it. When we were making a new series of *Dad's Army* in the studios, we arrived for rehearsal at ten o'clock, worked all day, left at four and didn't see each other until the next morning. When we went away filming for the exterior scenes, however, it was a different matter. We all stayed at the Bell Hotel, Thetford, and, for about three or four weeks, were forced into each other's company.

When not actually working, Arthur and I had something in common that none of the others had – we'd both done weekly rep. It's a thing that disappeared over thirty years ago. In those days there were dozens and dozens of theatres up and down the country who employed a company of actors who'd put on a different play every week, appearing every night in one play and, during the day, learning and rehearsing a different play for the following week. Now, both Arthur and I had done years of weekly rep and it was slavery, but wonderful experience. It gave actors that *edge*, and you've got to have a bit of an edge in this world. During breaks we'd talk about the hundreds of different parts we'd both played and how we'd tackled them. A very beautiful production assistant, named Kay Johnston, after listening to us rabbiting away, said, 'I don't know what you're talking about, you both live in a dream world!' Yes, we did a bit.

When we were doing the stage version of the show we opened at Billingham in Cleveland and spent several days of very tense rehearsals. I felt I just had to get out of the theatre for a short while and, passing an electrical shop, I saw, in the window, a lamp shaped like a mushroom, and inside was a family of rabbits sitting round a table having tea. On the spur of the moment I bought it and returned to the theatre. I showed it to Arthur. 'Look what I've got,' I said. 'I was so fed up, I felt I wanted to get in there and escape.'

He looked inside and said, 'Yes, I'd like to get in there as well.'

I never shared his enthusiasm for food, which was amazing; when we were filming he'd really tuck in. We'd have a breakfast at the hotel – his usual was the full English: tomato juice with Worcester Sauce, porridge, fried eggs, bacon, sausage, fried bread, mushrooms, toast and marmalade. In contrast John Laurie, having a bowl of porridge liberally sprinkled with salt and little else, would look across at Arthur's table and mutter to me, 'Will you look at that, James. It's gluttony, sheer gluttony. Yon Arthur will kill himself with his teeth.' Sadly, how right he was.

We'd arrive at location at about 8.30, start filming and, at 11.30, take a mid-morning break. This was really for the technicians, who'd probably have been there since 7 a.m.; tea, coffee and sausage or bacon rolls would be served and Arthur would dive in. 'Can't decide whether to have the bacon or sausage,' he'd say, so he'd pop both into a large bun, liberally cover it with mustard, and then bite into the greasy contents with a look of ecstasy.

At one o'clock sharp the cry 'Break for lunch' would come from the PA. As we always seemed to have 'David Croft' weather, as it was nicknamed, it was always glorious. The trestle tables and chairs would be spread out under the pine trees, Arthur would take a seat and his dresser would serve him. Soup, a main course – usually a roast and three veg – cheese – usually Stilton. 'I like the French style,' he used to say, 'having the cheese before the sweet.' Then, of course, a substantial pudding, which he'd wade through.

We'd film the rest of the afternoon until teatime. This was very special with dainty sandwiches and Mr Kipling cakes. Arthur was crazy about them. When a new floor assistant joined us just before we went away, Arthur rang me. He didn't want to know any of the details – what scenes came first and how long we'd be away etc. – he just asked one question,

'Have you told the new boy about the Mr Kipling cakes, James?'

'Yes, Arthur,' I said.

'Well, check again,' he insisted, 'and make sure he informs the caterers that we want plenty of almond slices. We ran out last time, remember? That girl went and got some different ones from a local shop. It was sheer chaos. We do not want any serious slip-ups like that again!'

The filming would usually be no trouble, David worked very fast, and we'd arrive back at the hotel about six. Arthur would disappear for a sleep and a shower, then reappear at the bar at precisely 7.30, immaculately dressed, and order a 'Gin Amazon' – his own invention:

gin, ginger ale and one – not two – slices of cucumber. Then, as he sipped it, the maître d' would bring in a pile of menus and Arthur would carefully peruse them for at least fifteen minutes. Then he'd go through the wine list. When dinner was ready we'd all troop in and it would take at least two hours. Finally he'd finish up in the lounge, sipping Guinness and that was his intake for the day.

Altogether, David and I wrote 80 episodes of *Dad's Army*, and there are still 77 in existence. The three missing ones were in black and white and, in spite of a nationwide search, they have still not come to light. People often wonder where all the plots came from. In truth, a lot of them were totally made up, although some, such as 'The Two and a Half Feathers' were based on real events. Another example of a fact-based episode was 'The Day the Balloon went up'. The idea for this episode came from a cutting in a Scottish newspaper, *The Bulletin*, dated October 1934. In the show, a barrage balloon has broken away from its moorings and comes down on the church hall. Mainwaring and the platoon grab the ropes and take it out into the countryside for safety. Due to an unfortunate incident they all let go of the ropes except for Mainwaring and, as the balloon soars up into the sky, he is desperately hanging on. Then the chase starts. Johnny Spriggs, the stunt man who doubled for Arthur, was filmed hanging from a rope suspended from a helicopter. It was great fun and made a classic episode.

Filming *Dad's Army* for television was a delight; it always worked – which is more than can be said about the making of the feature film! In 1970, with colour television in full swing, film producers were beginning to feel the chill wind of change, cinemas were starting to empty, a lot of them ignored it, others turned very nasty and did all they could to denigrate TV. A young director/producer, Norman Cohen, came to see David and me and asked if we'd like to write a

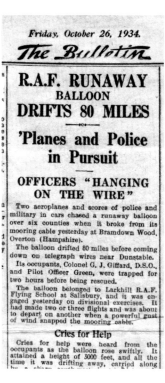

Friday, October 26, 1934.

The Bulletin

R.A.F. RUNAWAY BALLOON DRIFTS 80 MILES

'Planes and Police in Pursuit

OFFICERS "HANGING ON THE WIRE"

Two aeroplanes and scores of police and military in cars chased a runaway balloon over six counties when it broke from its mooring cable yesterday at Bramdown Wood, Overton (Hampshire).

The balloon drifted 80 miles before coming down on telegraph wires near Dunstable.

Its occupants, Colonel G. J. Giffard, D.S.O., and Pilot Officer Green, were trapped for two hours before being rescued.

The balloon belonged to Larkhill R.A.F. Flying School at Salisbury, and it was engaged yesterday on divisional exercises. It had made two or three flights and was about to depart on another when a powerful gust of wind snapped the mooring cable.

Cries for Help

Cries for help were heard from the occupants as the balloon rose swiftly. It attained a height of 3000 feet, and all the time it was drifting away, carried along

The film of Dad's Army
– not a happy
experience for me.

film script of *Dad's Army*. We weren't too keen but we followed it through and delivered. After some weeks he confided in us that, in fact, he'd not sold it and would I go with him to see one of the Boulting brothers? Like a sucker, I agreed. I can't remember which brother it was, but when we got into his office he put my back up straight away – his attitude was appalling. The script was in front of him on his desk and he poked it with his finger as if it were some disgusting object. 'What would you call this?' he enquired.

'It's a film script of *Dad's Army*.'

'Oh, no it's not,' he replied. 'It's not like any film script I've ever seen. I have watched a few of the television shows, and I have to say they are quite appallingly directed. *Are* they directed? They don't look like it to me; they look as though they've just been put together. The whole show's a slapdash mess!'

'They are directed by my partner, David Croft,' I said, starting to get very angry.

'Really?' said the Boulting. 'Well, you could have fooled me!'

I walked out of the office and Norman followed. 'Please don't upset him, Jim,' he pleaded.

'I'll upset him,' I said. 'I'll punch him on the nose! Who does that arrogant bastard think he is?' Norman was desperate; he needed to make that film. I always liked him so, being a sucker, I went back into the office.

In the end the film was made by Columbia, Norman directed it and I worked with him as technical adviser, for £20 per day. David, being wise, kept well and truly out of it. I've never known six weeks pass so slowly. Making TV comedy shows in front of an audience is what I do; making feature films is an entirely different cup of tea – East is East, etc. If you watch the film very carefully you'll notice Norman's way of direction encompasses many styles. The *Dad's Army* film has a bit of everything in it – John Ford and David Lean for the open-air scenes, John Huston and Hitchcock for the interior scenes and – just to make sure – Norman added a bit of the great Russian film director Eisenstein! As one famous critic wrote: 'The film was like the Curate's Egg – good in parts.' I was so angry that for many years I couldn't bear to look at it, but just recently I've watched it several times and – do you know what – it's not that bad. Apart from the sentimental pleasure of seeing so many old friends who played all the other parts and are no longer with us, it also reminds me of dear old Norman Cohen who joined them some years ago. Norman used to suck a small piece of a security blanket while he was trying to make up his mind which famous director's style he was going to use for the next scene. I thought he was the only adult who ever did this, until I saw Gene Wilder in the film *The Producers*.

Mum was in constant dread of the day when I would be conscripted into the Armed Forces. She suggested that I went to work in a munitions factory, which would delay my being called to the Colours. I hated the idea, I just couldn't wait to get killed but, in order to placate her, agreed.

My brother Charlie had been told, at an earlier Medical, that he had a heart murmur and so he would not be called up. (In spite of this he is still very much alive today at the age of eighty-three.)

When Charlie was young he was a very keen body-builder, which was quite a rare thing in the 1930s. It all started when he saw a magazine advertisement featuring a photo of Charles Atlas stripped to the waist, showing off his magnificent physique. Underneath the photo were the words, 'You too can have a body like mine'. Charlie sent for the equipment and, after six months working out, built his own magnificent physique. He was so proud of his body, and whenever we went to the seaside he would strip off at the drop of a hat to show it off!

So we both started training as makers of scientific instruments. The government training centre, in common with many all over the country, was a vast factory, which taught various simple engineering skills to hundreds and thousands of people, workers needed for the munitions factories. It functioned day and night, seven days a week, with a huge canteen that served terrible food, but we didn't care, we were so hungry we'd eat anything. There was always a *Worker's Playtime* during the hour's break, or some sort of entertainment – usually consisting of a sing-song of patriotic songs. It's amazing to think how Britain was geared up for total war; everyone, men and women, between eighteen and sixty, was conscripted, either into the Armed Forces, munitions factories, mining, on the land to produce food, and other vital war work. One day our instructor, Ken, called Charlie and me to one side and said, 'You boys are doing very well, you've got a natural eye for instrument making. How would you like to join my little syndicate?'

'What's that?' we enquired.

He lowered his voice to a whisper. 'Now, boys, what you're doing is very important and, as soon as your six months is up [the period of training] you will be equipped for vital war work. But meanwhile you need something to practise on. Now, you cannot buy cigarette lighters for love nor money anywhere, they are like gold dust, so my little syndicate makes them.' He produced a lighter from his overall pocket. 'These,' he said, 'are sold discreetly for five bob a piece and, once a week, we have a share-out.'

'Is that allowed?' my brother enquired. 'Brass is a vital material.'

A slight edge came into Ken's voice. 'And we are using it for vital purposes, Charles,' he said – he usually called him Charlie. 'You are perfecting your trade, people are getting fag lighters and we're all making a few bob at the same time as pulling our weight so that we can get this war over and done with.' Then followed a crash course in making lighters, not smart, chrome, modern models; but great big brass ones which, when you flicked the wheel, burst into flame like a blowlamp. When we were on night shift, Ken would give us our quota of half-finished lighters and we'd contribute our bit before they were passed on to another trainee for the next part of the process. One night shift, in the early hours of the morning, I was working away at my lighters when I saw a supervisor approaching and, in a desperate panic, I swept all my half-finished lighters into a tank full of filthy used oil.

He stopped by me and said, 'Hello, Jim, aren't you working on any lighters tonight?'

Of course everyone was in on it. Having said that, Ken, our instructor, was clever and bright and, by the time we passed out, Charlie and I were quite skilled instrument makers. When we'd finished our training we went to work at a small factory called Broadhurst, Clarkson & Sons at the top of St Albans Road. It had been quite a smart garage before the war and was now converted into a factory making naval telescopes, employing about thirty people. Working there was almost as boring as the carpet department at Waring & Gillow just before the war, but I was determined to get into the Armed Forces as soon as possible – all this I kept to myself.

As I think I've made perfectly clear, I was still obsessed with 'Going on the Stage' (as it was called in those days). I'd do anything to show off, but how? If only I could get behind those footlights (they don't use them any more), be an actor, a singer, anything! I was constantly mucking about and doing impressions of radio personalities of the day, but never in front of a proper audience.

Charles Laughton as Captain Bligh of the Bounty. My impressions of him probably saved my life.

Then it happened: one day, after a Home Guard parade, the sergeant announced that there was going to be a smoking concert and he asked for volunteers. 'You're always larkin' about, Private Perry. I'm goin' to put you down to do a turn.'

And that was the start of my entire career. It took me completely by surprise. 'Do a turn? What could I do?' I could scarcely contain my excitement. As soon as I got home I went to my room and got to work. I sorted out various jokes such as, 'An air raid warden shouted to a woman, "Madam, do you realise you've got a chink in your bedroom?" and she shouted back, "The liar! He told me he was a Japanese admiral!"' (This was, of course, before Pearl Harbor.) Then I went through my impersonations – Charles Laughton in *Mutiny on the Bounty*: 'Four thousand miles in an open boat? I'll see you hanging from the highest yardarm in Portsmouth, Mr Christian!', Ned Sparks in *Forty-Second Street*: 'We got the dames, we got the scenery, we got the costooms, but we ain't got the dough!', James Cagney: 'You dirty rat, etc. etc.' I decided to finish as one of my radio heroes, Izzy Bonn, with a jingoistic song he used, 'This Is Worth Fighting For'.

The show was held in the drill hall in Queen's Road, Watford, which, to the best of my knowledge, is still there today. And I was a hit! I brought the house down and I thought, 'I'm on my way.' But I soon realised that it was one thing to go down big with my drunken comrades in a drill hall and quite another to be a hit in front of people who didn't know me!

Now, every month the Gaumont Cinema in Watford put on an amateur talent show and I did an audition and passed. Came the night, as I stood in the wings, waiting to be introduced, I realised I'd made a mistake by deciding to wear my Home Guard khaki battledress. Millions of people were in khaki uniform; I should have worn something more glamorous.

Over thirty years later, when David and I were writing the stage show of *Dad's Army*, I said, 'This show is all khaki, David, we must have some colour in it.' So we put in a number, 'When Can I Have a Banana Again?'(bananas were impossible to get during wartime) with the entire cast wearing South American costumes. It was certainly colourful. The day before the opening at Billingham, we were having a final dress rehearsal. It was two o'clock in the morning and things were not going well. We were doing the banana number and when it finished Arthur Lowe, who was sitting in the stalls, beckoned me over and said, 'James, you want to cut all that crap.' (I think secretly he wanted to be a banana!)

Back to 1941. As I stood, waiting in the wings of the Gaumont Cinema, Watford, I looked out from the darkness at the vast auditorium packed with over 2000 people. The smoke from hundreds of cigarettes was swirling into the beams of the spotlights. And then it hit me for the very first time; a feeling that every performer gets – fear, panic, elation and nausea. It's more powerful than any drug and, once you're addicted, you can never break free from it.

I heard my name and rushed to the centre of the vast stage where the cinema manager was waiting for me. He adjusted the microphone and, with a thinly disguised sneer, said, 'Here he is – Jimmy Perry. Not very funny but a lot of charm.' He told me to stay and made a swift exit.

I looked out at the vast cavern of darkness, only broken by the glow of cigarettes and red exit signs. 'Don't applaud, just throw petrol coupons!' I shouted. (Petrol was rationed.) I got a faint titter. I ploughed on. 'I'm very depressed, my girlfriend's just got the sack. She worked in a furnisher's factory – kept losing her drawers!' Then it happened. I got my first really big laugh. It rolled out from the darkness and across the footlights, and washed over me. Once that happens you're done for. You can never return to being a real human being again. I was going well, I went on. And on. And then it happened: they stopped laughing, I'd lost my audience! My blood turned to ice, I did my Charles Laughton and the rest of my impressions, went into 'This Is Worth Fighting For' and got off quickly.

The next three days were a nightmare. I'd failed, what was I going to do? I'd had my chance and I'd missed it. And I'd thought it would be so easy.

Then suddenly, out of the blue, I got a letter from a Billy Cook. It was on cheap, lined notepaper in beautiful old-fashioned copperplate writing. He said he was a professional comedian who was doing war work but to keep his hand in ran a local amateur concert party,

'Hello, Watford, Hello'. Would I give him a call? I phoned and we arranged to meet. When he came into the saloon bar at the Compasses in Watford High Street I knew instantly he was a professional comedian, not only by his attire but by the fact that he left me to pay for the drinks. He told me he'd be pleased to have me join his concert party, which entertained wounded servicemen, factory workers and a local naval base. The concert party were all amateurs except for himself (he stressed this very carefully). They just got paid their expenses, which Billy collected and they had a share-out now and then.

He then started to mark my card: 'Saw you the other night at the Gaumont, son.'

'What did you think?' I asked eagerly.

'Bloody awful! What you wanna go on in a uniform for, unless you were trying to get sympathy? Wear evening dress or tails – Morry will fix you up. He's got that second-hand menswear shop on the bridge in North Watford. Won't cost you more'n about five quid at the most.' Then Billy really let me have it: 'Don't shout at the audience, son, you've got a mike! And don't keep lookin' at the roof – I can only see the whites of yer eyes, look like a bloody zombie! And what were yer doin' with yer hand in yer pocket?'

'Well, I was just trying to look casual,' I volunteered.

'Looked to me as if you were playin' with yerself. You don't wanna do that sort of thing in front of an audience, son.'

A few days later, recommended by Billy, I went to see Morry, on the bridge at North Watford. I'd always loved clothes, but it was Morry who really showed me how to dress.

During the war clothing was strictly rationed; tailors were not allowed to make double-breasted suits as they took up too much material, and also no turn–ups on trousers. The term for the resulting garment was a 'Utility Suit'. There were so many rules and regulations that some tailors just shut up shop but Morry was made of sterner stuff. He was the archetypal Jewish tailor; he loved clothes and I shared his obsession. He paraded and patted you when doing a fitting – just loved to feel the quality of the cloth. But even if he'd had the material, a new tuxedo was out of the question, I just couldn't afford it.

Before the war you could get a tailor-made suit for two pounds ten shillings; they were made by a chain of tailors called – believe it or not – the Fifty Shilling Tailors. There was also Montague Burton, which was slightly more 'upmarket': four pounds would buy you a three-piece suit, made to measure, with two fittings plus an extra pair

The William Powell look.

of trousers. This was known as 'The Full Monty', which is where the present-day expression originates.

Morry ran a tape measure over me and led me to the back of his shop; he whipped a dust sheet off a rack of suits to reveal a row of second-hand dinner jackets. 'These suits, son,' he said, 'all hand-made in Savile Row.' Taking one down, he slipped the jacket on me. 'By the time I've finished with it, son, this suit will fit you like a glove. What we're going for here is the "William Powell" look – sophisticated without being flashy.'

I looked on the inside pocket for the Savile Row label – there wasn't one. When I pointed this out to Morry, he threw up his hands in horror. 'A gentleman who pays ten guineas for a suit in Savile Row does not want a vulgar label in it, it would be showing off!'

So, for three pounds ten shillings, Morry said, he would alter the suit and throw in a shirt and a black tie – not a clip-on one, but one you tied by hand! – he would, personally, instruct me on how to do this.

Two weeks later I stood in his shop wearing the outfit. 'You look a million dollars, son,' he said. 'Anyhow, you got one thing over William Powell, you're very much younger.'

Morry himself was at all times immaculately dressed. Hints like, 'You must show a quarter to a half-inch of cuff below the jacket sleeve.' The shirt had to have a double cuff with cuff-links, a single cuff with a button was beyond the pale. 'Always have the bottom button of your waistcoat undone.' When I asked him why, he said, 'Lost in the mists of time, son, but it's just a thing a gentleman always does.' Even today, in my pathetic old age, I still follow most of his rules and feel somewhat ill at ease if I'm not immaculately dressed at all times.

The real thing – what style!

Sometimes when I enter a smart restaurant and look around, it seems that although quite a few of the women dress smartly, their male partners look as though they've just come in from doing the garden. Everyone seems to dress in black or grey. I know the fashion today is called 'dumbing down' but I just can't handle it. People keep saying to me, in restaurants and everywhere, 'Don't you want to take your jacket off?'

'No, thank you,' I reply. 'Why should I want to take my jacket off?' Fact of the matter is, having caught malaria in that rotten jungle all those years ago I always feel the cold. However, it amazes me how men rip off their coats, even in quite cold weather, to reveal underneath a short-sleeved shirt. To me short-sleeved shirts are the last word in naff. Please, if you want to look casual, wear a nice full shirt, with a long sleeve, and then roll the sleeve halfway up your forearm. It's amazing how smart and butch this looks.

PART THREE

CALLED TO THE COLOURS

1943 was drawing to a close. I worked all day in the factory, paraded with the Home Guard three nights a week and Sunday mornings, did two or three shows a month with the 'Hello, Watford, Hello' concert party and, if I had a spare night, went, of course, to the pictures. At that time there were six cinemas in Watford, with huge queues outside every one. Occasionally I'd go to the Palace Theatre, which had a weekly repertory company.

It was three weeks before Christmas; so far I'd heard no news about being called up, much to my mum's delight and my annoyance. About three months earlier I had reported for my Medical and, because of my hand, was graded B1 which meant I was pretty well fit for anything. There was such a desperate need for men in the Forces that they weren't very fussy.

And then it happened. I arrived home to be greeted by my mother with the words, 'It's come.' And there, on the mantelpiece, was the buff envelope that so many people dreaded. My calling-up papers. It's only now, after all these years that I can understand how my dear mother must have felt. Her three brothers had served in the First World War, one dreadfully wounded. But then, what did I know?

We had a wonderful family Christmas and then, on New Year's Day 1944, I reported to Mearnee Barracks in Colchester for six weeks' basic training. At Colchester station there were lines of army trucks to take us to the barracks. Always wanting to impress, I jumped up on one of them, slipped and fell flat on my face. A grizzled sergeant, who was rolling a cigarette, paused to lick the paper and said, 'Plenty of time, son, the war won't be over for a bit. Don't rush about.'

As we drove into Colchester some of the recruits started to sing, in a half-hearted way, 'Roll Me Over in the Clover'. I often wonder how many returned after the war. Lucky Jim – I've had over fifty years more life than a good proportion of the poor sods who were with me in those trucks on that day. Mearnee Barracks had been built in Victorian times and were long red-brick buildings; the lavatories were in a separate block. As we turned into the gates we stopped at the guard house for the driver to report. The building was long, with a veranda and huge, full-length mirror at the end; this was for soldiers to inspect themselves before leaving the barracks. There were three cells with the doors open, pale-looking prisoners were mopping out. 'Who are they?' enquired one of the innocents in the truck.

'They're on Jankers, mate, Jankers,' volunteered a dour, North Country man, who seemed much older than the rest of us. 'Take a tip from me and keep your nose clean, unless you want to end up like them. And keep clear of *those* bastards.' He pointed at a couple of Redcaps (Military Police). After driving down the grim lines of barracks we unloaded and filed into our quarters. There was a long row of two-tier bunks each side of the room; down the middle was a strip of brown lino, which was so polished it looked like glass, at the far end a coal stove that gleamed as though it was made of silver; beside it a bucket, also gleaming, in it lumps of coal that had been polished. Until then it had never occurred to me that coal could be polished; later in my army career I was in huts and barrack rooms where the coal had been whitewashed! In the series *It Ain't Half Hot, Mum*, Sergeant-Major Williams, played by the wonderful Windsor Davies, says to the concert party, 'You will whitewash the bottoms of all trees. I want to see this jungle gleaming, gleaming, gleaming!' It got a big laugh, but how many people realised that it was based on the truth? You may think, dear reader, being of logical and sound mind, 'How did they keep a barrack room warm if they couldn't burn the coal?' Simple – out of the way, under the stairs, was a wooden box full of dirty coal, which was brought in at night and taken out the next morning.

At the end of the room was a wooden table; scrubbed so clean it was almost white. Sitting at it, the sergeant who was to be in charge of us for the next six weeks. He was a tough Ulsterman and, if you look at him in the group photograph, you will notice he's pulled the stripes on his arms round to the front so that they can be clearly seen. This is, or was, a common practice and later, when I became a sergeant, if my photograph was to be taken I did exactly the same thing.

And so we queued up, gave our particulars and were allotted a bunk. Ex-members of the Home Guard had been told to report wearing their uniforms, which I duly did. I had by then achieved the dizzy heights of Lance-Corporal (one stripe) and without a word, our tough, macho sergeant, picked up a penknife and, with a few deft strokes, removed my stripes and, at the same time putting on a 'nancy' voice, whispered, 'I'll leave you to pick out all the loose bits of cotton!'

I looked round at my fellow conscripts. They seemed a very sad bunch; they'd come from all over the British Isles and reflected their backgrounds. There was the usual sprinkling from the well-fed middle classes, but the large proportion were painfully undernourished, products of the hungry Twenties and Thirties. That evening we were allowed out for just a couple of hours to phone our next of kin, as they were referred to. We patiently queued outside a phone box in the street and we scarcely spoke to each other. I finally got through to home: Dad answered and quickly put Mum on the phone. I could tell she'd been crying but all I could say was, 'I got here all right. Love you, Mum, I'll write.' The pips went and I shouted, 'I haven't got any more change!' Which was a lie, and that was that. Only a few of us phoned, the rest obviously had no phones at home – so few people had at that time – but they'd come out with us just to get away from the barracks. We stood around in the street for a bit, then slowly made our way back. With the exception of myself and a couple of others who were wearing our ex-Home Guard battledress, everyone was, of course, still in their civilian clothes.

As we went back in through the gates there was a roar and the duty sergeant came out of the guard house. 'What's the matter with you lot?' he barked. 'Stand up straight! Look at yourselves – you're a disgrace! It's a good thing you're still in civilian clothes and I can't touch you! But tomorrow, when you've been issued with uniforms, and I catch you slummocking about, I'll have you inside this guard house so fast your feet won't touch! Now, move yourselves!'

That evening was perhaps the gloomiest of my life. The bugler blew 'Lights Out' and we climbed into our bunks, hardly anyone spoke and, as I lay in the darkness, I could hear that a few of the others were quietly sobbing. I dropped off and the next thing I heard was a bugler blowing 'Reveille' as I slowly woke up. Then the corporal, whose bunk was at the end, leapt down and started screaming like a maniac, 'Get up! Have you all gone mad? Why are you lying in bed? Move! Move! Get up!' He ran up and down the bunks hitting them with an old battered cricket bat. Clearly, I was not in the army at all, but in a madhouse! Any minute now, aristocrats would be coming round and taunting us. Then I heard it: the most terrible sound of coughing and retching. Most of the comrades were now sitting on their bunks lighting fags. Our mad corporal, who had suddenly become sane, was doing exactly the same thing. Later I learnt that in the army, once you have both feet on the floor, this is considered 'up'.

And so my first day in the real army started. Before we marched to breakfast we were assigned our regular morning tasks, which consisted of cleaning and polishing everything in sight. I was handed a bunch of newspapers and told to clean the windows – were they mad? – but it worked. When I'd finished they gleamed like crystal. After breakfast it never stopped: haircut, showers, a visit to the dentist. For many of the men it was the first time in their lives they'd had their teeth examined. Then we were issued with all our equipment, followed by days of drill. At the end of the first week we were issued with our rifles, the good old reliable British Army Lee-Enfield. The magazine held ten rounds and it was much lighter than the old American Ross P14 and P17 we used in the Home Guard. Over the next six weeks we never stopped doing basic training – drill, taking weapons apart, putting them together again, physical training, assault courses, camouflage, drill, more drill – especially bayonet drill. This consisted of charging, bayonets fixed, at straw sacks made to look like Hitler, at the same time screaming our heads off. It was the instructor, another First World War veteran, who, for the first time, acquainted me with the phrase, 'They don't like it up 'em!'

There was also the poison gas drill. We were taken into a bunker, the door closed and told not to put on our respirators (gas masks) until given the order. Then they'd let in the tear gas and we'd instantly start coughing and retching. Finally the corporal, who already had *his* respirator on, gave us permission to put on ours. After about five minutes we staggered into the fresh air coughing our guts up. The final part of the drill was to experience mustard gas; we rolled up our sleeves and lined up, and an officer put one drop on our forearms and said, 'Right, men, if that mustard gas were left on your arms, in ten minutes it would burn right through to the bone. But we're not going to let that happen, are we?'

We all shook our heads. By that time the gas was starting to smart and rapidly getting worse.

'Right, men, take evasive action,' came the order. We quickly took out our little tins containing swabs and ointment, then pinched off the gas with the swab and applied the ointment. A very nasty business. To this day I still have a black spot on my forearm where they put that little drop of deadly poison. (Before you start to write and warn me – I have had the spot examined many times and it's quite harmless!)

As I had served two years in the Home Guard, apart from the poison gas drill all this training was a doddle. I thought I was well versed in the arts of war, but there was a rather nasty lesson I still had to learn.

One of my fellow recruits was a huge chap, nearly seven feet tall, a giant, he was just like Lenny in *Of Mice and Men*. (I refer, of course, to the black-and-white film version, with Lon Chaney Junior and Burgess Meredith – the best, without a doubt.) Our giant

Proper soldiers. I'm in the middle row, the second from left.

had a bad stammer and was quickly nicknamed 'Dumbo'. He was shown no mercy by the instructors. Poor Dumbo shouldn't really have been in the army at all, but at that time things were very desperate and every man who could just about stand was called up into the Forces. To complete our six weeks' basic training we were to experience being 'Under Fire'. This consisted of crawling across a field with machine-guns firing live rounds in a fixed line just above our heads. So we started crawling, the bullets were only about four feet over us and we desperately tried to get into the earth, away from the thousands of hideous hornets above. As the corporal, just before we started, said, 'This will learn you to keep your fuckin' 'eads down!' And how right he was.

We gradually covered the length of the field and the machine-guns stopped, then suddenly, for no reason at all, Dumbo leapt to his feet and shouted, 'Charge!' and at exactly the same instant the guns opened up again and Dumbo fell in a saggy heap. There was a long silence followed by frantic blowing of whistles and cries of, 'Stretcher bearers!'

We slowly raised our heads and looked at the disgusting mess that had, only a few seconds before, been Dumbo. I stared with fascination, thinking, 'Why is there so much blood? This doesn't happen in films; if people are shot they just fall over. When, in *Little Ceasar* (1930), Edward G. Robinson uttered his dying words – "Mother of Mercy, is this the end of Rico?" he'd been riddled with bullets and there wasn't a mark on him – no *mess*! This isn't right, why is there so much blood? Why have they shattered my dream world?' I was starting to learn about war.

There was an enquiry, of course. The warrant officer who had been in charge came into our barrack room the next morning and asked for volunteers to testify. At first no one moved, there was a long pause, he gave us a hard look and said, 'Now, you listen to me; my job is to train you to be soldiers. You all think I'm a bastard, well, that's all right, I'm used to it, but I'm determined that, by the time I've finished with you, when you go into action and the shit starts flying, you will stand your ground and take whatever you're up against. 'Cause that's my job, that's what British Army NCOs do – they make soldiers. Now, I'll ask you again; I want six volunteers as witnesses!'

After a short pause, we sheepishly raised our hands.

The Court of Enquiry was a very brief affair; the warrant officer was absolved of all blame and, a few days later, we were posted to various regiments all over the country. I was the only one to become a gunner. But first we were given a week's leave and so I arrived at Watford Junction and walked home to 237 High Street. I was given a rapturous reception, with my dear mum fighting back the tears, and Dad, standing in the hall with his beautiful white Persian cat under his arm, saying, as he stroked it, 'Look, Tibby, our Jimmy's home.'

Mum and Dad, summer 1944.

Even now, nearly sixty years later, I can still bring that picture to mind so easily. The next day I took my army-issue greatcoat to Morry the tailor.

'Is this the best you can get?' he complained. 'It's terrible!'

'Can you make it fit me a bit better, Morry?' I insisted. Then I told him I was being posted to the Royal Artillery.

'You're in luck, son,' he said, opening a drawer that was full of brass army buttons. He held one up. It was almost completely round, with a small Royal Artillery gun embossed on the front – perhaps a few old gunners will remember them, they are quite unique.

When I returned a few days later, to collect the coat, there it was on a stand and it looked fantastic. 'What have you done with it? It's amazing! It's like a German officer's greatcoat!'

'Yeah – bastards!' said Morry. 'Smart though, en' it?'

I put the coat on, paid Morry four pounds plus the cost of the buttons and walked home. I kept looking at myself in the shop windows. What had Morry done to it? It took me weeks to find out, but whenever I wore that overcoat on guard I always got stickman, I looked so smart. What's a stickman? I'll tell you: the guard for the night parades outside the guard house where they are inspected by the duty officer, and the officer taps the smartest man on parade with his stick − this means that the lucky bugger does not have to stand outside in the cold for his two-hour turn, he can get a good night's sleep in his bunk and only turns out in case of an emergency. Good old Morry, I can thank him for so many undisturbed nights' sleep. 'What was the secret of the greatcoat?' I can hear you asking. Well, it was hanging up, one night when I was on guard duty, beside another army greatcoat. I stared at it and realised that Morry had put an extra button on, so that when it was done up, it gave the coat an extra edge − as I constantly say, you've got to have that little extra edge in life. Why did I get on so well in the army? It's all a matter of acting. If you march briskly about the camp, smartly turned out, with a clipboard under your arm, banging up salutes to every officer you pass, no one questions you, because you *fit in*. But if you slummock, with baggy trousers, buttons not polished, dirty boots, you're in deep trouble. Every Saturday morning there would be a huge parade, which would be taken by the regimental sergeant-major, and it was always the same dialogue: 'Keep your 'eads up, stand up straight, don't look down. I was up at six o'clock this morning. I went all over that parade ground on my hands an' knees with a great big magnifyin' glass an', believe me, there is nothing on it, so why are you looking down? Don't you trust me? Keep your flippin' 'eads up or some of you will spend the night in the guard house and, take it from me, the room service is very bad, 'cos I organise it!'

Prior to that there would be the weekly kit inspection; every item issued to you had to be laid out on your bunk in a certain order, which you had to learn by heart. Of course, all the brass had to be gleaming, not to mention the boots – even the soles polished and the studs cleaned with silver polish.

As you read this, you're asking yourselves, 'Is this man mad? Why did he go along with it?' The answer is simple – no alternative. I certainly didn't want to join those pale-faced zombies in the cells of the guard house. Right at the very start of our training our sergeant from Ulster said, 'You can have it the easy way, or you can have it the hard way. The easy way is hard and the hard way is bloody hard!'

So, every Friday night I'd spend a couple of hours cleaning and polishing my kit and then laying it out. When the 'Lights Out' came I rolled in my blankets and slept on the floor. The next morning I was ready for inspection. At first the others jeered with derision but, within a few weeks, pretty well everyone was doing it. Promptly, at 9.30, the duty officer would carry out his inspection and, within a few weeks, he would walk down the bunks muttering, 'Beautiful kit layouts, beautiful!' I could swear he almost had tears in his eyes, which only shows: if you can't beat 'em, join 'em.

My first leave seemed over in a flash. I wouldn't let anybody see me off at the station; I just caught the Bakerloo tube train to Euston from Watford High Street. I was wearing FSMO (Field Service Marching Order) which consisted of large pack, small pack, gas mask – sorry, respirator – water bottle, ammunition pouches, bayonet and, of course, Morry's wonderful overcoat which, in point of fact, I was wearing for the first time. As I sat on the train, with my rifle between my knees, I knew that it would take nearly an hour to reach Euston

– plenty of time to slip into my dream world. I heard a voice saying, 'Major Perry, I'm sorry to have sent you to a unit as a simple gunner but, as far as the army's concerned, that's what you are. Your job is to remain under cover until you can unmask one of the officers in the unit who is a German spy.'

'Wait a minute!' I thought, 'I did this at Colet Court when I marched into the headmaster's study and denounced Mr Downes as a German spy!'

'This is much more serious,' said the voice. 'In any case, Mr Downes is dead. Everyone thought he had been killed when a bomb hit the school, but our Agent only made it look like that – he was "removed" and you got the credit for it.'

'Oh, good!' I thought, and suddenly I was in Wembley Stadium and thousands of boys were cheering, 'Good old Perry, he got rid of Mr Downes!'

'Not me, personally, gentlemen,' I protested. 'I just gave the orders.'

'Pay attention, Major Perry,' said the voice. 'There isn't much time. When you find out which officer is the German spy, you will leave a loaded revolver in his quarters and, if he fails to take the hint, you will use it on him yourself.'

Suddenly I realised the train had gone underground at Queen's Park and I could see my reflection in the train window. Although I was twenty, I looked much younger – a young boy, off to the Front, which is how my fellow passengers saw me. One woman was crying and saying to her friend, 'Oh, the poor young boy!'

A man leaned over and offered me a cigarette.

'No, thanks,' I said. 'I smoke a pipe.'

Another woman offered me a sweet. I wanted to say, 'Not on Active Service, madam, thank you.' But I just gave her a wry smile.

When I got to Euston the train to Chester, which was the first part of my journey, was packed. I found a corner and started on a new Scarlet Pimpernel book. Seven hours later, after many delays and changes, I arrived at Oswestry, in Shropshire, and reported to the First Mixed Heavy Anti-Aircraft Regiment. By now it was late at night and I was glad to settle in a hut. Something I could hardly believe was that there was central heating!

The next morning I woke to the sound of Glenn Miller over the tannoy. A bombardier appeared in the doorway and shouted, 'Right, breakfast in half an hour.'

'Thank you, corporal.' I said.

'I am not a corporal!' he replied. 'You're in the Royal Artillery now, in the Gunners. Two stripes is a bombardier, get it?'

It seemed a rather trivial thing to get upset about but never mind.

After breakfast we assembled in a lecture hall and waited. There were about forty of us and hardly anyone spoke, we just sat there. Then the door opened and a major appeared with numerous NCOs. We all shuffled to our feet and one of the sergeants, in a cut-glass accent, said, 'Right. Settle down. Major Smith will brief you about your training.'

The major took out a cigarette, fitted into a long holder and said, 'Good morning, gentlemen, smoke if you want to.'

We all looked at each other – sergeants with posh accents and majors acting like Noël Coward, calling us 'gentlemen'? What happened to all those rough NCOs who, during our six weeks' training, never stopped bawling and shouting at us?

The major put us in the picture: 'Now, you have been selected because, according to the tests during your basic training, you have shown yourselves to be intelligent. You are going to be trained as radio location operators.'

'Does that mean we get more money, sir?' piped up a Welsh voice.

The major didn't move a muscle, but you could see he'd marked the owner of the Welsh voice down as a potential trouble-maker.

'No,' he said, 'you will all remain gunners unless you are promoted.'

Then the sergeant with the cut-glass accent, who looked rather like an absent-minded professor, told us in simple terms how radar worked. He pointed to a large diagram. 'I'll just give you a brief outline. The transmitter sends out radio waves that hit the enemy aircraft and bounce back. They, in turn, are picked up by the receiver, and the information – height, speed, bearing etc. – is then relayed to the predictor by cables and, in turn, to the 3.7 heavy guns.'

That was nearly sixty years ago and I hope that any technical-type people who are reading this information and finding it incorrect will excuse me – I was never any good at understanding how things work. If I want to change the waveband on my car radio I have to send for the AA. Today I spent nearly an hour in my car with the handbook, trying to put the clock forward for British Summer Time, when I should have been writing this book. There is only one person who was worse than me and she's no longer with us. Her name was Pearl Binder, the famous costume designer. She was trying to make a phone-call on a payphone backstage and said, 'Do it for me please, Jimmy, I'm hopeless with machines!'

Having said that, after three months' intensive training, I became a very proficient radar operator but, to be fair, I only had to turn little handles, not do repairs.

When the sergeant had finished his lecture the major stepped forward and said, 'Now I want to talk to you chaps about sex.'

I thought, 'He's not going to nag us about wanking, is he, like the chaplain at Colet Court?' But I was wrong.

His eyes took on an evangelical look. 'This', he continued, 'is the First (Mixed) Heavy Ack-Ack Regiment. We are a training unit, but

I want you to concentrate on that word – *mixed*. For the first time in the history of the British Army, women are serving on active service, side by side with the men. The ATS won't actually be loading and firing the guns, but manning the fire control instruments: predictors, radar, height finders etc.'

By now, as usual, I was starting to get bored – I had no idea, at that age, what those wonderful, brave ATS women went through, I took it for granted. Even now, after all these years, there is so little information about them, so I'd just like to set the record straight.

During World War Two, 56,000 ATS women served in the Royal Artillery Anti-Aircraft Command. Now, there are four guns in a heavy ack-ack battery and the instruments are all in the area of the gun emplacement, so if enemy dive-bombers, or fighters, strafe the emplacement, there's a lot of crap flying about. Bullets and shrapnel cannot differentiate between the sexes so, of course, there were casualties, and ATS women were killed and wounded.

The ATS women served side by side with men on the Ack-Ack batteries.

The next morning we commenced our training as radar operators. In order to make everything work, a huge generator had to be started, and I was allocated that task, and what – as my old dad would have said – an ugly brute that generator was! No self-starter, of course, it had to be cranked and the handle had a kick like a mule. I cranked and pulled over and over again – nothing. Eventually the instructor gently pushed me to one side and gave it a quick flick; the brute roared and shattered into life. After that I just turned little handles and switches.

In the camp at Oswestry they had a concert party, which put on shows at the Garrison Theatre. I joined. By this time I had a quite polished act – or so I thought. I started off with a string of one-line gags, most pinched from Vic Oliver, who was on the radio a lot. I also copied his Jewish-American style, then I'd do impressions of famous film stars of the day: George Arliss, in a scene from *The House of Rothschild*, Ned Sparks in *Forty-Second Street* and, of course, Charles Laughton in *Mutiny on the Bounty* and *The Hunchback of Notre Dame*. I'd finish with the song I'd now made my own, 'This Is Worth Fighting For'.

After the war when so many would-be comedians queued up at the Windmill Theatre to audition, they all did the same impersonations and impressions – Peter Sellers, Harry Secombe, Tony Hancock and many others, who thought they were going to be great comedians, all did the same material at the start of their careers. Some made it, but a lot didn't.

Ten years later, in the early 1950s, I saw Tony Hancock in a show at the Adelphi, in which he did Charles Laughton as *The Hunchback of Notre Dame* and finished by saying, 'Here's one for the teenagers – George Arliss!'

In 1967, after an amazing career, just before Tony went to Australia and killed himself, I saw him in the last series he did on British television, and what did he do? George Arliss and Charles Laughton as *The Hunchback of Notre Dame*! What goes around comes around.

During March and April of that year, 1944, our training as radar operators continued. You may ask, 'Why, if the ATS were training as radar operators, were we also being trained for the same job?' Simple – we men were going overseas, ATS personnel were kept for the defence of the UK. There was an exception, however, when, in December 1944, the One Hundred and Fifty-fifth (Mixed) HAA

Regiment was chosen to go overseas to be the first (mixed) regiment to be deployed in the defence of Antwerp, then one of the major objectives of the German thrust in the Ardennes, and the target for a concentrated V1 and V2 attack, which surpassed anything London had ever experienced. Even under those bad conditions overseas, the efficiency, loyalty and good humour of those wonderful women of the ATS remained unchanged.

My comrade gunners came from a variety of backgrounds; there was 'Taff', a rather stroppy Welshman, who had been a schoolteacher in civilian life and questioned everything; Gerry, a cheerful cockney, who'd been a second-hand car salesman; Jock, the Scot from Glasgow who was Jewish; Bill, a heavy, pessimistic Yorkshireman whose one source of conversation was, 'This war'll go on for years and years, we'll never get out of the army.'

They were, in fact, like the cast of a typical British war film – stereotypes, most people would say, but they were real. The world is made up of so many stereotypes that the problem with writing comedy is how to avoid them. When David Croft and I started work on *It Ain't Half Hot, Mum*, we had a job in casting the part of Sergeant-Major Williams. We saw so many star and non-star actors, but none seemed right; then Leonard Rossiter came to see us. He'd been sent the script the week before, so David and I assumed he was well versed in it.

'You realise this part is a complete, stereotyped character?' he rather patronisingly informed us, then proceeded to demolish the entire script from start to finish. His attitude, to put it mildly, was a little arrogant but, in my book, he was downright rude. Why he bothered to come to see us, if he felt like that about the show, has always been a mystery to me. It's a strange thing about actors; they're so insecure that they want to tell everybody their opinions; they want power. It's amazing how, when a quite ordinary actor becomes a soap star, he or she is suddenly an instant expert on politics, religion, cookery, bricklaying – you name it, they know all about it, and they'll go from chat show to chat show, boring the arse off everyone.

A few days later Windsor Davies came to see us about the part. By now David and I were getting desperate. Windsor read the part in Cockney, as it was written, but it was just not right, his natural Welsh accent kept peeping through. We told him to go and get a coffee and come back in an hour, then rewrote a few pages of the sergeant-major's dialogue in the Welsh idiom. When he returned and read it in a Welsh accent the result was amazing: the whole character sprang into life; he'd taken it by the throat and made it 100 per cent real, even putting in 'lovely boy', which he created himself. So co-operation between writers and actor had done the trick, Sergeant-Major 'Shut up!' Williams became a TV legend.

Towards the end of the ten weeks, we went to North Wales for firing practice. The ATS didn't come with us – this was 'man's stuff'. The heavy guns would line up on the vast beaches and fire at cardboard cut-outs of enemy tanks, which ran on a little railway line. You may ask, why were anti-*aircraft* guns firing at tanks? We never found out; we radar and other instrument operators had nothing to do with firing the heavy guns. Instead we blazed away at the target with Bren guns (a light machine-gun). The target was an old windsock, towed behind a biplane, the pilot of which seemed totally unconcerned by the fact that the target was only about fifty feet behind him. One of us would fire the machine-gun from the hip and another gunner would stand behind him, in a very intimate embrace, to stop him falling over backwards from the kick of the gun. Each magazine held thirty rounds and we stuffed them with tracer bullets – we had a wonderful time! The plane flew backwards and forwards and we blazed away.

I've come to the conclusion that, apart from sex, the greatest thrill you can ever experience is firing a machine-gun. (Especially if you shout abuse at the same time!)

At the end of each day we would gather up thousands of empty brass cartridge cases, count them and hand them in. It must have cost a fortune, but war is an expensive business. After a session an officer brought over the windsock, which the pilot had towed behind the plane, and threw it on the ground in disgust – there wasn't a single bullet hole in it. It was then I realised why the pilot had seemed so unconcerned.

The ten-week training was nearly at an end, but during this time the eight of us became a unit and I have so many memories of them. I like to think I was very popular – they always laughed at my jokes – but perhaps there was another reason: once a week my dad would write to me, enclosing a pound note. It always arrived on Thursday, and on the following night we all went to the pub and blew the pound. (Remember that, in 1944, in present-day values, a pint of beer cost two and a half pence!)

We all realised that D-Day was approaching and, early in June, the names went up on the noticeboard of the various ack-ack regiments we were being posted to. Everyone except me.

I couldn't believe it. I went to see the battery sergeant-major. 'Why have I been left off? Why aren't I going?'

''Ow the hell should I know?' he said. 'Count yourself lucky, and keep yer fuckin' 'ead down if you don't want to get it blown orf!'

A few days later, as the camp emptied, I said goodbye to everyone with trite remarks, such as, 'Good luck, lads, I'll catch you up.' How,

I don't know – even they didn't know where they were going.

At last I managed to see the colonel, I was marched into the office by the sergeant-major. (The colonel was my inspiration for Colonel Reynolds, played so brilliantly by Donald Hewlitt in *It Ain't Half Hot, Mum*.) I asked him why I wasn't going with my unit for the invasion of France and the sergeant-major went apoplectic. ''Ow dare you!' he shouted. Who said anythin' about an invasion? Careless talk costs lives! I could 'ave you on a charge!'

'Well, Gunner Perry,' the colonel said, mildly, 'fact is, you're a damn clever feller. The chaps like the turns you do in the Garrison Theatre and it helps to keep up their morale, so I can't let you go. I mean, your Charles Laughton in *Mutiny on the Bounty* is fantastic. Have you seen it, sergeant-major?'

'Can't say I 'ave, sir.'

'Well, now's your chance – do it for him, gunner.'

And so, a few days before the greatest military invasion in history, with two million men and machines poised to cross the Channel, I stood in a battery office in Oswestry, and did: 'Four thousand miles in an open boat, Mr Christian? I'll see you hanging from the highest yardarm in Portsmouth.' And it most probably saved my life.

History rolled on and D-Day took place. A few weeks later, I was waylaid by the sergeant-major, who told me that my lot had had a bad time. When they landed, the cumbersome equipment had got bogged down in the sand, and they'd suffered heavy casualties. 'Take a tip from an old soldier, gunner, never volunteer, and keep yer fuckin' 'ead down!'

To this day I can still see their faces and I remember the Friday nights in the pub when we'd spend my dad's pound.

And so I spent most of the summer of 1944 at Oswestry. New intakes of gunners arrived, were trained, and sent over to join the Allied Forces in France. My frustration – that I was still in England – increased. I never heard any more about my comrades who had landed on D-Day and, for the first time in my life, I felt a deep sense of guilt.

I plucked up courage to ask the sergeant-major if there was any more news and he exploded, 'How dare you? What I told you was privileged information! How do I know what happened to them? There are a million men in the Royal Artillery. Do you think I know each of them personally? What's the matter with you? Are you mad? Do you *want* to get killed? You're on a cushy number here, gunner, doing shows at the Garrison Theatre. You may spend half your time up the colonel's backside, and he may think you're his blue-eyed boy, cos you talk posh and do a turn, but I'll tell you this for nothing: I think your impersonation of Charles Laughton is rotten – you haven't got the eyebrows for it. *Attention! Right Turn, Lef', Ri', Lef', Ri'!'* He marched me off, shouting after me until I disappeared out of sight.

Dear Mum, of course, loved the fact that I was still in England. When I went home on leave she always said, 'The war can't last much longer.' How could I be so insensitive as not to realise what she was going through – in common with millions of other mums all over the country.

One day I was doing my usual marching about smartly to keep out of trouble, when I heard the dreaded shout: 'Gunner Perry!' the sergeant-major appeared as if from nowhere. 'We've been looking for you everywhere. Where have you been?'

'I – er – I . . .' I flustered.

'Shut up! Follow me! The colonel wants to see you!' So I fell in behind him and, '*Lef', Ri', Lef', Ri', Lef', Ri*'' we stamped our way into the battery office.

The colonel looked up. 'Ah, there you are. You'll be pleased to hear, Gunner Perry, that it's been decided that you are potential officer material, so next week you'll report to the War Office Selection Board at Chester for three days. They'll sort of run a tape measure over you to see if you're up to scratch for a commission. That's all.' I was marched out.

The sergeant-major looked me up and down. 'Well, well, well – you must be pleased with yourself, Gunner Perry. How long you been in the army?'

'Er, seven months.'

He nodded. 'Seven months. Well, I've been in the bloody army thirty years. Took me fifteen years to make sergeant, and another five sergeant-major, and you roll into the camp and, within a few months, you're "*potential officer material*" – and why do you think that is?' he said, nodding his head towards the colonel's office. 'Cos you're one of 'im!' then he put on a terrible 'posh' accent. '*Dem good show lawst night, Gunner Perry, hey what!*' His eyes narrowed. 'I hate bloody officers. Now piss off!'

It was a sort of watered-down version of this attitude which David Croft and I wrote in some of the exchanges in *Dad's Army* when Mainwaring says to Wilson,

> MAINWARING: I started in the bank as a clerk, then chief clerk, then assistant manager and, finally, manager, and do you know how long it took me? Twenty years. But I still can't join the golf club and you, just because you've been to a tupp'ny-ha'p'nny public school, don't even *ask* to join, they ask you!

WILSON: If I didn't know you better, sir, I'd think you'd got a bit of a chip on your shoulder.

MAINWARING: I'll tell you what I *have* got on my shoulder, Wilson, three pips, which means 'captain' and don't you forget it!

A week later I arrived at the WOSBE at Chester. As soon as we had settled in we were summoned to a meeting. There were about twenty of us and we sat around a table with our examiners who, to quote the colonel back in Oswestry, were going to 'run the tape measure over us' for the next three days. We were told that name and rank would not be used; we'd simply be called by our numbers. As I arrived first, I was given an armband with '1' on it. Among the officers in charge was a snooty little Guards lieutenant who got up my nose from the very start. Several times during the meeting he said, 'Pay attention, Number One!' and it took quite some time before I realised he was talking to me – I was daydreaming. By now I was rapidly going off the idea of being an officer. The evening was spent in a sort of mock-officers'-mess atmosphere, and we were all encouraged to talk about ourselves. Some of the others had a problem with this, but it was no problem to me. After a few jokes – e.g. '*Waiter, what's this fly doing in my soup?*' – '*I think it's the backstroke, sir.*' '*Waiter, what's this fly doing in my ice cream?*' – '*They've taken up winter sports, sir*' – I realised that I was not making a good impression either on the examiners or on my fellow officer candidates. I decided against doing any impersonations and gave up.

The next morning we assembled in PT gear and the snooty Guards lieutenant – who, by the way, had a bit of a stammer – informed us that the morning would be spent finding out what sort of initiative and aggression we possessed. We formed in two lines facing each other and were issued with boxing gloves. As we were putting them on, I sensed trouble – it was clear to me that everyone assembled there that morning hated me. The idea was that as our numbers were called, we'd step in the middle and spar.

Straight away Snooty said, 'Number wa-wa-wa–One and Number suh-suh-suh–Seven! Commence!'

I stepped forward and, at the same time, so did

'Show some aggression, Number One!'

Number Seven, who must have been at least six feet tall and was built like a brick shithouse. He then proceeded to knock several different kinds of sherbet out of me. I ducked and weaved and defended myself as best I could to protect my face.

'Get sta-sta-stuck in! Show some aggression, nah-Number One!' shouted Lieutenant Snooty.

In those days one of my front teeth was very crooked – nowadays it's beautifully crowned, of course – and even the slightest blow caused it to cut my top lip, so the blood began to flow thick and fast.

The snooty lieutenant blew his whistle. 'Stay where you are, Number One. Number th-thu—'

I couldn't believe it! Number Three squared up to me and it started all over again.

I thought, 'Ah-ah, it's Spartacus time, is it?'

Only the copious flow of blood from my lip saved my bacon.

'Shu-shu-shu-show some aggression, Number One!' repeated Snooty. Then, as years ago in the assistant headmaster's study back at Colet Court, I had a strong desire to put my hands round Snooty's throat and 'just squeeze', but unfortunately, wearing boxing gloves, it was not possible. Also, striking an officer was a heinous crime.

Who can forget the scene in *The Charge of the Light Brigade* where a wretched soldier is being flogged for striking an officer? When the punishment is over the officer asks him, 'Well, my good fellah, what will you do with yourself now?'

'Re-enlist, sir,' gasps the wretched soldier, whose back has been cut to pieces.

'That's the spirit!' cries the officer. 'You've taken your punishment like a man. Here's a guinea for your trouble.'

An even more serious crime was an officer striking a private soldier – it meant instant court-martial – that's why soldiers would do all they could to goad an unpleasant officer into striking them. By lunchtime I just wanted to catch the next train back to Oswestry. I'd tell the WOSBE that I didn't want a commission; I'd stick to a straight salary. (Old Jewish joke, but very applicable in this case.)

Things got even worse in the afternoon. We had to go over the most horrendous assault course I've ever come across. At the end we fired five rounds rapid and I couldn't even hold the rifle to my shoulder – my muscles were like jelly. The next morning there were even more delights in store for us: we were shown a wire fence that was supposed to be electrified – actually it had little bells on it – and the idea was for a group of us to work out how to get everyone across without touching the fence and setting the bells off. We were supplied with some scaffold poles and wooden planks, and various groups of us spent the whole morning trying, without success, to get across.

In an episode of *Dad's Army*, 'We Know Our Onions', the platoon is sent to a special training camp for the weekend and put through all sorts of exercises to test their initiative. The Scots captain in charge (played by Fulton Mackay) is driven mad by their inability to understand the tests. They are given an exercise similar to the one I undertook, whereby they have to get over a wire fence without setting the alarm off, and they try again and again, without any success, until one o'clock in the morning. The platoon finally wins the competition the next day by using a load of onions – belonging to Hodges, the greengrocer – as ammunition, which repels an attack by a rival Home Guard platoon.

Even now, fifty years later, I still can't work out how we could have got over that fence. (It has just occurred to me that of course we could have gone *underneath* the fence – but that, I suppose, would have been too simple!)

At last the three days were over and I returned to Oswestry. My face was in a terrible mess and I had a very nasty black eye. The sergeant-major greeted me with the words, 'I know you've got a bad act, Perry, but there was no need for them to beat you up.'

'It was the WOSBE, they were trying to find out if I had enough aggression, sergeant-major,' I replied.

His eyes turned skywards. 'Officers – they're a load of c★★ts!'

There is a strange sequel to this story. Over the next three years, and for the remainder of my time in the army, a folder followed me all over the world, reminding me of my next appointment to attend the WOSBE at Chester. It even caught up with me in the jungle!

Back at Oswestry I made a fatal mistake – I started to feel secure. I forgot all about that nasty thing coming round the corner and hitting me in the balls. Our villain came onto the scene in October 1944; his name was Captain Dix – perhaps one of the most odious people I've ever come across. He fancied himself as a comedian and took over as compère in one of the shows at the Garrison Theatre. By then I regarded myself as one hundred per cent professional and I was appalled to find that when he turned up for the show he'd been drinking. He was under the impression that he was going well, not realising that soldiers will always laugh at an officer who makes a fool of himself.

I didn't say anything, but I was furious, and my anger must have shown because at the end of the show Captain Dix turned his bleary eyes on me and said, 'I'll get you, you little shit!' and within two weeks I was in the Quartermaster's Stores being issued with Jungle Greens (cotton uniforms for wearing in the tropics). Within another ten days I was sitting in a troop train with hundreds of others. The doors were firmly locked on the outside and Military Police patrolled the platform – there was no escape for anyone. Then Captain Dix looked in at me through the window, said, 'Bye-bye, Perry,' waved and drew his finger across his throat. What a bastard.

Perry and Waller:
   'My dog's got no nose'
   'How does it smell?'
   'Terrible!'
   'Kindly leave the stage.'

We were on our way to the posting everybody dreaded – the Far East. With me that day was another gunner, Harry Waller. We'd become pals during the last few weeks and did a double act in the Garrison Theatre. It was something we'd pinched off the radio from Arthur Askey and Richard Murdoch – 'The Proposal'.

'Your lips are like petals.'

'Rose petals?'

'No bicycle petals.' Etc. etc. . . .

It had gone very well and so we'd stuck together. For most of the day the troop train crawled and shunted and eventually reached the docks in Liverpool in the afternoon. The troopship, SS *Carthage*, was moored alongside the railway. The train doors were unlocked and, laden down with our kit, we staggered between two lines of MPs, up the gangplank into a hole in the side of the ship.

'Stick with me, Harry,' I gasped.

'Right behind you, Jim,' he replied. I followed the others up and down various iron stairways and right into the bowels of the ship. Eventually we reached our quarters, with rows of bunks, three deep each side. We took off our equipment and stared at each other; neither of us had ever been on a ship before and we'd certainly never left England. We went up on deck and I looked across the Mersey. There, scrawled on the side of a warehouse in huge letters, were the words, 'Fuck the Pope!'. It was the last sight I was to have of England for nearly three years. As it began to get dark we were ordered below and the hatches were battened down. We had a meal that surprised me, as it was so good – perhaps they were trying to keep us cheerful. We finally got to sleep. A few hours later we were woken up by the throbbing of the ship's engines. I'd never realised they could sound so loud but, over the next five weeks, they would hardly ever stop. It was obvious we were on the move, but most of us were too tired to care and went back to sleep.

Suddenly, in my dreams I heard a bugle, slowly awoke and I realised it really *was* a bugle and it was coming over the tannoy! 'How absurd,' I thought, 'you don't have bugles on ships,' but they did, and they never stopped blowing them, night or day.

And then it started. 'Hear this. Hear this,' over the tannoy, NCOs shouting and bawling at us. We were issued with life jackets and given the number of our lifeboat stations, then ordered up on deck. Eventually we found our station and stood there waiting. The convoy had assembled and it was amazing: everywhere, as far as the eye could see, hundreds of ships. Several NCOs pushed us into three lines and helped us on with our life jackets then an officer – who was rather like an enthusiastic scoutmaster – took the stage.

'Sorry to drag you up on deck without breakfast, chaps, but the convoy wants to move off, so you must know your lifeboat drill. I know the uppermost thought in all your minds is, what happens if we're hit by a torpedo? How many of you can swim?' Only about ten per cent of us raised our hands. He counted us. 'Well, chaps, let me assure you we have won the battle of the Atlantic. A couple of years ago I would not be talking to you like this, but I think it's safe to say the chances of a U-boat getting in among the convoy are pretty remote. On the other hand, one shouldn't be complacent. If the odd U-boat should get through and there's no room for you in one of the boats, and you find yourself in the water, make sure you join hands with your comrade and wait to be picked up. After all, it's unlikely you won't be spotted with all these ships about.'

Then, with those words of comfort, we were dismissed and went to breakfast, which, for some unknown, sadistic reason, was kippers. The combination of the smell of engine oil and those kippers did not go well together. Eventually the engines started up and the convoy was under way.

Conditions aboard a troopship for the ordinary squaddie can be very claustrophobic and most unpleasant – especially in the toilet department. We were issued with salt-water soap, as all the showers were sea water, so no matter how many showers you managed to get, you always felt sticky. As regards 'lavatorial arrangements' – as Arthur

Lowe used to call it – the loos were in rows, there were no partitions and the sight of twenty or so squaddies sitting in a line was, to me, quite horrendous. In the end I trained myself to go to the lavatory at about two o'clock in the morning when the loos were deserted.

For the first few days we were constantly expecting a big explosion as a torpedo hit us. Leaning over the side of the ship with Harry Waller, looking down, I said, 'It's a hell of a way to jump, Harry.'

I remembered a very early film, *Atlantic*, which was based on the story of the *Titanic*, one of the first talkies made in England. John Longdon, who plays the captain, says to a power-crazed multimillionaire these immortal lines, 'The ship has only four hours to live.'

Then Harry worked out that when we got into warmer waters, we could sleep in one of the lifeboats under the covers; then, in his words, 'If anything happened we'd be ready for off!'

After we'd been at sea for about five days, I noticed that one of my companions was always drawing lines on paper. I struck up a friendship with him; he was a Quaker and was so clever there was no subject you could fault him on. He reminded me of an old book we had at home: *Enquire Within Upon Everything*. Every night he went out on deck and worked out our course from the stars. He said, 'We're about halfway across the Atlantic on a course for New York.' And, as the convoy had to stick to the speed of the slowest ship, we were not making very good progress. The question was, why on earth were we going towards New York when we'd been issued with Jungle Green uniforms? But within another week, all would be revealed.

The next day I heard over the tannoy, 'Now hear this, hear this: will all volunteers for the ship's concert report to the main saloon at eleven hundred hours tomorrow morning.' A ship's concert, of course! Why hadn't I thought of doing one before? After all, we'd been at sea for nearly a week, but the fact is I'd been too busy worrying about U-boats and getting up at two o'clock in the morning to go to the loo. Of course, they would put me in charge. How wrong I was! The next morning Harry Waller and I reported to the main saloon, only to find that the man who was going to run the concert was the padre.

'Thank you for coming, everyone,' he said. 'Now, I thought we'd do the show like this: we'll all sit around on the platform in a half-circle and then perhaps we'll sing 'Happy Days Are Here Again' and then, taking it in turns, one of us will say, "I've got a story", and another one can say, "I've got a joke or two" and another one "I've got a little song".'

I could hardly believe my ears! 'It's amateur night in Dixie, Harry,' I hissed. 'I can't work with this man.'

'Keep shtum,' whispered Harry. 'If we're in the concert we'll get off duties.' Harry was from Liverpool and much more streetwise than I. Then the padre started to take our names.

I stepped forward briskly. 'Gunner Jimmy Perry,' I said. 'Professional comedian and impressionist. And this is my partner, Gunner Harry Waller – we do a double.'

I think the padre was rather taken aback by my brash approach, but I wanted to leave him in no doubt that I was a professional artiste.

We started rehearsals. One of the turns was an elderly man of about sixty – most unusual as nearly everyone on the troopship was young. He was a political officer in India returning from leave in the UK. He was going to sing 'The Laughing Policeman' and do some jokes. Now, there are two sorts of people I can't stand; one is property developers and the other amateur comedians. In spite of this, he was a nice man and, I regret to say, very funny (for an amateur, of course!). He wanted a police constable uniform but alas, where were we going get one on the ship? Then he got the idea of borrowing a uniform from one of the few Military Police on the boat. 'All I really want is the hat,' he said.

'Whatever you do, don't wear it,' I told him. 'You'll lose sympathy. That red cap will kill your act stone dead.' (Everyone hated Military Policemen.)

So come the dress rehearsal, he wore the following costume: a huge fisherman's wool jersey, huge wool socks turned over gumboots, an immense woollen scarf, duffle coat, woollen gloves and a woollen balaclava helmet, topped by a pith helmet. The rehearsal went very well and we were all set for the opening night. That evening my Quaker friend informed me that the convoy had turned due left and was approaching the coast of West Africa. The reason for our devious course was to avoid U-boats. The opening night came and went without a hitch. Harry and I did our double act. I did a solo – and added a new impression, Clark Gable in *Gone With the Wind*: 'Quite frankly, my dear, I don't give a damn.' To top it off I wore some cardboard ears I'd made. Then our friend the political officer came on . . . and brought the house down. He was a sensation! Now, as the main saloon only held about 300 people, we were going to have to perform the concert for several nights, and all the time the weather was getting warmer and warmer. By the third night I suggested to the political officer that he remove some of his woollens.

'No – they love it,' he said, perspiring. The following night he stood beside me, ready to go on. We were now well into the tropics. As usual, he'd kept all his woollies on and was pouring with sweat.

'I'm putting in something new tonight,' he said, holding up a cardboard truncheon. On he went, only this time he jumped into the audience and hit them with his truncheon. It's a sad fact that all amateur comedians are inclined to lose their judgement; the more laughs they get, the more 'stuff' they do. So this huge woollen figure singing 'Ha, ha, ha, ha, ha!' dived into the audience like a mad person, hitting everyone left and right. Suddenly he stopped and collapsed. The audience roared with laughter as the 'Laughing Policeman' slowly rose to his feet and staggered behind the screens.

The padre stepped forward and said, 'The next time, take more water with it!'

Twenty-four hours later we all stood on deck as the same padre conducted a funeral service over the Union Jack-covered figure of our political officer. We sang 'O God Our Help in Ages Past' and, as the ship couldn't stop, the body hit the water pretty fast. He was such a nice man.

Why does everybody want to be a comedian?

Some years ago, I wrote this song for a musical show I put on. Its original title was *Dirty Old Comics* and I lost my shirt backing it. In the end the song was never used, but it fits the bill perfectly:

> Everybody wants to be a comic,
> Everybody wants to be a turn,
> Everybody wants to get up on the stage,
> Be a hit, be a rage.
> Even an actor, playing heavy drama,
> Just can't wait to be a top banana,
> Cos everybody wants to be a comic,
> Everybody wants to be a turn!

A few days later we anchored at Cape Town. Harry and I looked over the side of the ship at the huge sharks circling, waiting for the food refuse to be thrown over the side. My reaction was, 'I don't think this is a good time to be torpedoed, Harry.'

He nodded and spat, and we watched the spittle go down and down until it hit the water. At last the ship's engines fell silent. We looked across at Table Mountain in the distance. We could see cars, like little Dinky Toys, moving along the road but there was to be no shore leave. The convoy was only going to remain long enough to refuel. Bumboats came alongside selling stuff and everyone bought bananas, which none of us had seen for over four years. Two days later we set off across the Indian Ocean on the last leg of our journey to Bombay. When we finally dropped anchor we'd been at sea over five weeks.

We disembarked on to a train bound for Kalyan. Kalyan was a vast transit camp for British servicemen and it was to be our home for the next six weeks. During that time we had so many inoculations – including one for bubonic plague, which you have in two lots, and the effects are so awful you're excused all duties for three days, most of which time you spent on your charpoy (bed). Now, in the British Army, if you're excused all duties, you really are bad. As soon as we could stagger to our feet we commenced jungle training – only the army would think up jungle training when there's no jungle. Kalyan is barren, dry scrub – nonetheless, we were given lectures on how to avoid being bitten by mosquitoes, how to survive with very little water, and how to make the jungle 'your friend'.

On parade one day the sergeant informed us we were going to the cinema. 'You're in luck,' he said. 'It's not often you can go to the pictures free, gratis, in the army's time! It's a wonderful film; it's in glorious Technicolor and it's such an exciting story – it's all about what happens if you go sticking your willies where they shouldn't be. *Attention! Right turn! Quick march! Lef', Ri', Lef', Ri', Lef'!'*

So we settled down in the camp cinema and waited. An army

doctor appeared in front of the screen and beamed at us.

'We're showing you this film today so that you can understand the full consequences of venereal disease.' The audience went very quiet. 'You've had several lectures on the dangers of unprotected sex with local women, but I think this film will underline everything that members of the Royal Army Medical Corps have been trying to drive home.' And then the film started. It certainly was in glorious Technicolor, with plenty of full close-ups. When the lights went up at the end there was a dead silence. Our friendly doctor came on, beaming.

'Well, I think that makes it plain to you all what will happen if you don't keep your private parts safe, and well tucked away in your Jungle Green underpants. So, let's have a laugh, men. Here's an old friend of ours. Right – roll 'em!' The doctor loped off and on to the screen came Mickey Mouse – I've never been so pleased to see anyone in all my life, but although poor Mickey worked his socks off he didn't get a single laugh; we were all suffering from shock. When it was finished we filed into the hard sunlight.

'Fall in in three ranks!' The sergeant's face was beaming from ear to ear, 'Well, well, what's the matter with you lot? Why are you looking so miserable? You had bad news from home or something? You don't know when you're well off. Heed the deadly warning! If, in future, you're feeling like a bit of what's-'er-name, I'm afraid it's the five-fingered widow or nothing.'

Things started to move very fast. Poor Harry Waller got a bad case of dysentery and ended up in hospital, and I ended up on a troop train heading east. Four days later we crossed the border into Burma and chugged down south to the Chittergong. Our final destination was a huge supply and air base. They had started transporting troops out East by plane, the base was a refuelling point, and we were taking

We never saw a single Jap plane.

over from one of the heavy ack-ack batteries defending the whole area. Considering we were relieving them, the gunners didn't seem overjoyed to see us. I suppose it was understandable, they were in a terrible state. The Fourteenth Army was called the 'Forgotten Army' and it was justified; they'd been fighting the Japs for years in the most appalling conditions and now, just as the tide was turning, we'd arrived from the UK looking well and fit. They called us 'Moon Men' because we were so pale and white. As they piled into their trucks the poor sods looked like scarecrows – they wished us luck and, with a few jeers, pulled away. Even then, I don't think they realised they were finally going home.

In spite of being on alert most of the time, we never saw a single Jap plane – what was left of their air force was in the Pacific fighting the Americans. The Japanese airmen were being trained as kamikaze (suicide) pilots. In spite of this, we had continual lectures on aircraft recognition. We'd crowd into an airless basha and the outline of enemy planes would be projected on to a screen. Because of the heat we always fell asleep and, to make things worse, the NCO giving the lecture insisted on showing us German, as well as Jap, planes. When I pointed out that the war in Europe was nearly over – and in any case the Germans had no planes left, and even if they had they were 5000 miles away – his reply was, 'You do your job, Bombardier, and I'll do mine.' (I'd been promoted in Kalyan.)

We were constantly being warned of Jap infiltrators; although the main Front was over forty miles away, there were pockets of resistance everywhere, holding out. Then we heard that the war in Europe was over – great news, but what about the Japs, they weren't going to give in? One day a party of Burmese irregulars brought in half a dozen Jap prisoners – this was quite a rare event. They crouched on the ground and hissed, which, I think, was the sign that they were humiliated – the code of the Japanese soldier is that he never surrenders. They were like skeletons; most of them had dysentery and were covered with lice. To us, they scarcely looked human.

One of them gestured that he was thirsty and a young Geordie gunner handed him his water bottle, as the prisoner reached for it, the others knocked it out of his hand. The Geordie went mad and started kicking the hell out of them. 'You disgusting, filthy bastards! You're shit!'

An officer stopped him. 'Leave them alone, gunner.'

'What use are they, sir?' he shouted. 'We should shoot them!'

'No. We need them for information,' the officer said coldly. 'Bring them along.'

And that was the attitude; the officer didn't reprimand the gunner for wanting to shoot them – he'd probably have done it himself – but we needed and wanted information.

'You're right, mate,' said one of the soldiers, 'they're filthy vermin.'

The Geordie's eyes were full of puzzled rage. He spat on the ground. 'What's the matter with them? Don't they know when they're beaten?' he shouted.

That night there was a film show in the cinema, it was the Victory Parade in London. All of us, sitting on the ground, clapped and jeered in derision. Lucky bastards! They were out of it and we were stuck here in this rotten, stinking jungle.

We spent most of the time keeping our equipment in order and having constant gun drills and lectures on aircraft recognition – and they were still showing us German planes! I tried to keep everyone's spirits up with some new impressions, but nobody was interested. We may have been bored out of our minds, but at least things were quiet. Then, around the corner *it* came once more and hit me in the backside: we were told that all heavy ack-ack units were going to be addressed by a general. Well, that'll be a novelty at least, we thought – we'd never seen one before. So we squatted on the ground and waited. They'd rigged up a sort of platform and a mike for the general. A junior officer shouted, 'Attention!' and we all shuffled to our feet. Then the general bounded on to the platform like a kangaroo – you have never seen anything like it in your entire life. It was the worst casting I've ever come across. You expect a general to have a ruddy complexion, bristling white moustache, bloodshot eyes and a monocle, and he should be short and fat and keep shouting, 'Eh, what!' This one was well over six feet tall, thin as a beanpole and round-shouldered. The costume was even worse. He should have been covered in red tabs and medals but this general wore a long khaki jumper, shorts that came down below his knees, and the whole effect was topped off by a bush hat pulled well down all round, which made him look like a mushroom.

They handed him the mike and he blew into it saying, 'Is it on? Is it on?'

'Oh, no!' I thought. 'Not *more* amateurs!'

Then he told us something that amounted to the fact that our anti-aircraft guns were completely out of date. By the time the radar and instruments had relayed the position of the plane to the guns, it would be out of their range before they had a chance to fire as it was too fast. In other words, all our training had been completely useless. Then the general added some words that made our blood run cold. 'There is one comfort in all this, men,' he said, 'three-point-seven ack-ack guns have proved excellent for dealing with Jap bunkers – so don't feel disappointed that you will not be used. In the next week or so there's going to be a huge push forwards on all Fronts and we're going to throw everything we've got at those Japs.'

There was a deadly silence until a thin voice piped up, 'What about us instrument operators, sir?'

'Good question, gunner. We just point the guns at the bunkers and blast away, so we won't need you for that, but there is a role for you in all this; you instrument chaps will be used to protect the gun crews from marauding Japs – so you'd better polish up your bayonet drill. That's all – dismiss.'

So the great push was on, then. We knew it was serious when planeloads of fresh mules arrived. Getting mules on and off Dakota transport planes is not an easy business; they don't take well to flying. In fact, they don't take well to anything.

Now, what I'm about to say is going to make a lot of you British people very cross, but I'm not much of an animal lover. I've never hurt, or ill-treated an animal in my life, but that doesn't mean I love them – they just bore me. Dogs, in particular, never leave me alone – they're such *crawlers* – they bound up to me and stick their noses straight up my backside, then roll around looking cute, but I turn away with a hard look in my eyes. This frustrates them even more and they try even harder to make me love them. Some years ago I went to see some friends who had two large Labradors. One of the dogs crashed up to me and licked my hand. I said, 'Excuse me, I must wash.'

'Why?' they asked.

'Do you realise how much bacteria a dog has in its mouth?' They looked at me as if I was some sort of idiot. There is one exception to the rule – I love cats: they are proud, beautiful and independent.

But to get back to the mules. It's not their fault they are neither horse nor donkey. They did a great job for us in that rotten jungle; the British Army has a lot to thank those mean, awkward, bad-tempered brutes for.

The big push was on and there was no way out for any of us, and then suddenly – oh, lucky Jim, how we envy him – on the eve of going into action, *it* happened. Let me paint the picture for you: it was about eight or nine o'clock at night and, in what passed for a canteen, in the dim light of the faint oil lamps, our faces looked pretty grim – even I had given up telling jokes – and we sat there drinking our one bottle of beer per night ration, and eating a plate of egg and chips. (The chips were made from sweet potatoes, and if you've never had them – don't try, they're awful!)

Suddenly, in rushed the battery idiot. He wore thick glasses and looked rather like Benny Hill's 'Fred Scuttle'; he shouted, 'Have you heard the news? They've dropped some huge bomb on Japan an' killed everyone and the whole country has sunk – Japan doesn't exist any more!'

Now we, even in our desperate state, didn't believe that! The messenger was pelted with ripe mangoes and treated to a chorus of 'Bugger off!' A short while later it came over the tannoy that the atom bomb had been dropped on Japan. We'd no idea what it was and for the next few days we held our breath; there was complete confusion but, thank goodness, no more stand-bys to move forward. Then it came: the war was over. How can one believe how we boys felt? We were going home, or so we thought, but it would be at least another two years before I got back to good old Watford. Strangely, when all the excitement had died down, I felt a terrible anticlimax.

Over the next few weeks I became slightly unwell. The MO couldn't find anything wrong with me, but I was losing weight and so I found myself on the train going back across India on to Kalyan. It must have taken about five days and I was feeling worse. When we arrived I suddenly started to vomit and became delirious; they carted me to a first aid post. By now I had a high temperature – I was in a

The army hospital – what a terrible place. I was dying by inches, but Major Loosemore, the surgeon, saved my life.

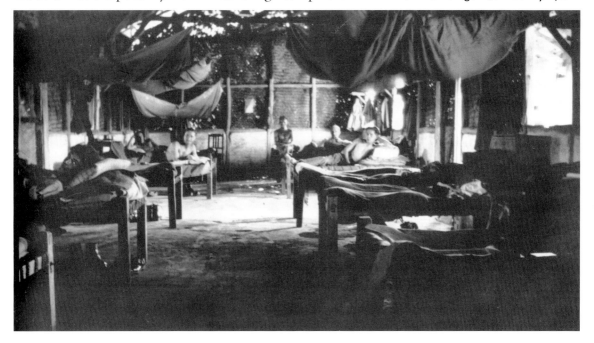

dreadful state. I remember being put into an ambulance and driven along a bumpy road to the army hospital. Each bump felt as though someone was sticking a red-hot poker into my tummy button. When we finally got to the hospital the only medic there was a young Indian doctor and two British nursing sisters – I was dying by inches.

In my delirious state I imagined I was tied to the front of a steam train and it kept hitting another one head on. I lost all count of time as I drifted in and out of consciousness, then, through a haze of pain, I heard the voice of the man who saved my life – Major Loosemore, a brilliant surgeon. I just caught the words 'For God's sake, get him ready for surgery!' before I passed out. How Major Loosemore got through so quickly, and how I survived a major operation and a burst appendix under such appalling conditions I'll never know.

From time to time various branches of the Armed Services are praised, but no one, as far as I can recall, says very much about the Royal Army Medical Corps. Without their care, I don't think I would have pulled through. Some fifteen years later I met Major Loosemore at a party. He was now a consultant working at the Peace Memorial Hospital in Watford. (All roads seem to lead there!) I reminded him of the incident. He didn't remember, but said, 'Show me your scar.' So I pulled up my shirt and revealed it. (Not a very polite thing to do at a cocktail party.)

He recognised it instantly. 'Oh yes, that was a close thing,' he said. 'What a terrible place the hospital at Kalyan was – you nearly bought it that day.'

I was in hospital for quite a few weeks and when I got out of bed I was transferred to a wheelchair. Slowly, very slowly, I started to recover, hobbling about on one stick. Eventually I was sent to a rest camp in Srinagar in Kashmir to get my strength back. After another interminable train journey I arrived, along with lots of other poor sods who really had been wounded – remember, the war had only been over for ten weeks.

I was dressed now in the standard British Army hospital gear: light-blue jacket and trousers, white shirt and red tie, topped off with my bush hat, and I was billeted at the Union Jack Club. The luxury of ad-lib showers and sheets on my bed was wonderful. I kept thinking, 'Was my operation serious enough to be a Blighty one (get sent home)?' Only time would tell.

Now, there was a big canteen and rest rooms, manned by members of the WVS – British officers' wives 'doing their bit for the war effort'. Most of their husbands were on duty, scattered all over India down in the plains.

This photo of me was taken by Edith – I was on cloud nine at the time.

One night I was queuing up for my cup of tea and statutory rock cake when I was confronted by a very formidable memsahib. 'Yes? What would you like?' she asked.

Well, there I was, twenty-two years old – I looked about seventeen – dressed in hospital blue, the standard Wounded War Hero. Suddenly she gasped, 'Oh, you poor boy!' burst into tears and ran into the back. 'What's the matter with the silly cow?' I thought and sat down. A few minutes later she came over and joined me, and started on that 'poor boy' stuff again. She asked me if I'd been badly hurt.

'I've had an operation,' I said. The scar was pretty horrific, and stretched from my ribcage down to my crotch.

'Where?' she managed to get out. I pointed downwards. 'Oh, no! Not that!' The tears came again.

'I haven't been wounded,' I said. 'I've had a burst appendix.' By now I was getting rather embarrassed. She started to question me – asking me my name and where I was staying – then, with a curt 'I must get back on duty', she left.

A Stupid Boy

The next morning I was told the warden wanted to see me. He didn't beat about the bush, 'One of the WVS ladies has offered to put you up on her houseboat. It would help us a lot if you went, we're very overcrowded. I'll check if it's OK with the doctor, right?'

A short while later an Indian bearer was carrying my kit down to the boat.

She met me with the words, 'I think you'll be much more comfortable here. You need to be properly looked after.' Now, the houseboats in Kashmir are really floating bungalows, and very comfortable.

Over lunch, she questioned me closely: 'You're not like most of the other soldiers, why aren't you an officer?' I dismissed this with a shrug.

'I'm a professional comedian, I'm in show business,' I said. It fell on stony ground.

'We can have a nice dinner tonight and you must get as much rest as you can.'

I'd no idea where all this was leading. I was twenty-two years of age and she must have been in her early forties. I had no knowledge of women at all and was completely naïve.

She told me her name was Edith and that her husband was a major, stationed down in the Punjab – the penny still didn't drop. It was rather like having lunch with a formidable auntie, even if she did look like a young Flora Robson!

Promptly at six thirty that evening I presented myself. I was wearing my best khaki drill bush jacket, which was starched so heavily it almost stood up on its own. The Indian bearer, Mohammed, told me that the memsahib would be with me very soon and, armed with a glass of *puggleparni* (gin and tonic), I waited.

Then the memsahib appeared. Gone was the matronly green cotton WVS uniform. It was replaced by an amazing sari covered with gold. She had rings on every finger, as well as some on her toes, and her nails were lacquered red. Her eyes were heavily made up with khol in the Indian style and as she came towards me I was almost overwhelmed by the strong jasmine scent of her perfume. Mohammed glided in behind, carrying the champagne.

'You may serve the champagne, Mohammed,' she said in a low, husky voice and with a '*Teekai*, memsahib' he opened the bottle. I'd never had champagne before; the only wine I'd ever tasted was sherry, and sweet martini at Christmas.

She led me out on to the balcony. 'Here's to us, Jimmy,' she whispered as we clinked glasses. 'You know, you're a very nice-looking young man.'

'Oh! Well – yes – you're nice too,' was my feeble reply.

'You've no idea how nice I can be,' she husked – she wasn't like an auntie any more – and suddenly the penny dropped. She wanted me to have sex with her! My mouth went dry, my heart started thumping. Mohammed saved the day as he bowed us towards the table. We ate and I turned the conversation towards films, which she liked. As the meal passed I felt more relaxed; perhaps at the end, she'd just say goodnight and that would be that, I thought. I was dimly aware that Mohammed had disappeared. Then she pulled me slowly to the sofa and we kissed. I'd never kissed like that before, her tongue was red-hot and everywhere – 'This is quite wrong,' I thought, 'it's all wrong!' – then she put her hand into my trousers and, within a few seconds, I exploded.

She didn't seem all that concerned, saying, 'That'll take a little pressure out of the situation, darling.'

I felt terrible, humiliated and ashamed. 'I'm sorry, I've never made love properly before,' was all I could say. She took me by the hand and led me into the bedroom. She let her sari drop as I half-heartedly undressed, then she pulled me to her. Her body was so amazing I just exploded again. We lay together for a few minutes. I felt so low it's just impossible to describe. 'What can I do?' I gasped.

'Have a little patience, and leave it to me.' I looked at her body in the faint light. I'd never seen a naked woman before, and it all seemed so very strange. 'Now, go back to your room,' she said, gently.

'Can't I stay with you?' I was amazed at my cheek.

'No. We won't sleep together until we've consummated our love.' I didn't even understand what she was getting at.

The second night was almost as bad.

'Perhaps I ought to go back to the Union Jack Club in the morning, as things don't seem to be working out,' I told her sulkily.

She sat up and looked at me, for the first time. She was really angry. 'You want to go, Jimmy? You want to join all the millions of other men who just don't know how to make women happy? You want to give up? Or, do you want to join the men who've been taught by women to understand them? You know what the Kama Sutra says: "The man who understands women and knows that they are the fountain of life, will indeed enter the gates of Paradise." Do you want to be one of those men?'

'Yes, please,' I managed to get out.

'Very well,' she said, turning back into the memsahib. 'We start tomorrow night.'

Edith was on duty most of the next day and I wandered about in a sort of dream, spending hours in the library, picking up books, glancing at them, putting them down, but my thoughts were on only one thing: what was the great secret I was about to learn?

When she came home she told me we were going out to dinner.

As a rule WVS officers did not socialise with BORs (British other ranks) but if they were in hospital blue they weren't bothered – after all, it was the duty of officers' wives to take care of our brave lads. There was to be no glamorous sari tonight. She appeared in a crisp, starched uniform, told me she had booked a table for two at a Chinese restaurant and offered me a wad of rupees. I refused it, and said I would pay, then she handed me a walking stick. 'Lean on it heavily as we go into the restaurant. I will support you by holding your arm and you will look as though you were badly wounded; then tongues won't wag so much – OK?' she said curtly.

'But I'm not wounded. It's nearly two months since I had my operation and I'm perfectly all right.'

'Don't argue,' she said, sounding like a hospital matron. A tonga was waiting outside. The driver whipped up the horse and we sped off to our romantic dinner.

So this was it, then. No wonder I used to hear my mother tell my sister that once men had got what they wanted, they didn't want it any more.

The Chinese restaurant was beside the lake and lit with coloured lanterns – it was very romantic. My first thought was, 'Have I got enough money on me?' We were shown to our table.

The waiter took my stick and handed us the menus, with the words, 'Ah. So sad.' I'm sure he was looking at my crutch. During the meal various people stopped at our table and, aside from a curt word, almost ignored me.

One woman leaned over and whispered to Edith, 'My dear, he's absolute heaven! You always have all the luck!'

When we got back to the houseboat I started to feel sick – it was either the excitement or the Chinese food. We undressed and lay on the huge cushions. Then she told me about foreplay and how vital it was. It seemed almost like those lectures on aircraft recognition. She continued – by now all thoughts of Japanese planes had gone out of my mind – and then she pulled me to her.

'Oh no,' I thought. 'I'm not going to make it.' Suddenly I felt the most terrible pain in my backside and then I felt it again. Edith started screaming and laughing, and then it happened – we consummated our love. She clung to me like a demented person and laughed with joy – she laughed loud and long. There was a gentle knock at the door.

'Tell him it's OK,' she hissed through clenched teeth. I pulled a towel round me and opened the door.

It was Mohammed. 'Memsahib OK, sahib?'

'*Teekai*,' I gasped. 'Memsahib pukka nightmare.'

'Ah. Memsahib aspirin?'

'Aspirin *neyhai*.'

He slid away into the darkness.

'We did it, darling,' she whispered.

I rushed out on to the veranda and was promptly sick over the side of the boat – it *was* the Chinese food! I cleaned myself up and returned to Edith. 'I'm sorry.'

'Was I that revolting, darling?' she teased. And then we laughed; the sheer joy in her voice was wonderful. I went to sit beside her and I felt a strange pain in my backside. I touched it and there was a spot of blood on my hand.

'Sorry, darling, it was the only way,' she cooed. 'Don't worry, I sterilised the darning needle.' Far into the night she explained: it was a man's natural instinct to climax almost at once. The only way he could overcome this was to train his subconscious brain that it was wrong, but to do so he was fighting the whole male psyche. Now, the first step in controlling his natural instincts was to introduce a pain that was so intense it would counteract his natural desire. Hence the needle applied to my rear! Another instinct was for the male to leave his partner and fall asleep as soon as he had achieved climax – this had to be fought and conquered until the male would actually enjoy a postcoital cuddle.

Just a few years ago I watched a TV series about the Edwardian beauty, Lillie Langtry. The part was played by that beautiful actress Francesca Annis. In a scene, set the morning after her wedding night, she was sitting up in bed eating breakfast and her husband was putting on shooting clothes. She looks at him, pats the pillow and says, 'Come back to bed, darling.'

His reply is 'Are you mad? What's come over you?' and he stamps out of the room. You see a close-up of her face. It is the expression of so many women who have been let down by so many so-called 'men'.

For the next three weeks my 'training' continued. Edith taught me about many Oriental and Eastern cults – the Tao Art of Love, the Kama Sutra – all of them devoted to sex. She told me she'd read that the Aga Khan could make love for hours on end, provided he had both elbows in a bucket of ice. I didn't know if she meant one bucket or two, but by then I was almost hysterical with happiness. On our last night together she took my hand and told me a terrible, terrible story: 'A husband and wife decide to go on a second honeymoon, the room has single beds. The husband says, "Come to my bed, darling" and, as she crosses, she trips on the carpet. "Oh dear, you poor little girl. Did you hurt yourself?" coos the husband. After they had made love, she goes back to her bed and trips again. "Watch where you're going, you clumsy cow!" he shouts.' It sums up what so many women have had to put up with since the beginning of time.

I sat in the train as it wended its way south – my four weeks' convalescence leave had ended. I'd said goodbye to Edith and we'd spent the last night in each other's arms crying, it seems, for most of the time. We'd watched the fingers of dawn creep across the ceiling and I'd thought at the time of how many lovers had been in that position – the last brief hours together, then never to see each other again. I'd never seen anyone so upset as Edith and now she'd gone out of my life for ever. It took a long time to sink in.

Filming a scene from the episode 'Monsoon Madness' – the actors are digging trenches for the rain.

I was posted to Deolali, which was a huge Royal Artillery base. At one time it had been a mental hospital for British soldiers – hence the expression 'doolally-tap' for anyone who is off their rocker. I arrived just as the monsoons were about to break. During the 200-odd years the British had ruled India, this was always a very tense couple of weeks. There were stories of soldiers who had run amok and shot their officers, husbands who had shot their wives, wives who had shot their husbands, as the tension built up and up, and the heat increased until the monsoon finally broke.

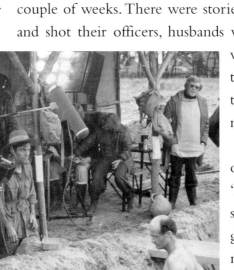

David and I wrote one episode of *It Ain't Half Hot, Mum* called 'Monsoon Madness' which was set in it; Gunner Sugden ('Lofty') goes out of his mind and tries to murder Sergeant-Major Williams (Windsor Davies).

The first person to greet me when I arrived at Deolali was Harry Waller. He'd seen my name on the posting list. It was over three months since I had last set eyes on him and he looked as thin as a rake. He'd spent six weeks in hospital and the dysentery had been quite serious. 'You'll never believe it, wack,' he said, 'they've got a concert party here!'

And that was how I heard for the first time about the famous Royal Artillery Concert Party. They also had their own band and theatre – it was paradise! We wasted no time in applying for an audition. We performed the 'proposal' sketch and we were in – at last I was working with professional artistes. Most of them had been in show business before being called into the services and the man in charge was Lieutenant Rankin who, in Civvie Street, had been the director of the Glasgow Orpheus Choir. An excellent pianist and far too highbrow for this job, it was his first experience of working with common comics, popular singers and female impersonators, but he loved it.

Most of the artistes had seen service with the Fourteenth Army in Burma. Stanley Axham was the female impersonator – not 'Drag Queen', he had far too much dignity. He made all his own dresses and used a turban, which did away with the need of a wig. He was far too lifelike, and frequently went, in costume, down to the officers mess in the evenings – he was the only 'female' company they were going to get!

With monsoons about to break, all shows were suspended as everyone frantically dug deep ditches round the edge of our bashas. Bashas were the huts we lived in. They consisted of a brick wall about

The Royal Artillery Concert Party, 1945. Back row: Stanley Axham, me, unknown, Les Booth, Ken Ryland, Ken Smith, Ev Mansbridge, Cliff Bishop. Front row: Roger Bourne, Jeff Myers, Lieutenant Rankin, John Barber, John Barlow.

Standing outside the Royal Artillery Theatre in front of the poster for 'We Couldn't Care Less' – my first show as producer.

four feet high, the rest of the wall being made up of dried rushes – the roof was tiled. The only trouble was that chipmunks (sort of squirrels) pinched bits of the rush walls to make their nests so that all of the buildings had the appearance of being moth-eaten. The Royal Artillery Theatre was also built in this way.

Then down came the rain – it was the first monsoon I'd experienced. All shows were cancelled – the rain made so much noise on the roof no one could hear anything. The trenches we had dug round our bashas filled up very quickly and, within two days, Deolali, which had been a dry, dusty cauldron of heat, rainless for nine months, completely changed. Vegetation sprang up like magic from nowhere, thousands of frogs appeared and lots of nasty little snakes (including the *krait*, a small black and yellow little sod, which is very poisonous). We used the time to prepare a new show and it was then that I started writing comedy material; I'd never tried it before. Most of it I remembered from radio shows I'd heard over the years. Roger Bourne was a comedian and tap dancer, and far older than the rest of us. I wrote a 'spiv' character for him (pinched from Sid Field), which worked very well. This was long before Arthur English did *his* spiv.

Many years later I used Roger as a member of the platoon in *Dad's Army*.

After a few weeks the rains eased off and we resumed our shows – the Royal Artillery Concert Party went on tour. We took a portable stage with us that was far too heavy, plus a mini-piano which, because of the humidity, was always going out of tune – Norman Mail, our pianist, had to learn quickly how to tune a piano, but he mastered it. We'd set up the stage and do shows over several nights before moving on. We were billeted in various camps and some of the living conditions made us long for the comfortable bashas back at good old Deolali. We sometimes had audiences of over 1000 and, at other times, just a handful. Troops came from miles around and were always very enthusiastic – but what else could they be, they had nothing else!

There were so many problems performing in the open air. As soon as the stage lights came on, it started – thousands of flying creatures were attracted by the glare: moths, as big as small birds, instantly committed suicide and the floor of the stage became so slippery with the corpses of small insects that every so often it had to be swept. I worked out a comic routine for this: two members of the concert party quickly swept and the spotlight moved in front of their brooms. Finally they'd get the light into a corner where it grew smaller and smaller as they swept it, until it finally went out. Years later I saw Marcel Marceau, the famous mime, do this routine in London – fancy pinching it from us! I can't remember ever seeing him in the audience . . .

After the show our shirts would be soaked with sweat; they'd be promptly collected by the dhobi wallah and brought back the next day, clean, starched and beautifully ironed. Unfortunately, bashing them on a rock in the river was inclined to wear them out. Lieutenant Rankin kept telling them to use soap flakes – their reply was, 'Sadly, Sahib, not enough soap flakes to fill river.'

When we got back to Deolali, Stanley Axham found that his demob had come through and he was off to Blighty, and I was told that I was to take charge of the concert party and was promoted from bombardier to lance sergeant – a rank that I don't think exists any more – you wear the three stripes without the little gun on top.

So far I've not mentioned the *original* sergeant-major: the character we wrote for *It Ain't Half Hot, Mum* really did exist. The only thing was he was cockney, not Welsh. The colonel was all in favour of the concert party, also the adjutant – the sergeant-major hated us. 'You are a bunch of poofs' was his regular saying. 'No man who puts on make-up and ponces about on a stage is normal – what are you?'

'A bunch of poofs!' we'd reply.

Unlike the sergeant-major in *It Ain't Half Hot, Mum*, ours was a pathetic creature. Now I was a sergeant I could use the mess, and one night I saw him on his own; the place was empty and I bought him a drink. He pointed to my Burma Star (they'd just started to issue service medals). 'You, and all those poofs in the concert party have got Burma Stars,' he slurred, 'an' I've got nothing.'

I pointed to his chest: 'You're wearing an Indian Service Medal.'

'But it's not on *active* service, is it?' he said. 'Apart from a few bouts of leave, in Blighty, I've been in India eight years and never heard a shot fired in anger!'

'Well, I never saw any *real* action,' I said sympathetically. 'The only Japs I came across were prisoners. I was just there.'

'Oh, is that a fact?' he shouted and, mimicking me – badly, 'You were "*just there*" – how jolly brave!' and with that he staggered out.

I started to put together a new show call *We Couldn't Care Less* (what a rotten title! – I was never any good at them.) I got forty-eight hours' leave to go into Bombay to pick up some new music and I took Harry Waller with me. We stayed the night at the usual Union Jack Club. Bombay was a seething mass of humanity. Beggars and street vendors were everywhere. Amazing contrasts; there were so many magnificent buildings erected by the British over the years, not to mention imperial statues. Up until then I had had no idea of the problems between Muslims and Hindus that were building up which, within just over eighteen months, would lead to the division of India and Pakistan.

Now, the music shop was in the smart part of Bombay and was kept by an enthusiastic Anglo-Indian who frequently had copies of new sheet music sent in from the UK. Opposite the shop was a new cinema called the Metro – Indians just loved cinema and it was always packed, especially in those days. Shows would start in the morning and go on all day until late into the night. Harry and I were going through piles of music when we heard what sounded like

The Metro Cinema, Bombay, where a gunman opened fire into the crowds as they came out of a showing.

firecrackers. We looked out of the window and some madman with a revolver in each hand was shooting into the crowd who were coming out of the cinema. People ran screaming in all directions, a tram came round the corner and stopped. I always had my camera with me, and I ran up to the first floor to take a picture. Although it was only a few minutes after the shooting, the street was almost clear. The owner quickly put up the shutters and closed the shop; his wife came out of the back with a tray of tea, which we drank in silence. How typically British!

The time came for Lieutenant Rankin to go home, and to take his place as entertainments officer Lieutenant Joseph O'Conor came into our lives. Now Joe was very much a straight actor. (Incidentally, he played the part of Old Jolyon in the original BBC television series of *The Forsyte Saga*.) He was always worried about raising the standard of the show and called us together and presented us with a script for what he thought was a very funny play. It was called *Two Gentlemen of Soho* and was a send-up of Shakespeare's *Two Gentlemen of Verona*. It was written by A. P. Herbert and was very clever and sophisticated – but not suited for an audience of hairy gunners. To appreciate the wit you had to be a devotee of the Bard – which our audiences certainly were not. It was only a short one-act play and Joe said the second half of the evening's entertainment would be a variety show compèred by me.

In vain I protested, 'It's not suitable for our audiences.'

'We have to raise our standards,' insisted Joe. 'If we don't try, we'll never get the chaps to appreciate the more intelligent stuff.'

I was desperate. I tried everything: 'What about the new show I've got together *We Couldn't Care Less?*'

'Oh, we can do that later,' Joe said.

And so we started rehearsing for *Two Gentlemen of Soho*.

In spite of the fact that the war had been over for some considerable time, there were still a lot of servicemen eager to get home; there were not, however, enough troopships to deal with such huge numbers – but it was no use telling them that.

The opening night of *Two Gentlemen* drew nearer. We all sensed disaster, but it was no good – Lieutenant O'Conor was determined to give the troops 'something intellectual to lift up their minds'. Sixty paratroopers had just arrived in Deolali to await transport home. They'd had a tough time in Burma and had been overseas for years – they were due for demob. They'd been constantly promised they'd be drafted back to the UK but the plans were always being cancelled.

Things were boiling up – those tough jungle fighters were in an ugly mood; they'd had enough. To calm them down, the colonel decided to invite the paratroopers to the first performance of *Two Gentlemen*. Came the opening night, there was a tense feeling among the concert party. Another circumstance was to come into the picture – the mango season was in full swing and the fruit wallahs were selling them to the audience. They weren't like the mangoes you buy at Sainsbury's, but twice the size and very squashy.

Eventually the curtain went up on *Two Gentlemen of Soho*. We held our breath, but for the first five minutes we could hardly believe our luck; the audience were listening attentively . . . then it happened. There was a loud raspberry, followed by a low hum that was slowly swelling louder – I can only describe it as being like the noise the Zulus made in the film *Zulu* just before they were going to attack. Then the first mango came flying through the air and hit the scenery, its contents trickling down. Within seconds the air was full of flying mangoes. The cast was manfully struggling with their lines, but it was impossible to hear them above the shouts of the audience. The stage was covered in slippery mangoes, plus the odd pineapple or two. Joe O'Conor appeared in the wings and shouted, 'Keep going! You'll win them over!' By now the noise was deafening and the curtain came down. Joe pushed me through them, shouting the immortal line, 'Go on and tell a few jokes!'

The sight that greeted me was horrendous; the paratroopers were not only fighting the other soldiers in the audience, but pulling down the flimsy rush walls – they were destroying the theatre. At last the Military Police arrived, lead by the provo sergeant, who shouted in vain, 'You're all under arrest!'

Nobody took any notice. Finally reinforcements of MPs arrived and things were gradually brought under control. Within forty-eight hours the paratroopers were on their way home, no charges were made.

The Colonel called the concert party on parade and said, 'Now listen, chaps, I've just had a signal from GHQ about the little disturbance the other night. The *Times of India* may be sending a reporter down and this is what I want you to say: there has been no mutiny. British troops do not mutiny; they are a disciplined force and will always behave. Have you got that?' We all nodded. He went on, 'You will say the show went down so well that the audience got a little overenthusiastic. Is that clear?' We all nodded. 'That's all. Dismissed.' Within days the walls of the theatre were quickly repaired and we started on the production *We Couldn't Care Less*.

Of all the TV series that David Croft and I have done together my favourite, without any doubt, is *It Ain't Half Hot, Mum*, which was, of course, based on the Royal Artillery Concert Party. There was something about it that was so totally different from any other TV comedy series – apart, of course, from the fact that it was set in India – since it was also based on fact: the last days of the British Empire. When it first came out, in 1973, although it was a comedy show, it set the pattern for many other TV plays and series about the British Raj. What David and I were trying to do was to explain why we had so many Asians living in the UK and how we became a multiracial society; it was the effect of the aftermath of Empire. But when people started to dismiss the show as racist it filled me with despair. The people who said this were all British and it was purely based upon ignorance. Some years ago a BBC executive bluntly said to me that they wouldn't repeat the series 'because it's racist'. Obviously he knew nothing about the history of the British Empire and had never been to India. The strange thing is that British Asians loved it – and still do – they call it 'our programme'.

Michael Bates, who played Rangi-Ram, the bearer, was a joy. In 1972 there were very few Asian actors and, sadly, not one experienced enough to play a leading comedy role (today, of course, there are plenty and it would be easy to cast). During the series David and I were responsible for starting off, and encouraging, many Asian actors who have since become well known. Michael was born in India and spoke fluent Urdu, and the part fitted him like a glove. He had been an officer with the Gurkhas during the war and served with the Chindits behind the Japanese lines in Burma. When he contracted cancer during the series he refused to let it interfere with his work and survived for two years, managing, between bouts in hospital, to make two more series. He knew he was terminally ill but, somehow, kept going. After a while we used an actor, Michael Beavis, to double for him in the long shots when he had to run about. His sense of humour never left him; one night he threw a small party after the show in his dressing room and we were greeted with the words, 'White wine, gin and tonic, or plasma?' The last series was so difficult for Michael. By now he was extremely ill, unfortunately, and when we were in the studio making the show in front of an audience, he could not take painkillers because they made him too dizzy. But as soon as the show ended his dresser would be standing by with the tablets and a glass of water, Michael would gulp them down and sink into a chair. He was one of the bravest men I've ever known.

Michael Bates, one of the bravest men I've ever known.

I shall never forget the night we recorded the pilot of *It Ain't Half Hot, Mum* in front of a live audience. It was an extraordinary experience. The effect on the people in that studio audience was wonderful as they met the characters like the Char-Wallah and the extras – they were enchanted. Colonel Reynolds and Captain Ashwood, played by Donald Hewlett and Michael Knowles, were a perfect comedy duo, each one playing off the other. Ashwood is the typical English silly ass but, as played by Michael, he is very real. In one episode he is waiting for Colonel Reynolds who has gone to GHQ; the Colonel arrives back late at night and is greeted by Ashwood:

> ASHWOOD: Where have you been? It's nearly one o'clock in the morning, I've been worried to death.
>
> REYNOLDS: Why didn't you go to bed?
>
> ASHWOOD: You know perfectly well if I'm woken up I can never get back to sleep again.
>
> REYNOLDS: Oh, don't start nagging.
>
> ASHWOOD: Have you been drinking?
>
> REYNOLDS: Yes – what's it got to do with you?

David and I had written a sort of husband and wife scene for them and it worked to perfection.

The casting of Don Estelle as Lofty happened almost by accident. While we were still doing *Dad's Army*, Arthur Lowe recorded a show for Granada Television during a break in production. One of the small-part players came up to him and said, 'How can I get into situation comedy?' It was Don Estelle, he was under five feet tall and rather round. 'I'm a singer you know,' he persisted. Whether Arthur's sense of humour got the better of him, or whether he was serious, we shall never know, but he said to Don, 'Write to David Croft and mention my name.' Which Don promptly did, also sending a tape of his singing. As luck would have it, we were looking for a very small man for a small part in the next series of *Dad's Army*, so David booked him. When we came to cast *It Ain't Half Hot, Mum*, we wanted a singer who was out of the ordinary. Don had a very pleasant voice, reminiscent of Dick Powell, and the character of Lofty was born.

In 1975, Wally Ridley, the record producer, arranged to make an LP of the show with all the characters doing various numbers. He wanted something for the sergeant-major and Lofty together, but was completely stumped. The recording was made at Abbey Road, the famous studios where The Beatles recorded so many of their songs. On the day it was to take place, Wally had still not found a suitable number for Windsor and Don. I was in the shower in my flat in London, listening to Pete Murray in *The Morning Show*, when he announced the Inkspots number, 'It's a Sin to Tell a Lie'. As I listened it suddenly hit me – it would suit Windsor and Don perfectly. I rang Wally Ridley at home, but was told he'd already left for the studio, so I phoned Abbey Road early and caught him as he arrived.

'Nobody's heard of the Inkspots for twenty years,' he said. 'I'll think about it.' And that was it.

'Well,' I thought, drying myself. 'Sod 'em. They'll just have to do one number short on the record.'

I didn't hurry to get down to Abbey Road, but when I arrived the recording was well under way. Wally was in the sound gallery. When there was a break he mentioned to me, quite casually, 'That was a good idea, Jim. I dug out a number, another Inkspots song. "Whispering Grass". We've already recorded it – it only took about ten minutes.'

And that's how a hit was born. It became a huge success, topping the charts for many weeks, and Windsor and Don were overnight stars. By the way, it was Windsor who put in several lines, including, 'I will not have gossip in this jungle!'

Towards the end of 1946, after all the years it had been in existence, the Royal Artillery Concert Party was disbanded. The few remaining members were posted to the far corners of India and, to make matters worse, Harry Waller got another bout of dysentery and was taken into hospital.

The 1982 reunion of the Royal Artillery Concert Party. Joe O'Conor, front row, second from left.

About twenty years ago one of the Sunday newspapers wanted to do an article on 'Where are they now?'. They decided to get together the original members of the Royal Artillery Concert Party. We assembled at the BBC Television Centre, had photographs taken and gave various interviews. Looking at all those faces today, I'm afraid that I'm almost the only one still alive.

I was posted to the Gordon Highlanders. The camp was about five miles from a town called Coimbatore in southern India. I left Deolali on Christmas Eve and, after travelling most of the day and night, arrived on Christmas morning in Madras. I spent Christmas Day 1946 on Madras railway station, eating my Christmas dinner alone in the European dining room – eggs and chips, and crème caramel. Now, I don't want to sound an old misery, but somehow this experience put me off Christmas and I've hardly enjoyed one since.

Eventually I got another train to Coimbatore and arrived, about five or six hours later, at the Gordon Highlanders' camp. The first thing that happened was they took one stripe away, reducing me from sergeant to bombardier. The officers and most of the NCOs were Scottish, and about eighty per cent of the other ranks English. It's almost impossible to describe how toffee-nosed the Scottish officers were – they looked down on us Sassenachs as if we were some sort of native troops and treated us accordingly. Me, a gunner, in an *infantry* regiment? As soon as possible I went to see the adjutant.

'The whole thing's been a mistake,' I pointed out. 'I shouldn't be here. I'm not an infantryman, I'm a gunner! I used to run the Royal Artillery Concert Party!'

His hard eyes had no sympathy. 'What did you do? Fish a rabbit out of a bloody hat?' he asked.

I just repeated, 'I shouldn't be here! The whole thing's a terrible mistake!'

It was the same scene, as in so many films, where Our Hero is wrongly accused – he shakes the bars of his cell and shouts, 'I'm innocent, it's all a mistake!' Then he's hit on the hands with a truncheon by a brutal guard.

'I think I've got a job for you, corporal—'

'Bombardier,' I corrected the adjutant.

'Och aye the noo!'

He totally ignored me and ploughed on, 'I'm putting you in charge of the armoury. That's all. Dismissed.'

The armoury was a large army marquee, stuffed full of rifles, machine-guns, anti-tank guns, grenades, and huge cases of ammunition. There were two charpoys in the far-end corner, which were the living quarters for me and my assistant. Miles of chain was threaded through the trigger guards of the weapons and fastened with huge padlocks, but as I lay under my mosquito net listening to

185

my assistant snoring his head off I thought, 'Supposing we were attacked, there are enough weapons to equip a small army!' But no one came anywhere near us in the few weeks I was there. I would even have welcomed an attack – I would probably have died with a Union Jack wrapped round me. I hated that place and everyone in it, they seemed so cross and bad-tempered. That an artiste like me should be reduced to such straits!

I was in charge of the armoury, which had enough weapons to equip a small army!

Although there were about 500 men in the Gordon Highlanders' camp, there were in fact only eight kilts to go round. Normally this didn't bother anyone, as kilts were only for ceremonial parades and we'd never had one . . . up until now. Then, one day on parade, the colonel told us that a general would be making a 'surprise' inspection of the camp in two days' time. He'd heard about this on the grapevine. We would, therefore, make the eight kilts we had go a long way.

'This is a fine Scottish regiment,' he shouted at us wretched Sassenachs. 'Unfortunately most of you are not Scots, you are' – he could scarcely get the world out – '*English*!' (Of course nowadays the colonel could have been had up by the Race Relations Board.) 'Now, starting today you are going to learn to wear a kilt because, when the general arrives, he will be greeted by a guard of honour in kilts. As we only have eight, as soon as he has inspected the guard and moved on, they will whip off their kilts, which will be rushed to the other end of the camp where there will be another ceremonial guard who will put the kilts on and be inspected – clear?' For the next couple of days we were treated to the sight of two guards of honour on parade, practising pulling on and off kilts.

The day before the general arrived, the colonel briefed us for the very last time; after we'd gone through all the kilts procedure he talked about 'Chads'. Now the camp had an outbreak of Chads. They were very popular at the time and consisted of a cartoon of the top half of a little man's head looking over a wall. The caption below would be 'Wot, no Leave?', Wot, no demob?', 'Wot, no women?' As everything was covered in fine dust, the Chads were everywhere. The Colonel shouted, 'This camp is covered in Chads! When the general arrives I don't want to see a single Chad anywhere! The camp will be Chadless!' The next day there was not a Chad in sight. We all turned out for the general, he inspected the first guard and, as he moved on, the kilts were whipped off and rushed to the other guard in a jeep; the whole thing passed off without a hitch. At the end we all lined up to give three cheers as the general's staff car moved out through the camp gates – drawn in the dust on the back of the car was a Chad, and underneath the words; 'Wot, no Chads?'

WOT? NO KILTS!

Every evening I'd deliver a report to the office that everything was normal in the armoury and that no one had stolen any guns. It only took up a few lines – pointless really, but just one of the things the colonel insisted upon.

Once, as I crossed the square, the bugler played the 'Last Post' and a small detachment lowered the Union Jack. I stood to attention with all the others until the last notes had died away. Suddenly there was a shout of rage from the duty sergeant as he charged over to a group of char wallahs who were getting ready to sell their tea and cakes. 'How dare you rattle your char irons while the "Last Post" is being played? You should be standing to attention!'

'Sorry, sergeant, sahib,' pleaded the char wallah. 'Not possible to get tea ready and stand to attention at same time.'

'Just watch it!' he shouted and disappeared into the office.

Let me tell you about the char wallah – played so brilliantly by Dino Shafeek in *It Ain't Half Hot, Mum*. The character was taken from real life. There were thousands of them in the army in British India. The tea in the urn came out very thick, in the bottom of the urn was a small fire of charcoal and so it stewed for a long time. Condensed milk and sugar had already been added but, in the blistering heat, the mixture that came out tasted like nectar.

I have often wondered over the years whatever happened to all the thousands of Indians who earned a living by waiting on British troops after we'd left India: char wallahs, toenail wallahs, dhobi wallahs and – of course – barber wallahs. Just before "Reveille" they would go down the beds of the sleeping soldiers; one would lather the faces and the other would shave them without any of them waking. Young British soldiers, when they first arrived in India, could never understand

Char Wallah, as played by Dino Shafeek.

Below left: Fruit Wallah
Below right: Ear Wax Wallah

what had happened to their beards. They were told by the old sweats that in the hot climate your beard stopped growing – and they believed it.

As I left the office one evening, having delivered my report, a small truck came in through the gates and in it was Harry Waller, out of hospital once more. As he got down, he looked thinner and paler than ever, with his matchstick legs sticking out from the

Barber Wallah

bottom of his shorts. I was so pleased to see Harry and would have put my arms round him – but, of course, British soldiers 'don't do that sort of thing' (especially in the tropics).

'It's come, Jim,' he said. 'It's come!'

'What are you babbling about, Harry?'

'It's our audition!' he shouted.

Later that evening we had a celebration meal; goat steak with a fried egg on top and plenty of chips – not sweet potatoes, but the real thing. As we tucked in, Harry explained that when we'd left Deolali and he'd been taken into hospital, he'd read in *SEAC* (*South East Asia Command News* – the services' newspaper) that, because of the civil unrest, ENSA artistes who were civilians would no longer be sent out from the UK as it was too dangerous. A new outfit had been formed: Combined Services Entertainment and they were advertising for members of the Armed Services to go to Delhi for an audition. Harry had sent in an application on behalf of us both and now, after all these weeks, it had come through. Good old Harry had saved our lives. Next morning we presented ourselves to the hard-eyed adjutant. He said he'd send a signal to Delhi to confirm it, and we waited for ten tortuous days until finally it came and I was asked

189

to report once more to that hard-eyed adjutant.

He read out: 'Bombardier Perry and Gunner Waller will report to CSE headquarters. [My blood was racing with excitement.] On the way, Bombardier Perry will pick up two sailors and a Military Police Corporal – details enclosed – at Madras station RTO. The party will then report to Squadron Leader Fletcher at CSE headquarters in New Delhi for an audition. In the event they are not up to standard, they will return to their units.' He looked up from the paper and sneered, 'You and Gunner Waller had better pass that audition, Perry, because if you are sent back here, I personally will make sure that you learn what being a soldier is all about. All that way for an audition, what a waste of bloody money.' The man was clearly not a theatre lover.

Within forty-eight hours Harry and I were loading our stuff on to a jeep outside the office.

'Don't look up, Harry,' I whispered. 'In case they change their minds!' I turned to the Indian driver, Abdul, 'Let's go – slowly, very slowly.'

As we crawled out of the gates the soldier who raised the barrier shouted, 'Jammy bastards!'

As soon as we were out of sight of the camp Harry and I went mad – we were free!

'Step on it, Abdul!' I shouted.

'*Teekai,* Sahib!' He put his foot down and huge clouds of dust swirled round us. We sang,

> There was a brave old Scotsman
> At the battle of Waterloo,
> The wind blew up his petticoat
> And showed his cock-a-doodle-doo!

We were on our way.

After a four-hour train journey from Coimbatore, we arrived at Madras railway station. Harry and I picked up the two sailors plus the MP and boarded the train to New Delhi, which was exactly 1200 miles away. As we were British we travelled in a carriage with Indian officers. The journey would take over three days. The train did a steady 40–50 miles an hour and, twice a day, it was shunted into a siding for an hour while we ate in the station restaurant. As night approached the sliding doors in the carriages were pulled open and the officers changed from their uniforms into dhotis (sort of white robes), and out came the hubble-bubble pipes and Harry and I were invited to smoke. The hubble-bubble has the bowl of lighted tobacco at the top and the smoke is drawn down through the water and up through a tube, which is held in the fist to avoid contact with the mouth, the tube is then passed round the circle. So the evening passed peacefully as, with a soft breeze coming through the open doors, we chugged through the night across the vast Indian plains. The two sailors and the MP were in their bunks fast asleep. Then, for some reason, Harry started giggling. I kept asking him what he was laughing at, but he just giggled. I realise, after all these years, that we must have been smoking hash.

During the next few days the Military Policeman confided in me that he was a bit nervous about doing the audition, but he thought he had a natural flair as a comedian. He then proceeded to tell me a string of the filthiest jokes I'd ever heard, which he punctuated with, 'Good, eh? Eh? Eh? Good. What do you think?' I was so embarrassed I just nodded. He also did a routine of 'Famous People on the Toilet', which I used, many years later, as an act for Ted Bovis (Paul Shane) in the *Hi-De-Hi!* series.

The two sailors kept insisting on showing Harry and me their act, which they described as 'Knockabout Comedy' – but it was completely unfunny. All they did was to slap each other round the face and stamp on each other's feet. They were really hurting themselves. As I remarked to Harry when we climbed into our bunks, 'I don't think we've got much competition here.'

On the third day we woke up shivering. It had turned very cold, needless to say the carriage doors were firmly shut and it was then I realised why we'd been issued with warm battledress uniforms. The next day we arrived in New Delhi and, as we pulled into the station, I was amazed to see snow on the ground. Snow in India! Who could believe such a thing? We had left Madras in sticky tropical heat and three days later arrived in what looked like a typical English winter. We unloaded our kit and went into the waiting room to get out of the cold. By now the two sailors and the MP were starting to have second thoughts. The MP kept asking which of his jokes I liked best. And our two knock-about sailors were really starting to damage each other – it was plain that all three were just trying to get a cushy number. We eventually arrived at Combined Services Entertainment in Cornwallis Road and, as the truck deposited us, I could hear an accordion being played very well and someone singing; it sounded professional and made our three companions turn slightly green. There were several other servicemen hanging around, who had come from all over India for auditions. That adjutant back at the Gordon Highlanders was quite right – what a waste of money! Midday I was told to report to Squadron Leader Charles Fletcher, who was in overall charge of CSE, which was originally the RAF Gang Shows.

Every time I'd reported to an officer until then an NCO had marched me in, but when I got to the outer office there was just an RAF corporal sitting at a desk typing. 'Oh, hello,' he said. 'Squadron Leader Fletcher will see you now.' I paused. 'What are you waiting for?' said the corporal, pulling out a nail file and starting to give himself a manicure.

'Isn't anybody going to march me in?' I enquired.

'You'll be lucky, sunshine,' he purred, flashing his eyelashes. 'Just turn the handle and walk in.'

I did exactly that and in the room saw three men sitting at a trestle table. I halted, did a right turn and banged up a salute, with the words, 'Bombardier Perry, Royal Artillery, reporting, sir!' I stood at ease.

Squadron Leader Fletcher threw up his hands in protest. 'Oh, please don't do all that banging around; this is Combined Services Entertainment, not the Coldstream Guards. Now, let me introduce everybody: I am Squadron Leader Fletcher – I look after the RAF – and here, on my right, is Lieutenant Peter Ashby-Bailey, Royal Navy – he looks after the sailors, and, on my left Captain Staite, Royal Army Service Corps – he looks after the soldiers and is in charge of discipline.' The Captain laughed à la Ted Heath (the ex-Prime Minister, not the bandleader) and, as his shoulders went up and down, started to light a huge pipe. I could hardly believe my eyes – even my naïve, unsophisticated eyes could detect that the Squadron Leader Fletcher and Lieutenant Peter Ashby-Bailey (Royal Navy) both had make-up on, albeit very subtly applied.

'Ready for Action' rehearsal. Squadron Leader Charles Fletcher sits on the front row, far left.

'Now, I see from your papers that you ran the Royal Artillery Concert Party,' said Charles Fletcher. 'I don't want to upset you, but could you sing a little song or something? I'm sorry we haven't got a piano.' And so I launched into the good old Royal Artillery Concert Party tried and true –

I'm getting matey with Katie,
Katie's a wonderful girl,
Biggest blue eyes, wonderful touch,
She's got two of everything
And nearly twice as much!

I took her to a movie,
It really was a wow,
We saw Frank Sinatra
And we had a dreadful row.
Cos Katie jumped up on the seat,
Said, 'Frankie, take me now!'

Katie's a wonderful –
She's so wonderful –
Katie's a wonderful girl!

I followed it with the usual impersonations of Charles Laughton, Ned Sparks, Rob Wilton – I didn't do Clark Gable because I hadn't got my cardboard ears – and when I'd finished they all applauded.

'Ah, yes!' Charles Fletcher purred, 'I think you're going to fit in very well here, Perry.'

'Do you want to see Gunner Waller?' I asked.

'Is that the nice chap with the ginger hair I saw you arrive with? I just happened by chance to be looking out of the window,' the squadron leader quickly added. I told him everything about Harry, our double act and our time with the Royal Artillery Concert Party.

'Oh, we can see him later. I'm sure he's all right if you say he is,' said Lieutenant Peter Ashby-Bailey. 'By the way – you brought a couple of sailors and an MP?'

'Nothing to do with me,' I quickly corrected him. 'I just picked them up in Madras.'

'Those sailors were terrible!' Peter added.

Captain Staites suddenly came to life and banged the table. 'And that MP was a disgrace! I've never heard anything like it – disgusting! We gave them short shrift, they're already on their way back to their units. We don't want anybody like that here.'

'And we don't want any filth,' added Charles Fletcher.

'Thank you,' I said and left the office on Cloud Nine.

'Got some applause, did we?' said the RAF corporal, busy with his nails. 'That's a rarity. A word to the wise – watch that Lieutenant Peter Ashby-Bailey, RN, you're just his type.'

'But he's an officer. Royal Naval officers don't behave like that,' I said naïvely.

'Wanna bet?' said the corporal, returning to his typing.

Well, I didn't see very much of Lieutenant Peter Ashby-Bailey after that. As soon as we had rehearsed the show we were out on the road and only returned to Delhi every three months or so.

This story has a sequel to it: in 1950, when I was a jobbing actor, in common with many others I spent a lot of my time going up and down Charing Cross Road, doing the rounds of all the agents. In those days there were dozens and dozens of them, all scratching a living. They were usually women who looked like Margaret Rutherford. You climbed those rickety stairs and knocked on a glass panel. It would slide back, you gave your name and back would come, 'Nothing for you today, dear' or 'Fancy going up to some godforsaken hole? Twelve pounds? As it's such a long way away, I'll only take five per cent commission.'

I'd met Kenneth Williams the previous year. He'd also been in a services concert party in the East and we had a lot in common. We'd meet, maybe once or twice a week, in the Express Dairy in Charing

Cross Road. It was always full of pros – actors, comics, singers – and it was in the Express Dairy that the great Max Miller paid Sam Kern ten shillings for the song 'Mary from the Dairy'. Kenneth told me he was going to Newquay for the summer in a repertory company run by Peter Ashby-Bailey.

'Peter Ashby-Bailey?' I exclaimed, then told Kenneth all about him in Combined Services Entertainment in India. 'Do you think he'd take me on?' I asked.

'Not a chance,' said Kenny. 'It's a fairy grotto down there. They'll never take a butch ome like you!'

I lost touch with Kenny in the 1960s and only ever saw him once again. He was an amazing man, brilliantly clever, but strange, difficult, with a dark side to his nature. In the early days, when I knew him, he was wonderful company, the funniest person I ever met; there was a talent that perhaps was never realised. He spent so many years camping it up in *Carry On* films. When I read his diaries, as far as I could see the only two people he had anything pleasant to say about were Barbara Windsor and myself. A couple of years before his death I met him in Joe Allen's, the restaurant – he looked straight through me and walked past without a word.

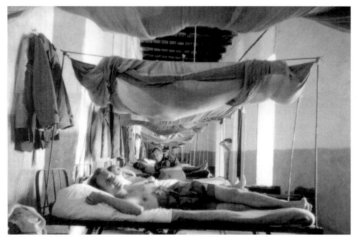

The living quarters on the racecourse in Delhi – sheer luxury!

And so, Harry and I were fully fledged members of Combined Services Entertainment. Our living quarters were on the racecourse at Delhi. They were sheer luxury, with flush loos and electric fans – we couldn't believe it. I was promoted back to sergeant, then Harry was promoted to sergeant – in fact, everyone became a sergeant. All this was getting a bit rich for our blood. After about a week we started rehearsals for the show, *Ready For Action*. Charles Fletcher was a great producer who really knew show business. He'd been in musicals before the war. Tall, good-looking, he was every inch a leading man, if a trifle old-fashioned. Our opening chorus was,

Ready for action, so on with the show,
Ready for action, so here we go,
With music and laughter
To help you on your way,
To raising the rafters with a
Hey, hey, hey.

So getting around and going places,
Getting around wide open spaces,
Getting around, we're mental cases,
Yes – we're getting around!
From Bangalore to Singapore,
From Rangoon to Bombay,
And if you really liked our show
We'll come again another day.

So getting around to show our faces,
Getting around wide open spaces,
Getting around, we're mental cases,
Yes – we're getting around!'

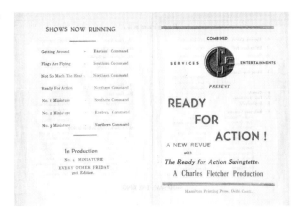

The 'Ready for Action' programme.

Charles Fletcher used to drum into us, 'Eyes and teeth, boys, eyes and teeth! Let them have it! Project it! Project yourselves!'

197

A Stupid Boy

There were ten of us in the show and every one a good performer. Charles refused to accept anyone who wasn't a hundred per cent. One night Harry and I were having a meal in our usual Chinese restaurant in New Delhi, when he brought up something that had been worrying him for a long time. Over the spring roll and chips he broached the subject. 'Jim,' he said, 'how many of the members of the show do you reckon are irons?' (Iron hoofs = poofs.) Now Harry was 110 per cent butch. His battle cry was, 'Hairy pie!' He was suspicious of anybody who didn't share his views.

'Forget it, Harry,' I reassured him. 'This is show business – what do you expect? There's bound to be a few of them that are like that; so what? Would you prefer those butch Gordon Highlanders?'

A strange, sad look came into his eyes. 'Jim, you're not on the turn, are you?' he said.

After three weeks' rehearsal we were ready for the opening night. None of us realised it was going to be quite such a social affair. Charles Fletcher was well in with all the High Society of Delhi and, as the audience filed in, we peeked through the tabs; we were amazed to see how many were in white dinner jackets or dress uniforms. I'd done very well in rehearsals and thought I was the star of the show. I'd been chosen to do a solo right at the start. After the overture I was supposed to come on stage and sing;

An invitation for the opening night.

> We're off on a new show,
> To make your blues go [I did *not* write these words],
> And we're very much all alive
> With rhythmical beats please,
> Hold on to your seats please,
> While happiness round you thrives.

198

Then the tabs go back and on come the rest of the cast singing,

> From the north, south, east and west of everywhere,
> We appear to make you laugh and bring good cheer.

Then we go straight into 'Ready for action, so on with the show', etc.

I was really cocky that night . . . and then that thing came round the corner and hit me in the balls – and, boy, did I deserve it! The footlights came up, the houselights went down, I stepped into the spotlight, Derek and the trio played the music, I opened my mouth to sing, 'We're off on a new show' and nothing came out! I stood like a rat hypnotised by a snake, I had dried! *Dried!*– D–R–I–E–D! I couldn't remember a single word. After what seemed like an age – actually it was twenty seconds, later I timed it very carefully – on came the rest of the cast, everyone singing (thank God) 'From the north, south, east and west of everywhere we appear . . .' I remembered. It came back to me. I joined in and then I went on to automatic pilot – 'Good evening, ladies and gentlemen,' I pattered.

(*Enter* ALF *with suitcase.*)
> ME: What are you doing with that suitcase?
> ALF: I'm taking a case to court.
> ME: Kindly leave the stage.
> (ALF *exits and reappears with a ladder.*)
> ME: Now where are you going?
> ALF: I'm taking it to a higher court.
> (*Exits. Enter* BERNIE.)
> BERNIE: I can prove to you I'm not here.
> ME: Impossible.
> BERNIE: I'm not in Manchester and I'm not in

Birmingham, am I?

ME: No.

BERNIE: Then I must be somewhere else. If I'm somewhere else, I'm not here.

(*Exit. Enter* HARRY)

HARRY: They tell me that your dog has fleas.

ME: That's quite correct.

HARRY: I know how to cure that; get some whisky and lots of very gritty sand. First of all rub in the sand and then rub in the whisky.

ME: Does that work?

HARRY: Wonderful! You see, the fleas get drunk, and throw stones at each other!

Those are what we in show business call 'Crossovers' and boy, was I grateful for them that night! The laughs came thick and fast, and the show was off to a wonderful start. All my stuff worked. When the show was over, with all the usual congrats, in spite of everything I felt

Guarding the props.

dreadful – *I had dried*! I had dried on the opening night in front of all the glitterati of Delhi.

The next day I waylaid Charles Fletcher. 'I'm sorry about last night,' I stumbled.

'What was that, dear boy?' he asked.

'Well – at the start.'

'I didn't notice anything,' he said quietly. 'I was chatting to the Viceroy's aide. You were excellent last night, Jimmy, working so very well. One day you're going places.'

Now, when my time comes and I conk out, if I meet him, still doing shows upstairs, I shall say, 'Thank you, you dear old queen, for saving my life.' I learned a lesson on that night that

I've never forgotten – don't ever get cocky and do not take anything for granted.

The *Ready For Action* roadshow left for a tour of northern India, which was, of course, to become Pakistan. It was 1 March 1947; the rule of the British Raj in India would only last another seven months. After over 200 years we, the British, were leaving. The show worked its way north, performing for the various garrisons of British troops, in Ambala, Amritsar, Lahore, Rawalpindi. British officials were getting ready to pack up and go back to the UK. Some had been born in India and had no idea what life was like back 'home' – as they always called it. There was a gloomy atmosphere everywhere, except, of course, among the British troops, who were delighted.

To my mind, the 'End of the British Empire' was rather like the end of a summer season in the UK: you've been playing in a concert party on the pier and, as the summer draws to an end, the holidaymakers start to go home and the audience drops off. You look out across the windswept promenade and find it impossible to believe that only a month ago it was packed with people.

So many suffered when the British left: the Anglo-Indians were shamelessly deserted. I tried to explain to somebody once exactly who they were.

'Oh, you mean people of mixed race,' she said. Their origins were certainly of mixed race but they were a community on their own. They ran the railways, they were civil servants and held various government posts. They were fanatically loyal to the British; their greatest ambition was for a daughter to marry a British soldier but, apart from that, they always married one of their own kind. Despised by the Indians and looked down on by the British, they were an isolated community. The women were cruelly referred to by British

On the road again.
Reality...

...and the TV version.
Dorothy Lamour
(Melvyn Hayes) and
Bing Crosby (George
Layton) stand to my
right, David Croft stands
on the ladder at the
back.

soldiers as 'chi-chi girls' – derived from the Hindi *'chi-chi'*, 'Shame on You!' 'Don't let one of them get their hooks in you or you're done for,' soldiers would warn their comrades who became too friendly with any of them. The only concession they had was British passports. After Independence a lot came to the UK, some took Welsh names like Williams, or Jenkins, to account for their dark looks and sing-song accents. Quite a few went to Australia. The rest, who couldn't afford to leave, were left to fend for themselves. Over the past sixty years they have disappeared into the British population.

And so we chugged north, blissfully unaware of the frightening violence that was about to erupt. We spent most of our time in railway trains. The Indian railways are amazing, but you can have too much of a good thing. We worked on the show constantly, experimenting; taking stuff out, putting new stuff in, always thinking up different ways to get a laugh. Alfie Summers, whom I still keep in touch with today, was an amazing man and he really cared about people. One of our venues was a small British garrison and getting to it involved a journey of nearly 100 miles over rough mountain terrain. We did the journey in army trucks driven by Indians. The weather was cold and it was Alfie who saw to it that they got greatcoats, food and somewhere to sleep. When we arrived there were perhaps not more than 200 Brits but we always got a great reception. We never stopped mucking about; we'd take photographs of each other, trying to think up new wheezes. Bernie Ismay and Alf Summers always tried to outdo each other with gags and jokes.

It was when we got to Peshawar that the laughing stopped. Full-scale riots had broken out between the Muslims and Hindus, and the few British troops who were trying to stop them killing each other were in the thick of it. Nevertheless, it was our job to try to entertain our comrades and there was no question of doing anything else. We were staying in barracks just outside the town and were asked to do a show in the Cantonment, right in the thick of everything. We went in in army trucks covered in heavy-duty wire mesh and drove slowly through the narrow streets with furious mobs abusing us. I find it difficult to forget that look of terrible hate in their eyes. The wire protected us from solid objects but there was no proof against liquids – I shall never forget Julian Pepper, sitting on a prop box doing his nails, looking out at the hysterical mob, who would have happily torn us to pieces, and saying, 'Take no notice, they're only jealous cos they're not in show business.'

We arrived inside the Cantonment and got ready to do the show. There were about 500 men of the King's Own Scottish Borderers, the rest were on patrol or other duties. We set up the piano and bits and pieces. In more peaceful times it had been the governor-general's garden, but now it was flattened. We changed in a sort of large pavilion, which had been mainly glass, but now all the panes had been broken and replaced with cardboard. We swung into *Ready For Action* and the show was under way. As we were singing 'I'm Getting Matey with Katie' there were distant small explosions and numerous shots from all over the city. Suddenly there were shouts of 'Take cover!' and, in common with everyone else, we ran across the apology for a lawn and dived into a slit trench. About a hundred yards away, on top of a high building, there was a mullah (Muslim leader) shouting, 'Death to the Hindus! Death to the Faringee!' (That was us.)

An officer came along the trench, pausing only to say, 'The show was going so well, chaps – sorry we had to stop it. Never mind.' Then

'I'm getting matey with Katie'
Back row: Bosh Lacey-Moody, me, Harry Eighteen, Harry Waller, Derek Taverner, Cliff Walton. Front row: Leslie Litton, Bernie Ismay, Danny Willis (centre), Neville Bunn, Alf Summers.

he said to one of the soldiers, 'Duffy, you're a crack shot. See if you can get that chap up there,' pointing to the mullah on the top of the building. 'There's a drink in it for you if you can do it.'

'Leave it to me, sor,' replied Private Duffy. He took careful aim and fired. The figure in black toppled and fell, looking like a bundle of old rags as he disappeared from sight.

Instantly the crowd quietened down as our brave officer punched the air and said, 'Well done, Duffy! That certainly deserves a double scotch!'

I shall never forget standing in that slit trench, wearing full costume and make-up, listening to an English officer in a Scottish regiment congratulating an Irishman on killing a man.

We went back to the show and picked it up from 'I'm Getting Matey with Katie'.

The next morning, before we left, we were standing on the roof of headquarters and things seemed to have quietened down, but how wrong we were. I was looking down and I saw a group of demonstrators with banners at the top of a narrow street. At the other end was another group. Both ran forward and clashed. There must have been

Below: The Scottish Borderers returning from patrol.
Left: Looking down on the street below.

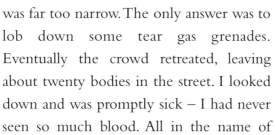

600 of them. None of the Scottish Borderers could do much, the street was far too narrow. The only answer was to lob down some tear gas grenades. Eventually the crowd retreated, leaving about twenty bodies in the street. I looked down and was promptly sick – I had never seen so much blood. All in the name of

religion. Even today, after fifty-five years, I can still remember every detail of that terrible morning.

The next day we left for Landi-Kotal on the Khyber Pass, which was about fifty miles away. We did the journey in army trucks over

Our heroes on The Khyber Pass.

terrifying mountain roads with a sheer drop on the edge that seemed bottomless. As I stood on the Khyber Pass, looking at the awesome sight, I thought of all the adventure stories I had read about it over the years – G. A. Henty's *Frontier Days* and of course, 'Clickeybar' in the 'Wolf of Kabul' featured every week in the boys' paper, *The Wizard*. Of all the places I've ever been to, the Khyber Pass is the only one that has completely lived up to my expectations. It was quite stunning. Unfortunately, when we got there, there were no British troops and, after a couple of days, we were curtly told by an official that there was no one to entertain, so we got back in the trucks and went to Kohat – no one there to entertain either, so we asked for a signal to be sent to Delhi for instructions.

Back came the reply: 'Return at once to headquarters – very urgent.'

No problem. After all, Delhi was only a mere 700 miles away! We had a conference with an Indian railway official at the Kohat station. We pointed out that we were in a hurry.

'No problem,' he said, 'you can leave on an express tonight; it will only take three days.'

'Why so long?' we asked.

'Well, sometimes it has to turn from an express train into a slow train.'

'Why?'

'Because of the people riding on the roof. If the train goes too fast they fall off and we get so many complaints.'

That night we piled into the train and prepared for another three-day journey. Now, you may wonder why we didn't get on each other's nerves, but the fact of the matter was they were a great bunch of blokes. We'd all come safely through the war and we knew we'd soon be going home. On top of that, we were doing something we loved – performing. To help pass the time on our constant train journeys, Alf Summers devised a wonderful game. After he got home, Alf went into the rag trade and he was always telling us 'how to be a good salesman' – he'd hang up an old bush jacket and say, 'This is a thirty-guinea suit.' (A lot of money in those days.) Then one of us would be the customer, and the other, the salesman. Alf would referee. It would usually go like this:

'Good morning, sir, can I interest you in this suit?'

'No, no, no!' Alfie would shout. 'Be positive. Say, "This suit is for you, sir, and only you!" Now go out and come in again.' Sometimes things could get very heated but mostly we'd laugh and send the wretched customer and salesman up. We'd rattle across the Indian landscape for hours while dear Alf tried to turn us all into super-salesmen.

Alf Summers could sell you anything.

Three days later we arrived back in Delhi and found the riots had spread there too. Our headquarters in Cornwallis Road were surrounded with barbed wire and sandbags and – horror – we were expected to take our turn on guard! Female impersonators and comics in steel helmets and carrying rifles with fixed bayonets was just too much.

Squadron Leader Charles Fletcher was furious. 'What *are* those natives playing at?' he protested. 'We are artistes! Let them have their Home Rule, see if I care. I mean, what can you expect from a nation that has no show business? As far as I know there isn't a single Indian concert party anywhere!' He pointed to a holstered revolver he was wearing in his belt. 'I mean, I have to walk about all day with this great heavy gun strapped to me, it's . . . it's just too much!'

The next day he announced we were leaving for Simla – there was to be a high-level conference to discuss the partition of India and we were going to provide the entertainment in the evening. After three days of rehearsals we climbed on the train, once again, and chugged north. A day and a half later we arrived in Simla, which is right in the mountains. The town was rather like Worthing: full of British-looking buildings and churches. During the great days of the Raj it had been the summer capital of the government – when the fierce heat set in on the plains, everything was moved up there from Delhi. We were to do our show in the Vice-Regal lodge, a magnificent building where the conference was to be held. Attending were the Viceroy of India Lord Louis Mountbatten, General Slim, Pandit Nehru the Hindu leader, and Muhammad Ali Jinnah, leader of the Muslims, plus various toadies and hangers-on. I don't think any of us realised what earth-shattering events were taking place – talks were going on to discuss the future of hundreds of millions of Hindus and Muslims, and we were discussing how many verses of 'I'm Getting Matey with Katie' to put in the show. They had already rigged up a stage for us in the sumptuous ballroom, so all we had to do was wait.

Pandit Nehru who, after the show, told me I was a very talented young man. I was delighted, despite the reprimand for 'mocking the afflicted'.

208

The conference had attracted the attention of the world's press and the next day we were briefed by a major who looked like Boris Karloff. 'Gentlemen,' he began, 'I cannot stress enough how important this conference is. It is my responsibility to see that there is nothing of a dubious nature in your show, and so will you kindly perform it for me at fourteen hundred hours this afternoon.'

'You don't want costumes, do you?' asked Alfie Summers.

'Yes, please,' said Boris.

'What about make-up?' I ventured.

'I want everything,' he said. 'That will be all, gentlemen.' With that, he went.

'All right, fellers,' said Alfie. 'Let's work out exactly what we're gonna do.' Now, the strange thing about Alfie was everybody thought he was in charge – even me – he was so bright and sharp. I based the character of Bombardier Solomons in *It Ain't Half Hot, Mum* on him – beautifully played by George Layton. Unfortunately, after the first series George left the show – he said he wanted more funny lines. In vain I pleaded with him to stay, pointing out that he was the linchpin of the whole series, but he insisted on going. Just a few years ago he said, 'I should never have left the show, Jim, but I was young and ambitious. I didn't realise how important the part was.' George was not only a good actor but, as a comedy writer, was responsible for many hit series, including *Don't Wait Up*.

Simla: just like Worthing.

That afternoon, in Simla, we were all ready in costume and make-up to do our show. The audience consisted of Major Boris, armed with a huge notebook, and no one else. We went right through and when we'd finished he congratulated us. 'That was first class, gentlemen,' he said. 'I can find no fault in it. I have no notes. Perhaps you'd like to join me in the Mess when you've changed.'

And that's where we made our big mistake. The major was just another wannabe comedian and regaled us with an endless stream of stories. Somehow, with his lugubrious appearance and sinister voice, it didn't quite come off – as he remarked, 'Of course, I missed my chance. I should have gone on the stage instead of to Sandhurst.'

On the night of the show we were all tense. They had laid out over 500 chairs in the huge ballroom and it was packed: Lord Louis, General Slim, Pandit Nehru and Muhammad Jinnah, dress uniforms and gold braid everywhere, several rajahs in amazing robes and jewels – it made the opening night of the show in Delhi look like *Workers' Playtime*. The curtain went up and on we went.

'We're ready for action . . .'

'I'm Getting Matey with Katie . . .'

Then the crossovers – taking a case to court etc. . . .

Now, I'd like to say the audience went wild, but they didn't. They tittered, they applauded very politely and were well-behaved. My solo spot was number thirteen in the programme. I called it 'The Lull'. (Don't ask me why – bad title again.) I went on and worked my socks off: mother-in-law jokes, wife jokes – I was determined to win.

I was reminded of this just a few years ago when my all-time favourite and hero, Ken Dodd, was doing a spot in the cabaret at the Water Rats Annual Ball at Grosvenor House in London. The audience was dire, but Ken never let go. After about an hour he shouted, 'Do you give in?' and give in they did.

But I was no Ken Dodd, especially when I was only twenty-two. Then I came to the impressions and finished with Charles Laughton in *The Hunchback of Notre Dame*. I gave it everything: 'The bells . . . arrh, the bells . . . arrh, I'm so ugly, ugly!' I dragged myself across the stage and slobbered at the audience. When I'd finished I got off quick, almost to the sound of my own footsteps. We came to the finale of the show and took our curtain calls. Major Boris had asked us to remain on stage to be presented, and so we lined up and waited. Lord Louis went down the line, nodded and was very gracious as always.

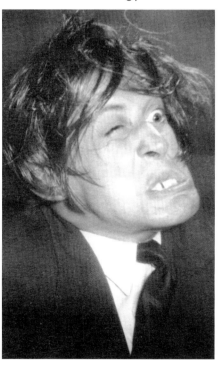

My impression of the Hunchback of Notre Dame – a true classic! 'Oh the bells, the bells! I'm so ugly!'

Then came General Slim, he stopped in front of me. 'I remember you. You were in the Royal Artillery Concert Party.'

I nodded. 'That's right, sir.'

'You chaps do a wonderful job,' he puffed. 'Great for morale.' I was on Cloud Nine, General Slim remembered me!

Finally I was presented to Pandit Nehru. He said, 'You know, you are a very talented young man.'

'Did you enjoy my *Hunchback of Notre Dame*?' I crawled and oozed.

'I will give you a word of advice, young man,' he said. 'It is wrong to mock the afflicted!'

The next day we got a signal from Squadron Leader Fletcher congratulating us and were told to return to the North-West Frontier. We held a meeting; we'd already played all the Frontier dates, but what could we do? We packed up and got on the train for another 600 miles to Bannu, to indulge in more lessons from dear Alfie on how to sell a suit. After all, what was distance? By now there were very few British troops to play to, but we managed to scratch up audiences of government officials and Anglo-Indians. At last we arrived at Bannu.

Above: Bannu!
Below: We break down on the way to Razmak – an adventure that formed the plot for one of the It Ain't Half Hot, Mum episodes, 'The Road to Bannu'.

This adventure formed the plot of the episode of *It Ain't Half Hot, Mum*, which was nearly all true, that we called 'The Road to Bannu'.

Now, the idea was to take our show to a fort called Razmak, which was right in Warizastan on the border of Afghanistan. In the good old days it had been the site of many skirmishes between British troops and tribesmen. The road from Bannu to Razmak was just over fifty miles; it was only opened once every two weeks. In order to stop the tribesmen firing at the convoy, the district commissioner would set up a table and the chiefs would line up and be paid, in gold sovereigns, not to shoot at the trucks. Waiting in Bannu were two soldiers who belonged to the Army Kinematograph Unit, whose job was to travel all over the place showing films to British troops. They had a projector and two films with orders to proceed to Razmak to give a show – could they come in the convoy with us?

'Of course. The more the merrier.' And off we went, escorted by two armoured cars.

Now, you may say the expense of it all – just to entertain a few troops – was ridiculous and I would reply, 'The show must go on, there's no business like show business and you can't beat a live show.'

We'd gone about twenty miles on the road to Razmak when one of the armoured cars broke down. There we were, in the open, surrounded by mountains – helpless – for all we knew with hundreds of savage tribesmen sitting up in those hills about to open fire. We waited as one of the Indian soldiers tinkered with the engine of the broken armoured car. The officer in charge was a young, fresh-faced lieutenant straight out from the UK, who was certainly brave. He strode over to us and said, 'We must reach the fort before nightfall, men.' (What a wonderful line!) After about an hour the sun was getting really hot and we were crouching in the shade. Suddenly there was a series of flashes from one of the hills and answering flashes from the hill opposite.

'All right, gather round,' said the young lieutenant coolly. We did so. 'It's a good job', he went on, 'that you're all armed. I've worked out that there are about twenty-eight of us who can make a field of fire, and of course we've got the machine-guns on the armoured cars, so we should be able put up a pretty stiff resistance.' No one said a single word; we just looked at each other. At this point the engine of the armoured car sprang into life and we all turned our eyes upwards to say thank you.

'All right, chaps,' said our hero. 'Let's get going. We've just got to reach the fort before nightfall!' (*Still* a great line.)

The time was 11.30 and we'd less than 55 miles to travel, so we should easily be there in time for lunch, but no one pointed this out to our young officer. I think he'd also read the series in *The Wizard*, 'The Flaming Frontier'.

In the TV version, 'The Road to Bannu', in order to get the maximum amount of laughter we took a lot of artistic licence; the concert party were all in one truck with a sign on it: 'The Royal Artillery Roadshow'. The tribesmen capture them and the chief says, 'I've seen all the Roadshow films – *Road to Morocco*, *Road to Singapore* – show me Bing Crosby!' They try to convince the chief they haven't got Bing. The tribesmen point their rifles at the concert party and the chief says, 'If no Bing, we go bang!' Suddenly Bombardier Solly (George Layton) comes out of the back of the truck dressed as Bing

Filming It Ain't Half Hot, Mum *in the sand quarry at King's Lynn. This time it serves as the north-west frontier of India!*

Crosby, singing 'Moonlight Becomes You'. The tribesmen go mad with joy and fire their rifles in the air.

But to return to real life. As we bumped along the dusty road to Razmak, the brave young lieutenant explained that since the British started paying the tribesmen gold sovereigns not to fire on the convoys to Razmak there had been very little trouble.

We finally arrived at the fort in time for a terrible lunch – tinned stew. After we'd unloaded our props we took stock; apparently there were only a handful of British personnel in the garrison. They consisted of some Royal Artillery, with a couple of field guns, and the rest – Royal Army Service Corps, a few other odds and sods and quite a big political staff. The rest of the garrison was made up of Gurkhas and Indian troops. Had we come all this way just to entertain a few British? As Julian Pepper remarked, 'When I think what we went through to get here! If those tribesmen capture you, they cut your balls off.'

'Well, it wouldn't have bothered you, Julian,' said Cliff Walton, our super-butch ex-paratrooper.

Later that day we had a meeting with the colonel and he enlightened us. 'Well, chaps,' he said, 'First of all, thank you for coming all this way, you do a damn good job. Now, I've arranged for you to do two shows, one for the British personnel and one for the Gurkhas and Indians.'

'But they won't understand us,' ventured a bright spark.

'Ah, I'm coming to that,' said the colonel. 'Now, as you know, all the British Gurkha officers speak fluent Urdu and one of them is a damn funny fellow – plays the giddy goat and keeps us all in stitches every night in the mess. So what he's going to do is to stand at the side of the stage and translate the show into Urdu as you go along. You've really nothing to worry about, the chap's damned clever and might even add a few bits and pieces himself!'

We stared at the colonel open-mouthed. 'Oh, no, not another one! Not another amateur comedian!' As Julian remarked later, 'We don't interfere with their soldiering, why do they have to interfere with our show business?' I pointed out the fact that we were also soldiers and he was highly insulted.

Well, as usual, we were all wrong. We did the first show for the British personnel and, the next night, the one for the Indians and Gurkhas – they loved it. The British Gurkha officer translated the jokes and they howled with laughter. But there was silence when our singer did Ivor Novello's 'We'll Gather Lilacs'. His voice echoed from the fort and into the mountains – you could have heard a pin drop. The British garrison was so pleased to see us that we scratched together another show for the following night. Then we had to wait a week for the convoy to return to Bannu. There was nothing we could do but hang about. We couldn't go more than a hundred yards outside the fort, there were notices everywhere – 'Beware Snipers'. If one of the tribesmen got bored he would settle down behind a rock and while away the afternoon sniping at the fort. Their great ambition was to possess a British Lee-Enfield rifle. There were small factories all over the North-West Frontier that made a complete replica of this. Unfortunately they couldn't harden the rifle barrels enough, so after firing about twenty rounds they were useless.

Razmak – keeping out of the snipers' range.

Nowadays, of course, they all have Kalashnikov automatic rifles.

The colonel decided that the two soldiers from the Army Kinematograph Unit would show their only films – *The Lost Weekend* and *Diamond Horseshoe*. As soon as the news got out, the colonel received a deputation of local chiefs; could they come and see the film? They only liked two sorts of pictures: 'Fighting' or 'Women', so they didn't want to see Ray Milland in *Lost Weekend*. What they wanted to see was Betty Grable. The colonel called us together and said, 'As you realise, we don't want to upset the tribesmen. We shall be leaving India in three months' time and I want to steer clear of any trouble, so I'm going to let them into the fort to see Betty Grable.'

'Excuse me, sir,' I piped up. 'Isn't that rather dangerous? In that film *The Drum* the tribesmen lured the British into a trap and opened up with machine-guns.'

This rather upset the Colonel. 'I'm not a complete fool, you know, sergeant, I saw that film as well. I know you can't trust these Pathans, so they're just jolly well going to have to leave their weapons outside the gates. They won't even be able to bring in as much as a toothpick. Of course, there will be Gurkhas posted around the walls and if those chappies start any trouble, they'll jolly well regret it!'

And that's how, in the final months of the British Raj, a hundred tribesmen sat down with the British – against whom they had been fighting for centuries – and watched, in glorious Technicolor, Betty Grable, clad in tights, in *Diamond Horseshoe*. After the film ended they paid their respects to the colonel and filed out through the fort gates to retrieve their weapons. They all looked slightly downcast; I think

216

they were a bit sorry to see the British go. Everyone thought that the Russians, who were only a couple of hundred miles to the north, would cross the border into Afghanistan – which they subsequently did, after 33 years, in 1979.

A few days later we were ready to leave. All the British in the fort would also be leaving in a few weeks' time and the political officer and his staff were burning government documents.

We got back to Bannu without any trouble, and then on to Rawalpindi, where there was a signal from Charles Fletcher to say we could take two weeks' leave in the Murree Hills before we finished our tour. Now, the Murree Hills were right up in the mountains and the climate was not unlike Scotland, with a lot of mist. It was either Harry Waller, Alfie Summers, or both, who booked us into a sort of nightclub called the Ambassadors. This of course was unknown to Charles Fletcher down in Delhi as, being in the Services, we were

Gala night at The Ambassador in the Murree Hills!

not allowed to work for money, but they were 500 miles away and we were on leave. The resident bandleader at the club was a Russian, Slavia Tiroff, a fanatical anti-communist, who was always afraid that KGB spies were going to kill him. The band consisted of Anglo-Indians and they were excellent musicians. Our ten days went very well but towards the end, one of the less worldly of our merry band said, 'Why do men keep going upstairs? I think it's one of those places!' to which we all said, 'No!'

'If my mum knew I'd been working in a knocking shop she'd be most upset,' he said. Well, I don't think my dear mum, Dolly, would have liked it very much either.

At the end of the ten days we went to collect our money. The proprietor of the Ambassadors, who looked rather like Genghis Khan, smiled, displaying a mouthful of 22-carat solid gold. 'Sorry,' he said. 'You only half as funny as you said you were. I only pay you half money.' When we protested with that old-fashioned saying 'That's not fair!' his reply was, 'You make trouble, I report you to Military Police.' Well, as Genghis Khan was not a member of the Society of West End Theatre Managers and Equity, the actors' union, was 5000 miles away, we couldn't report *him* to anybody, so we took the money and left.

David and I worked all this into an episode of *It Ain't Half Hot, Mum* entitled 'Cabaret Time'. Sergeant-Major Williams is constantly thinking up ways to get the concert party posted back up the jungle. He reads a report from HQ that the shady Kharma Sutra Club is out of bounds and that any British personnel found there will be arrested. He therefore sets a trap: he contacts the owner of the club and says he'd like to arrange a very special show for some friends, and that he wants to use the Royal Artillery Concert Party. He gives him some money to pay them. The members of the concert party are delighted with an offer of work from the club, but Solly, being a bit more streetwise than the others, has his doubts. On the night of the show, after a tip-off from the sergeant-major, the MPs arrive at the club to find the Concert Party dressed as Military Police! Solly tells them that they have the situation under control, the real MPs leave, and the concert party are free to do the show. One of the lines we used from real life is when Lofty says, 'Solly, soldiers and sailors keep going upstairs.' And Solly replies, 'Take no notice, sunshine, they're just going up to have a lie-down.'

When we got back to Rawalpindi our instructions were waiting for us, with details of the rest of the tour. We were to proceed straight to

Karachi, train to Lahore, change at Multan, down into the Punjab on the North-Western India Railway, and across the Sind Desert, to Karachi – a mere 1000 miles! I forget exactly how long it took us but it was a great tribute to our comradeship that we didn't end up killing each other. We were incarcerated in a small carriage with bunks, in perhaps the hottest place on earth. Every so often, at various stops, a huge block of ice would be thrown into the loo. We had one electric fan overhead, which sometimes packed up working, and at night dozens of cockroaches would emerge. When we finally staggered out of the train at Karachi – after what must have been about four days – we were in a terrible state. We were met by an RAF officer who had fixed all our dates. So a few days later we played a big cinema right in the middle of Karachi. It was packed with British and American sailors. As we started (with 'Getting Matey with Katie') a huge Yank shouted, 'What a bunch of fairies!' But after that they settled down and the show went very well.

Later, as Harry Waller and I were doing the 'Proposal' scene, I looked across at him; he was wearing a white jacket and on it a slide was projecting part of an advert, which read 'Showing Tonight – Ray Milland in *Lost Weekend*' – we never seemed to be able to get away from that film! The Indian cinema proprietor was losing no chance to advertise. We finished the show and the audience gave us a great reception.

The harbour in Karachi was full of British and American ships, and we spent the time on and off landing craft doing shows on board everything from an aircraft carrier to the slightly more intimate destroyers. By the time we finished we'd had enough of playing to sailors!

And so our tour was almost over. It was now July and we knew, come rain or shine, we'd be going home as soon as India and Pakistan got their independence. We'd run out of dates; there was nowhere else for us to play. No signal came from Delhi and so we just sat and waited. A couple of days later our RAF liaison officer burst in and said, 'I've got another date for you, chaps!'

'Where?' we asked.

'Oh, it's quite a way,' he said. 'It's in Baluchistan on the Iranian border, a place called Jiwani – it's a refuelling depot for transit planes. There are about 500 RAF chaps there who never get any entertainment. They've got nothing and I'm sure they'd enjoy your show. It's about 400 miles away and we'll fly you there by Dakota.'

Flight to Jiwani – real life. Here we are, boarding the plane.

A few days later we arrived at the RAF base, with our props, for the flight – we even had to take our mini-piano. Hunched in the plane, we flew for hours over the most desolate terrain I had ever seen. As we flew low we could just see the shore of the Arabian Sea and endless desert for hundreds of miles. About three hours later we finally arrived. They had nothing in Jiwani; everything had to be flown in – food, water, petrol – planes just landed, refuelled and took off. The RAF personnel had no entertainment whatsoever, except for a small radio station and stacks of primitive long-playing records. They were so pleased to see us they'd even built a stage. The following night we did the show and, when we'd finished, they were very rowdy and the wing-commander asked us, as a favour, to do the show all over again – which we did. Then somehow the rumour got around that one of our female impersonators was in fact a real girl. By now we'd realised that most of the RAF airmen who manned the base had been isolated for so long they were quite potty. We were due to return to Karachi the next day but the CO begged us to do another show that night – anything would do as long as it had plenty of girls.

'But we haven't got any girls,' we protested. 'We're all men.'

'I know you haven't,' said the CO. 'For God's sake, I know a girl when I see one, but you've got to understand that my chaps have been stuck in this dreadful place for so long that anybody — anything – that looks even *remotely* like a girl will do!'

What a tour! We worked out that in six months we had travelled the same distance as if we had gone to London and back.

We agreed to stay another day. We held a council of war and decided to put in as many 'female' numbers as possible – 'A Pretty Girl is Like a Melody', 'Dames', 'The Ballet' etc. By now, however, we were getting a little worried – the CO seemed just as potty as all the others. Nevertheless, we had to go ahead and so, that night, we gave it all we'd got. The RAF chaps just sat there, quietly, with tears streaming down their faces. They were so pleased – anything that looked, even remotely, like a girl was all they wanted.

Next day, as we breathed a sigh of relief, the Dakota took off and as it circled the airfield we looked down and saw a small bunch of airmen giving us a feeble wave.

Those were the facts. David and I used this trip as the basis for perhaps one of the funniest *It Ain't Half Hot, Mum* episodes we did; it was called 'Flight to Jiwani'. In the TV version we took the story much further. The airmen are convinced that Gloria (played by

'Flight to Jiwani' – the TV version.

By now, Bernie and Alf would do anything for a laugh.

Melvyn Hayes) is a real girl, and will not accept he's a man. Colonel Reynolds and Captain Ashford try to convince the airmen that there are *no* women in the show, but even the CO at the base doubts their word. 'Why are you hiding Gloria? You're trying to keep her for yourself!'

Things start to get very ugly and there is only one answer – they will have to prepare a lot of numbers with the whole concert party dressed as females. The idea is that they'll look so awful that (surely) this will convince them. But the poor sex-starved airmen still refuse to believe them and shout, 'Gloria! Gloria! We want Gloria!'

In the end the concert party make a run for it and are chased across the airfield – they get on the plane just in the nick of time.

Our tour was over – six months on the road, or perhaps I should say on the rail. We must have covered thousands of miles. We prepared to start our journey back to GHQ at Delhi – only a mere 700-odd miles away – and began to work out our route.

Julian Pepper put his foot down firmly. 'You others can do what you like,' he said, 'but I'm not going back across that Sind Desert – it took me a week to get the sand out of my hair last time.'

A compromise was agreed upon: we'd travel to Hyderabad, change on to the Jodhpur railway, change at Jodhpur, on to Jaipur, change for Agra, then on to Delhi. And so we started on the long road home. It was only a matter of weeks before we would all return to the UK and we should have been on top of the world, but a terrible anticlimax set in; we started bickering among ourselves.

Looking back, after all these years, it's easy to see that this was the end of their careers as performers. Maybe one or two would end up as professionals, but within a year or two most would have wives and families to support. Of all the original members of Combined Services Entertainments I only kept in touch with a few. When *It Ain't Half Hot, Mum* first came out on television I had some letters from ex-members of the show. Perhaps the only one who'd made a successful show business career was Derek Taverner, our rather temperamental pianist. He was a brilliant musician and the one upon whom I based Mr 'La-Di-Da' Gunner Graham. In 1966 I did a musical with John Hanson, based on the play *Smiling Through* and called *When We Were Young*. John had written all the songs and I played opposite him as Doc Owen, his lifelong friend. Derek had worked for John as his musical director for some years. Later Derek helped me with the music for the signature tunes of *Dad's Army* and *It Ain't Half Hot, Mum*. Alfie Summers is well and we still talk on the phone. But two of the others I kept in touch with over all the years, Ken Rylands and Harry Waller, sadly died some years ago.

After about three days – which seemed like three years – we arrived, at last, in Agra, only to find that we would have to wait six hours before catching the train to Delhi.

'Listen, chaps,' I said, 'the Taj Mahal is quite near – why don't we go and see it?' No one wanted to come. In the end I persuaded Harry Waller and we caught the bus. It took about half an hour and what a sad sight greeted our eyes. Owing to the war, very little had been done to maintain the glorious tomb. The lily ponds were stagnant and the building itself was peeling, but in spite of this, there it was in front of us – what I thought had to be the eighth wonder of the world.

Harry turned to me and said, 'Have you brought me all this way just to look at that?'

'It should be seen by moonlight, Harry,' was my feeble excuse.

'Are you *sure* you're not on the turn, Jim?' he said, then asked, 'Want some nuts?' as he crossed to a nearby fruit wallah.

When we got back to the station they all asked, 'What was it like?'

'Falling down,' said Harry . . .

Saying goodbye to Harry Waller.

Ten days later, back in Delhi, I was packing up to leave. I was a year or so older than the others so I was going back earlier. We said goodbye, and I embarked on yet another 700-mile journey. As I got on the train it didn't occur to me just how dangerous the current situation was – millions of Hindus were moving down into India, and a similar number of Muslims up into Pakistan – I was the only British person on the train and it was packed with refugees, quite a number armed with swords or highly decorative daggers, and one giant Sikh was carrying a large ornamental spear. I was feeling decidedly nervous and, with nowhere to lie down, I sat upright for just over two days pretending that everything was normal. As regards 'lavatorial arrangements', we'll draw a veil over that. I bought food from vendors through the window; I didn't dare leave the carriage in case someone took my place and I couldn't get on again. None of the Indians travelling with me showed any hostility when, in their present mood, there was nothing to stop them tearing me to pieces. It was with a sigh of relief that I got off the train at Poona – regardless of the fact that it was a hundred miles out of my way – my destination was the transit camp at Deolali where I was to join with all the other Blighty-bound men waiting for the next troopship out of Bombay.

At last, after more than two and a half years, I was going home. The old Royal Artillery depot was no more, it was derelict. I was billeted in the transit camp about half a mile down the road and one night, unable to resist it, I took a tonga for just one last look at the Royal Artillery Theatre. I told the driver to wait and peeked into the building – it had been completely stripped out; all the wooden benches, that our audiences sat on, had obviously been used for firewood. It was lit by two dingy oil lamps and, in the gloom, I could see a group of Indians crouching round a charcoal fire, smoking a hookah pipe. If this had been a film you would have heard faintly in the background, the Royal Artillery Concert Party singing 'I'm Getting Matey with Katie' with a bit of echo on it. But it wasn't a film, it wasn't my dream world, it was real life. I'd had enough. I closed the door and quickly returned to the tonga.

The driver said, '*Teekai*, sahib?'

I said, '*Teekai*.'

He shook the reins and we sped back to the transit camp lines.

Three days later the troop train was pulling into the docks in Bombay alongside the ship that was to carry us back to Blighty – SS *Franconia*. What a different atmosphere from the trip those years before! Things were very relaxed and, having settled my kit in, I changed into a civilian shirt and took a last look around Bombay, bought a cheap wristwatch in the bazaar, went to the cinema to see *A Matter of Life and Death*, and finished up at a Chinese restaurant

Bless 'em all, Bless 'em all, the long and the short and the tall.
Top: Next to the SS Franconia.
Below: Our last look at Bombay.

where I had my last meal in India – lemon chicken.

Next morning we cast off and moved out of the harbour. Everyone seemed so solemn. I wanted to jump up and down and say, 'Hooray, hooray, we're going home today!' But they looked so gloomy. Perhaps, after being abroad for such a long time, the fact that we were going home had not entirely sunk in.

I looked at my new watch and saw we'd been at sea for twenty minutes and I'd done nothing about organising a concert party! So I went down to the purser's office, saw the adjutant and a few days later I was holding auditions. We were going back through the Suez Canal so it would only take three weeks to get home – I hadn't got much time to lose. I was delighted by the talent we had on the boat – an officer's wife who played the musical saw and a brilliant young Indian who was a violinist and going to England to study at the Royal Academy of Music.

On top of that all sorts of odds and sods but – thank goodness – no comedians. I would take care of that! I gave myself a fifteen-minute spot in each half. By the time we reached Aden I'd pulled together a neat little show. We rehearsed all the way through the Suez Canal and, when we moored at Port Said, the show was ready.

While the ship was taking on supplies the adjutant sent for me, and introduced a Captain Smith. 'He's just boarded the ship,' said the adjutant. 'He's a professional entertainer and comedian and is taking over the concert party.'

'That's right,' said Captain Smith in a cockney accent. 'You see, I do a spiv act.' I could hardly believe my ears. 'I'll take over, son,' he said, 'and I'll do two spots. In one of them I'm a nancy-boy dress designer . . .' I shrank from him '. . . and I'll need half a dozen men to put on drag – I'll introduce 'em as flowers. Then I'll do my spiv. So leave it all to me.'

'Well, I'll just do my two spots,' I said.

'Wrong, son,' he replied. 'You'll just do one spot in the first half – right?'

I went off and sulked, and left the captain to it. I was white with rage. 'How *dare* this man get on the ship and take over the concert party!' *I* was the one – the professional entertainer, ex-member of Combined Services Entertainment and the Royal Artillery Concert Party. Anyway, two days later we opened the show and what can I say? It was a hit. Everybody loved it. For his camp dress designer the captain had borrowed clothes from the officers' wives and dressed up six hairy soldiers, and he minced about in front of them. It was crude and vulgar, but the audience roared with laughter. In the second half he did his spiv act, with plenty of jokes about knicker-elastic. 'Knicker-'lastic is impossible to get back in Blighty,' he leered to the audience, 'but there – you can't keep a good man down!' I shuddered with anger. My own turn was greeted with polite laughter.

I later found out that our cockney captain had his own concert party with the Eighth Army and it was quite well known.

Earlier on in this book I said that you'd find out I was a bit of a nerd – well, now's the time.

We did the show for a couple more nights with great success. I would have let the whole thing pass, but after the show the captain said, 'I'm gonna give you a bit of advice, son. You'll never be funny with that posh accent of yours – you're too tight-arsed. And believe me, when it comes to show business I know what I'm talking about!'

'How *dare* this man tell me what to do,' I thought. 'What does he know about show business?'

Every morning the officers organised three-legged and egg-and-spoon races with 'the ladies'. One of them acted as a bookie, chalking up odds on a black board, all 'jolly fun, eh, what?'. That part of the deck was out of bounds for us BORs until the races were over. Later on that morning, when they'd finished, as I was walking along still boiling with anger – 'How *dare* that captain tell me I couldn't be funny with a posh accent!' – I looked down and there was a large piece of chalk that had been dropped by the bookie. I quickly put it in my pocket – an idea was forming in my warped brain. By now we were halfway through the Med and the weather was very hot, most of the men slept on deck and, that night, so did I. At about two o'clock I woke and looked at the hundreds of sleeping soldiers. They looked like flies on flypaper, emitting all sorts of snores, grunts and groans. I tiptoed over them with my chalk and wrote. *'NO COMMON MEN AS OFFICERS!'* on bulkheads, tarpaulins – anything where the white chalk would show up. I managed to cover most of the obvious parts of the ship, then I threw the tiny remaining piece of chalk – the evidence – overboard and crept below.

The next morning all hell broke loose and at about two in the afternoon everyone was paraded on deck. There must have been about 1000 men and the CO addressed us through the intercom

'Very well,' said the CO, 'I hope that man can live with his conscience.' I certainly could – revenge is sweet.

mike. 'Men,' he shouted, 'we are all bound for Blighty, soon to join our loved ones in Civvy Street, and a spiteful individual has maligned an officer. I'm going to give the person responsible the chance to own up – whoever it is, take one pace forward now.' I made a great show of looking around at the others – no one stepped forward. 'Very well,' said the CO, 'I hope that man can live with his conscience. Now, I want to say just one thing: the British Army has no class barrier. When a man has three pips on his shoulder, he has earned that commission and he is entitled to respect, even if he is com—' He stopped, realising what he'd been about to say. There was a pause for about three seconds, then the whole deck exploded with laughter.

Ah! Sweet, sweet revenge! I looked across to the coast of Morocco, which we were passing at that moment, and thought, 'If I were a civilian I'd be paying money for a boat trip like this.'

The rest of the voyage was quite uneventful.

A few days later ss *Franconia* dropped anchor in Southampton and there it was – England – on a beautiful autumn morning: everything looked so small and neat and clean. Still not much emotion from my comrades. Perhaps they were thinking of their pals who didn't make it back and were buried somewhere in that rotten jungle. One thing that struck me was the silence. We all just stood along the deck rail and watched the ship tying up. A couple of hours later we filed down the gangplank, loaded with kit. I'd rehearsed this moment for years. I'd always intended to go down on my knees and kiss the ground, but now the moment had come, all I wanted to do was get home. On to the train – they didn't lock the doors this time – and then, next stop, Aldershot. Believe me, it took nearly four hours with constant stopping and shunting onto sidings. Our poor old country was shot to pieces; the railways and the roads were in a terrible state, we were nearly bankrupt and food rationing was even worse than during the war. True we had won, but what a price we'd paid. Comparisons are odious, but perhaps in comparison to the Russians, who had suffered the deaths of 20 million people, we were well off.

As soon as we got to Aldershot I phoned home. I kept it as brief as possible – the usual stereotyped conversation: 'See you tomorrow, Mum and Dad.' Then I hung up.

That evening a few of us went to the Aldershot Hippodrome to see a variety bill. As we walked in we were greeted in the foyer by the commissionaire, wearing a uniform that had seen better days – on his chest he wore medals from World War I. 'Welcome back, lads,' he said. 'I wish I'd been out there with you.' He shook me warmly by the hand. I felt a complete liar and a cheat – as the assistant headmaster at Colet Court had once called me – after all, what had I done to earn the Burma Star? Ponced about on the stage, keeping up the morale of my comrades. The only Japs I'd seen were those few wretched scarecrows just before the war ended. As we settled down to watch the show my mind went back to those Jap prisoners. I could see the Geordie gunner kicking them and the captain stopping him saying, 'We need them for information' and then they were taken away. No one spoke Japanese, how could they get information? Had they been shot? I would never know. As I sat through the show I was feeling more and more depressed. To make things worse the turns were awful, not a patch on the Royal Artillery Concert Party or the *Ready for Action* roadshow. Later, in the pub as we sat over a pint, things brightened up a bit. It's so strange how, for years, you look forward to something only for it to turn out an anticlimax. I remember my brother-in-law, Harold – who was a Japanese POW working on the Burma–Siam railway – after three and a half years of terrible privations and torture, saying that when they were finally released he'd never felt so low.

The next morning everyone woke early; it was Demob Day. After breakfast we were each issued with a dreary demob suit and all accessories, a ration book, pay book, army discharge book, money and railway tickets. We then signed off and were ready to go home.

At the station I was surprised to see Boy Scouts waiting to help us on to the train with our luggage. I offered one of them half a crown and his answer was, 'Oh, no, sir, you helped to win the war. Thank you.' That was it; I just burst into tears. 'Are you all right, sir?' enquired the bright little face.

'I'm just so bloody glad to get home,' I said.

When the train finally arrived at Waterloo there was a large orchestra, made up of members of the Railway Workers Union, playing its socks off. I thought it was to greet us, but it was a standard Sunday morning procedure. Suddenly I felt wonderful. The crowds that passed were shabby and thin-faced, but there was a spring in their step. It's difficult for people today to understand how glad everyone was that after all those years of war they'd survived.

In keeping with all proper film clichés I'd arranged to meet Mum and Dad under the clock. When I saw my dad standing there, the first thing I thought was, 'Doesn't he look old?' I hadn't seen any British old people for nearly three years. I shall never forget the looks on their faces as they turned and saw me. Strangely, I was embarrassed – why do you never get the feelings you expect? We seemed quite shy of each other; we just kissed and stood there. There were so few cars about that my mum had parked right inside Waterloo Station, which would seem quite absurd today. I piled all my kit in the back and, with Mum at the wheel and Dad beside her, we drove home to Watford. Sitting in the back, I could see her face in the driving mirror and every time we stopped at a traffic light she looked at me

– I was safely home with her at last. Lunch that Sunday was unforgettable: my sister Mary had been married for two years and she'd waited patiently for over four years for her husband Harold to return from the Japanese prisoner of war camp, never knowing if he was alive or dead. It was the start of many joyous family gatherings. The following year my brother, Charlie, got married, and I was his best man.

Charlie's wedding.
Left: Me, as best man, with Charlie.
Centre: My sister, Mary, and her husband, Harold.
Right: Mum and Dad (looking rather camp), with a strange relation – Cousin Dolly. There were some funny ones in our family.

PART FOUR

WAITING IN THE WINGS

Now, on the boat on the way home, the one thought that was never far from my mind was 'How can I get into show business?'

Every young, hopeful comedian returning from the war tried to get into the Windmill Theatre. It ran continuous shows all day and, during the war, was famous for its motto 'We Never Closed'. Apart from comics it featured young girls who posed nude, which was allowed by the censors providing the girls in question did not move. The man who ran the Windmill was called Vivian Van Damm and was famous for all the comics he'd discovered. I wrote for an audition and was surprised to get a quick reply. Apparently he gave returning ex-servicemen priority. What should I do? I decided to try something new and wrote a rather camp routine about a carpet salesman – wrong! To quote from *Hi-De-Hi!*: 'The first rule of comedy, – when you do an audition, stick to material you know well.' In the letter I'd been given a very precise time and when I arrived at the theatre I realised why – there were at least fifty or sixty would-be comics, most of them wearing their idea of a funny costume, about half of them dressed as spivs. A new young comedian called Arthur English – who later became a very good friend of mine – had made a huge success at the Windmill with a spiv act. His outfit was usually a large, broad-shouldered jacket or overcoat, white scarf, very loud kipper tie and, of course, a snap-brimmed trilby hat. The character had sprung out of wartime shortages when a spiv, for a price, could get you things that were in short supply. The comedian who originally created 'The Spiv' was the great Sid Field in a show at the Prince of Wales Theatre. After that many comics did a spiv act, including that 'common' captain who'd got on the troopship at Port Said.

Later David Croft and I revived the spiv in the character of Joe Walker, played so well by James Beck in *Dad's Army*.

As Arthur English had become a star at the Windmill as a spiv, everyone else thought they'd do exactly the same. I gave my name to the stage doorkeeper and he told me to go down the stairs. I pushed my way past the dozens of waiting spivs and on down into the wings. 'Why does everyone want to be a comic?' I thought, thinking of the poor political officer, on the ship going out to the Far East, who had killed himself trying to be funny. I stood there, waiting. A voice from the stalls called out the names of the hopefuls and on went the spivs.

'Anybody want to buy some knicker-elastic?' they called.

'Thank you,' said the voice from the stalls. 'Next.'

'Anybody want to buy any nylons? You just can't get 'em.'

'Thank you,' from the stalls.

''Ere, listen, I can get you some petrol coupons,' says yet another spiv.

'Thank you.'

One after the other they went on, only to be callously dismissed within a matter of seconds.

There was also a vogue for Al Jolson. His records were constantly played on the radio – due to the huge success of a film about his life called *The Jolson Story* – so among the spivs there was quite a smattering of 'Jolsons', all (dare I say it?) 'blacked up'.

(This is terribly politically incorrect so I'll get it over with as quickly as possible. Al Jolson wore a black make-up, which had started in his Minstrel days.)

So there I was, waiting in the wings of the Windmill, surrounded by spivs and Al Jolsons.

The Windmill Theatre – the Mecca for so many would-be comics returning from the war. But not for me.

When I heard my name I rushed to the centre of the stage and started: 'My name's Jimmy Perry – not very funny, but a lot of charm. Don't applaud; just throw petrol coupons.' Then I slipped in 'Sorry I didn't come dressed as a spiv,' and got a laugh. Then I started on the carpet jokes …

Disaster! After about fifty seconds a voice said, 'Thank you very much.'

I made a swift exit, pushed my way past the spivs and Als on the stairs, and rushed out into the sunlight of Archer Street. I was numb with shock. I crossed the road and went into the Swiss Miss Coffee Bar and sat up at the counter nursing a coffee.

'Where had I gone wrong?'

That was the start of a lesson in comedy that was to take me eighteen years to learn. The reason the line 'Sorry I didn't come dressed as a spiv' got a laugh was because it was *real* – the place was full of spivs, everyone could identify – the carpet jokes didn't come off because how many people had worked at Waring & Gillow eight years before?

A few days later I went to see Joseph O'Conor in a play he was appearing in at the Playhouse Theatre, called *Cockpit*. Joe had been demobbed at least eighteen months before me and was doing well. I went round afterwards, gave my name to the stage doorkeeper, then climbed the stairs to his dressing room. He greeted me warmly. Later, over a drink at the Sherlock Holmes pub just round the corner, I poured out my story and told him about my disastrous audition as a stand-up comedian at the Windmill.

'The Windmill Theatre?' he gasped, 'that dreadful place? Thank God they turned you down! Dear boy, there's only one thing for you to do – you must study at the Royal Academy of Dramatic Art. I will coach you for the entrance audition. As an ex-serviceman you are entitled to a government grant to pay the fees. Come round and see me at my flat in Barnes.'

I didn't waste any time and the next afternoon saw me getting off the bus at the Sun Inn. I'd not been to Barnes for nearly eight years and got a very weird feeling as I walked to Joe's flat along Kitson Road where, all that time ago, I'd helped the boy carry his sack of driftwood. Joe's pretty Canadian wife opened the door, greeted me warmly and later, as we sat over a cup of tea, Joe repeated that he would coach me for my audition pieces for RADA. I sent in my application and after a week received a time and a date for my audition, along with a selection of pieces to choose from. I settled for the suicide scene from *Othello* and an excerpt from *The Plough and the Stars* by Sean O'Casey.

Joe O'Conor – a very generous man.

I shall never forget Joe O'Conor's kindness. He gave so much of his time to coach me and I don't think I ever properly thanked him. In later years I tried to use him in many shows but he was always working on something else.

The next question was what to wear. I paid a visit to Morry the tailor on the Railway Bridge in St Albans Road in Watford. I'd not seen him for three years and we embraced each other affectionately. Then he prodded me, saying, 'There's nothing of you, son.'

We chatted away and finally I explained that I was doing an audition for RADA in ten days' time and I wanted something really smart. I also showed him the stack of clothing coupons I'd been issued with when I was demobbed.

My sister wearing the new look, and me in my three-piece Harris tweed suit, just to go shopping!

'What a lot you got, son,' he said. 'Now listen, it's lucky for you that I can work fast.' He looked around furtively and took a bundle of cloth from under the counter. 'I've been saving this for you, specially,' he whispered out of the corner of his mouth, 'and I've got a set of leather buttons that'll go with it – it's perfect.'

I kept that suit for years and always enjoyed wearing it.

The great day came at last. I was due at RADA at 4.30 in the afternoon. I dressed carefully in my Harris Tweed suit and a bow tie.

I arrived at Euston two hours early and started to walk towards Gower Street. It was late November and a fog was coming up. Don't forget, this was before the Clean Air Act – nowadays the only London fogs (pea-soupers) you see are in American films about Jack the Ripper, but fifty years ago they were a reality.

I thought, 'Poor old London.' Everywhere there were huge bomb craters from German air raids, and there was also a power cut so only a very few street lamps were lit. I started to walk down Gower Street past the medical schools. A bunch of students came out of one of them and they looked so full of fun, swanking in their white coats with stethoscopes sticking out of the pockets. For a moment I envied them – they really looked like medical students, and what did I look like? I caught my reflection in a shop window – that silk bow tie just did not go with the Harris suit, but it was too late to do anything about it now.

One of the pieces that Joe and I had chosen was the suicide scene from *Othello*, where the unfortunate Moor stabs himself. I was muttering the lines over and over again as I approached the entrance

238

of RADA:

'I took by the throat the circumcisèd dog and smote him thus!'

And then I stabbed myself. I couldn't quite work out whether to stab myself on the word 'smote' or 'thus'. The entrance loomed up. There it was – my destiny!

The vestibule was gloomy and lit by a single light bulb; a commissionaire with a chestful of medals was organising young men and women into lines. Could we never get away from the Services? I was sick with nerves. I looked at the watch I'd bought in the bazaar in Bombay only weeks earlier – it had stopped. There was a clock on the wall above the entrance and I peered in.

'Yes?' barked the commissionaire.

'I'm too early,' I said, pointing at the clock. 'An hour and a half. I'll come back.'

I felt an enormous sense of relief as I walked back down Gower Street. There was an ABC on the corner. Now the Aerated Bread Company were the sort of tea shops-cum-bakeries that have long disappeared from the London streets. I went into the gloomy interior.

'Yes?' said a woman behind the counter.

'Tea, please, and – er – any cakes?'

'You an ex-serviceman?'

'Yes.'

'You can 'ave *one*,' she muttered out of the corner of her mouth as she rummaged under the counter for a bakewell tart. 'Where you been?'

'The Far East.'

'Well, you don't look very brown – more *yellow* I'd say.'

'I've had malaria,' I confided.

Tears welled up in her eyes and she sobbed, 'Oh, you poor boy!

There's nothing of you! You'd better 'ave another bakewell.' She plonked another one on the plate and I took them, with the cup of tea, and sat in the corner.

I was still muttering, 'I took by the throat circumcisèd dog . . .'

Suddenly, looking across to the other tables, my heart missed a beat. Sitting alone was an amazing-looking girl. It really was love at first sight. Who was she? I wanted to rush over and sit with her but I was far too shy. She gave me a half-smile and went back to her book. For the moment I forgot all about taking the circumcisèd dog by the throat and drifted into a daydream . . .

It's the Russian Revolution and she is the mysterious countess whom, as a British agent, I've been ordered to smuggle out of the country to safety, but she's devoted to the Revolution and is a Moscow tram driver. She refuses to come with me.

'My duty lies with The Cause!' she declares.

'But I love you, countess,' I protest.

'Don't ever call me that, comrade. We must go our separate ways. Now, if you'll excuse me, I have to start up my tram.'

'Does that mean that when you walk out of here I shall never see you again?'

'That's right, comrade – farewell!'

We embrace in a passionate kiss . . .

'Did you enjoy your bakewell tarts?' a voice cut in.

I looked up: it was the woman from behind the counter clearing the tables. Then I saw that my mysterious Russian countess had gone.

'Are you gonna do an audition for the Radar?' asked the woman, piling up cups on a tray. I nodded. 'We've had 'em in 'ere all day long. Are you gonna be a film star?' she added, wiping the table. I shrugged. 'I must say, you don't look like a film star – you're too yellow! I'd say you look more like a farmer!'

An hour later, full of numerous cups of tea and bakewell tart, I found myself sitting outside the audition room of RADA with a dozen or so other young hopefuls. The commissionaire, in the patronising manner usually adopted by sergeants when addressing officer cadets, said, 'Remember, ladies and gentlemen, you have five minutes only, so do not go over your allotted time.'

By now the cups of tea were having their effect on me and I was a bit restless.

'Do you want to go to the toilet, sir?' barked the commissionaire.

I nodded.

'Down the hall on the left,' he pronounced, barely concealing his sneer.

The loos were in the basement and deserted, so I thought I'd have a final practice: 'I took by the throat the circumcisèd dog!' Should I stab myself on the 'smote', or on the 'thus'? I still couldn't decide. My voice bounced off the brick walls and sounded great.

'I'll just have one more go,' I thought, then panicked. How long had I been down here? Had they passed me by? I quickly sorted myself out and hurried upstairs and sat down. Only three people in front of me now. I was numb with fright and went into a sort of trance.

Suddenly I heard, 'Mr James Perry?'

I turned. A trim secretary was standing in the open doorway.

'Oh, God, it's me!' I felt like a paratrooper just before he launches himself through the door of the plane into space.

I charged into the room, nearly knocking the secretary for six. At the far end three people were sitting looking at me: Sir Kenneth Barnes, the principal, Dame Irene Vanbrugh, the grande dame of Edwardian theatre and, sitting in the middle of them, Edith from Kashmir. What on earth was she doing here? Then I realised it was

Dame Flora Robson

Dame Flora Robson (although I don't think she was a Dame then). I braced myself – as though for a force 10 gale – and waited.

'Thank you, Mr Perry,' said Sir Kenneth, 'you may commence.'

And off I went:

And say besides – that in Allepo once,
Where a malignant and turban'd Turk
Beat a Venetian and traduc'd the state,
I took by the throat the circumcisèd dog
And smote [*stab*] him thus! [*stab*]

Just to make sure, I'd stabbed myself twice on both 'smote' and on 'thus!'. I then sank to my knees, emitting a low moan.

The silence was finally broken by the dulcet tones of Flora Robson: 'Have you got something a little *quieter*, dear?'

I started on my next piece, from Sean O'Casey's *The Plough and the Stars*. The play is set during the Easter Uprising in Dublin in 1916. In my impassioned speech I described how I'd run through the streets under heavy fire and, scrunching up the jacket of my immaculate blue suit, I said the final line, 'Will you look at the way the machine gun bullets have torn me coat?'

A week later a letter arrived marked RADA. I tore it open and dashed in to my mum and dad. 'I've passed! I've passed!' I shouted. 'With honours!'

They couldn't believe it; they couldn't believe that I'd actually passed an *exam*, let alone with honours. My father almost had tears in his eyes: 'Congratulations, Jimmy,' he said. 'You're going into a very fine and noble profession.' (How naïve my poor dad was.)

What a Christmas we had in 1947. I know I said earlier that the one spent on Madras railway station had put me off them, but this was special. An American woman, Mrs Elliott, who kept an antique shop in Los Angeles and had been a customer of Dad's before the war, sent us an amazing food parcel, with rich fruit cake, tins of spam *and a box of chocolate Hershey bars*. Not a patch on my beloved Cadbury's Dairy Milk, but even two years after the war sweets and chocs were so heavily rationed that the Hershey bars tasted like nectar. If my memory serves me right, owing to rationing and restrictions, chocolate firms were not allowed to make full-cream choc − it was called 'half-milk'.

What a wonderful day it was when sweets came off the ration in the early Fifties. I bought a half-pound bar of Cadbury's *Full* Milk, unwrapped it, and just stared at it for a full five minutes before diving in and devouring it like a demented madman.

On top of everything else, Mum had reared some ducks for the Christmas dinner and made a sumptuous feast. Relatives came from far and near, it really was a Christmas to remember. That night during the height of the festivities I noticed that Mum was missing. I went upstairs and found her sitting on the bed, sobbing. 'You all right?' I asked, putting my arms round her.

'I'm just so happy,' she said, 'so happy that you're home safe and sound.'

A couple of weeks later came my first day as a student at RADA. We gathered in the small theatre below ground. The large one, the Vanbrugh, had been bombed, leaving just a huge hole in the middle of the building. Looking around at my fellow students I suddenly saw my mysterious 'Russian countess' from the ABC tea shop. My heart sang! What an idiot I'd been not to notice that she too was doing an audition on that day. The principal, Sir Kenneth Barnes, came on to the stage and bade us welcome. I don't think that at any time in its

history RADA has produced so much talent at one particular period. Most of the men had been in the war and were in their twenties and a large proportion of the girls were just seventeen or eighteen. Quite a few of the men had been through bad war experiences that gradually came out as we got to know each other better. One in particular was Harold Siddons, who'd been a bomber pilot. He'd been shot down over France and interrogated by the Gestapo. Harold had a lisp, which was inclined to worry Clifford Turner, our voice production tutor. He'd talk very little about the war, but his eyes had a haunted look that I shall never forget.

There was Warren Mitchell – who subsequently became 'Alf Garnett'. I was never very close to him but I always admired him tremendously.

Dorothy Tutin was an amazing talent: fine actress, delightful singing voice and a flautist to boot, very pretty in a sort of elfin way. At a party I noticed a young man who was desperately in love with her declaring how he felt. After he'd poured out his heart she looked at him very seriously and said, 'The only advice I can give you is that you should see a psychiatrist.'

Top: Harold Siddons
Above: Warren Mitchell
– the never-to-be-
forgotten Alf Garnett.

Then there was Lionel Jeffries, with whom I became very friendly; he showed a lot of talent very early on and quickly took off after leaving RADA, appearing in many films. To my mind his best performance was as the Marquess of Queensbury in *The Trials of*

Top left: Dorothy Tutin — so talented, so young.
Above: Lionel Jeffries.
Bottom left: Robert Shaw, in Jaws.

Oscar Wilde. He later became a sensitive film director and screenplay author – his *Railway Children* is a classic. After that he went on to write and direct several other films.

Robert Shaw was quite extraordinary. He had everything: looks, blazing talent as an actor and he was also a successful writer. His greatest hit as an author was *The Man in the Glass Booth*. I always found him rather frightening and a little mad; he used to sit in the canteen banging the table, going red in the face, and saying, 'I'm going to be an international star within three years!'

Well, he achieved his ambition, and then

245

one day he banged the table once too often, and keeled over with a fatal heart attack.

Lynn Reid-Banks became a very successful novelist, best known for her book *The L-Shaped Room* among many others.

The extraordinarily wild Welsh Rachel Roberts was there too.

Another amazing student was Nigel Green. Tall and handsome, he subsequently went into films, one of his great triumphs being the part of the sergeant in *Zulu*.

Below: Rachael Roberts with Albert Finney in Saturday Night and Sunday Morning

My lovely 'Russian countess' from the ABC tea rooms was called Pamela and, during the first couple of terms, we sort of had a rather strange, on–off, boy–girl relationship. Her sister, Eileen, was a gorgeous girl who later did well in films.

And this is only a smattering of the students at that time. There was an air of desperate ambition. The tuition was inclined to be old-fashioned and, to anybody working in television or theatre today, would seem absurd. There was very little encouragement. Students were told, constantly, how wrong or bad they were. This harsh criticism was prone to bring out a lot of tension among so much highly charged talent. Many of the tutors at RADA simply did not understand what was

Above: Nigel Green (left) in Zulu.

happening – for the first time ever, young men and women were being given government grants to study there. They came from working-class families and spoke with a variety of different accents. The voice production and diction classes were something to behold.

A man I had a lot of time for was Clifford Turner who, unlike some of the other tutors, was very successful in his own right. He'd written a book on Voice Production and Diction and, some years before, had been asked to try to get rid of King George VI's bad stammer. Being a gent of the Old School, he would never discuss it. His lessons were extraordinary: he liked to give us nursery rhymes. We'd all sit round in a circle and, when my turn came, it was always, 'Now, come along, James – "Lavender blue, Dilly-Dilly, lavender green, I'll be your king, Dilly-Dilly, if you'll be my queen."' I'd repeat it after him, then, 'No, no, no, dear boy,' he'd moan as if I'd just slapped him in the face, 'we must get rid of those flat vowels – now, now, now, not ow, ow, ow!' And so it went on. He was always polite and would show great patience. It was amazing what he could do; at the end of two years cockney, north-country and rural accents had completely disappeared.

'You can always revert back to your roots,' he'd say.

When I told this to Joan Littlewood, who had pioneered actors using their natural accents, she went mad. 'How dare he?' she spluttered, 'making an actor lose his own voice!'

I went along with all the lectures and classes because I had a strong desire to please. For the first time in my life I was in a semi-academic situation where I found it relatively easy to keep up. I no longer dreaded classes, I looked forward to them.

My brother Charlie had a lifelong friend, Michael Arnold, who was a doctor and during the Easter holidays he arranged for me to have an operation on my hand to tidy it up. The result was good, but the fact that I had a missing finger still bugged me – how was I going to be an actor, especially in films? People would say they never noticed, but I did and was constantly aware of it. Sometimes I'd wander round London theatres looking at the photographs on display outside. Did

A STUPID BOY

the actors' hands show? Of course they did. It sometimes filled me with despair, but I was determined – somehow – to overcome it.

Top: Wally Goodman, Butlin's Entertainments Manager
Below: 'Spivs'

As the summer term was coming to an end, I thought, I must earn some money during the forthcoming long holiday. I'd seen a film called *Holiday Camp* a few months before and suddenly thought, 'Why not try for a job at Butlin's?' I rang up Roger Bourne, late of the Royal Artillery Concert Party, who had been a Redcoat. He was now touring with an act called 'Bourne and Barbara'. They mimed to gramophone records – at that time everybody was doing it. He told me to get in touch with Wally Goodman, who was in charge of the entertainment staff at Butlin's. I phoned and made an appointment. A few days later I left RADA early and took the bus to the Butlin's GHQ in Oxford Street. As I sat on the top deck looking down, I thought it was so sad; the street had suffered a lot during the war, there were gaping holes where the bombs had fallen, the buildings were grimy and depressing, and every few yards were the traditional spivs selling Black Market goods. They would use two suitcases, one for a base with the other opened on top to display the goods – ladies' stockings, or nylons, jewellery, little men you wound up who would go round in circles on the pavement. There was such a desperate shortage of stuff that people would buy anything and were often sadly disappointed when they got their purchases home – stockings with one small and one large foot, watches that stopped, knicker-elastic that didn't knicker (had no stretch to it). There would be lookouts up and down the street and if a copper came in sight they would tick-tack to their companions; instantly the suitcases would snap shut and all the spivs would be gone, only to reappear quickly once the police had passed.

As the bus approached the stop I looked down and saw Frank Muir and Denis Norden walking down the street. They were both wearing beautifully tailored double-breasted suits (the shirt cuffs poking out of their sleeves half an inch, no more, no less). They were both over six feet tall and carried off the whole effect most magnificently. They were at the height of their careers, not only as radio entertainers, but as the authors of the hit radio show *Take It From Here*.

'Real stars!' I thought. 'I wonder if I'll ever be as famous as that?'

Butlin House was brightly painted and the foyer was filled with life-sized cardboard cut-outs of girls in swimsuits holding beach balls with provocative captions such as 'Come to Butlin's for the time of your life!' and 'Butlin's make your dreams come true!' After the demure girls at RADA, these girls looked much more interesting and saucy.

Wally Goodman greeted me with the words, 'Come in son. So you want to be a Redcoat?'

'Yes,' I said.

'I'm a bit worried, son, about that posh accent of yours.'

'Well, I'm a student at the RADA and I'm going to be an actor.'

Wally was not impressed. 'I can use you as a sports organiser. Are you a friendly sort of person?'

'Rather!' I said, thinking of the saucy cardboard girls in the foyer downstairs.

'A super Redcoat' – Billy
Butlin's words, not mine!

'I'll start you at eight pounds a week and the cakes.'

'What sort of cakes?' I asked.

'Food and keep – you sleep in a chalet. Is it a deal?'

I nodded. Wally spat in the palm of his hand and we shook on it.

I arrived at Pwllheli in north Wales a few weeks later when the term at RADA broke up. I hardly had time to unpack when the entertainments manager sent for me. 'Listen, son,' he said, 'I've got a problem [why did everybody keep calling me son?]. A Polish football team have arrived. They're on a goodwill tour and they're playing a match against the Butlin camp's staff. They're all bloody commies and I don't want any trouble so you're going to referee the match!'

My blood turned to water. I'd forgotten I was supposed to be a sports organiser.

(I should point out that in 1948 the Iron Curtain was well and truly down. Except for sports and the arts.)

After a sleepless night, I went out on the pitch to greet the Poles. I shook hands all round, hoping that a miracle would happen to put an end to my agony. The political officer, who was a heavily built man wearing a baggy double-breasted suit (with *no* cuffs showing), shouted at the team and pointed in my direction.

The interpreter turned to me. 'He is telling them to listen to the coach and follow instructions at all times.'

'What coach?' I asked.

'You, of course!'

The interpreter droned on. 'There are several hours before the match starts,' he shouted at the team, 'so you will commence training straight away.' They looked at me with rapt attention.

I picked up the ball, closed my eyes and threw it at them. During the next ten minutes I fell over, was knocked over, the ball hit me in the face, and I blew my whistle and charged up and down the pitch, waving my arms about. Suddenly the team stopped kicking the ball and gathered in a sullen knot with the political officer in the middle. They stared at me, muttering, then the political officer and interpreter advanced on me yelling, 'Take us to the official in charge!'

I led them to the entertainment manager's office where the interpreter shouted, 'This is a capitalist plot to discredit the glorious Polish Socialist Republic! The coach is acting like a fool and a clown, but in reality he is a spy! I warn you, unless we win this afternoon by a large number of goals this matter will be taken up by our ambassador in London.' They stormed out, shaking their fists.

'I'm sorry,' I said. 'What are you going to do?'

'Simple,' said the entertainments manager, scratching his backside. 'I'll offer our team a day off and ten bob each, and you'll be amazed how many goals those Poles will put past them!'

'You mean they'll throw the match?' I gasped.

'Your mouth's hanging open, son,' he grinned. 'By the way, I've just found out that you're not a sports organiser. You're a drama student at RADA, studying Shakespeare and Greek plays.'

I nodded.

'You should have said before. You can organise the campers' concert on Thursday. Then I want you to compère the Ugly Face competition, the Nobbly Knees competition and the Glamorous Grandma competition. So far you have, without doubt, been the worst sports organiser I've ever come across. This is your last chance.

*The ugly
face competition.*

'If you mess up you'll be on the train by the end of the week.'

And so I became a holiday camp fanatic. I was issued with a bike, painted bright yellow, and went from competition to competition compèring everything. I shouted, 'Hi de hi!' and the campers shouted back, 'Ho de ho!'

As regards the campers' concert, I really went to town. Having auditioned about half a dozen hopefuls, instead of just bringing them on, one at a time, I borrowed some chairs and tables, hung up some balloons and made the whole set look like a Viennese beer garden. Unfortunately the only backcloth available was New York, but it had to do.

I compèred the talent show, of course, and dragged the poor contestants up from their seats. If they went on for too long I'd shout, 'How about that? Let's hear it!' and the applause would drown them out as I shoved them back into their seats. The show certainly had plenty of pace!

The entertainments manager was over the moon: 'You didn't learn to do that at RADA,' he said.

'No,' was my cocky reply, 'I learnt it on the North-West Frontier of India and all points east.'

Many of my contemporaries thought I was mad working at Butlin's, but the joy of making people happy has always given me a kick and if you're blessed with that knack, believe me, you are very privileged. Some years later when I was in weekly repertory, I was sharing a dressing room with an old character actor, Harold Wilkinson. One Saturday matinée for old age pensioners I came into the theatre and started to get ready. 'I don't want to do it this afternoon, Wilkie,' I moaned. 'All those old people out there give me the hump.'

He stopped making up and turned slowly round. All his life he'd been a working actor, just about making a living. He lived in a small flat in Brixton and, after a lifetime's work, had virtually nothing.

'Listen to me, son,' he said. 'You're still a very young man and you're lucky. But out there, sitting waiting in the theatre, are 400 or so old people. Most of them have worries, some are very ill, some have lost their lifelong partners, and it's your job to go out there on that stage this afternoon to make them laugh and forget their troubles, just for a short time. That's what you do, son, that's your trade.' Dear Harold Wilkinson, he taught me so much.

Holiday camps were really booming just after the war, and if you look at the photographs in this book you will notice several things: how thin people are, how they are dressed (no one has any special holiday clothes) and the happiness on their faces. Everyone had come through six years of war – after that, everything else was a bonus. Billy Butlin was a brilliantly clever man; he gave the public what they wanted. The camp at Pwllheli was amazing: two theatres

He's a larf – what a berk!

which housed a revue company and a repertory company, Eric Winston and his band, Ronnie Munro's band for dancing, a theatre orchestra for the shows – there seemed no end to the amount of entertainment. The resident repertory company was run by J. Baxter Somerville and all plays were cut down to an hour – it was Billy Butlin's rule that nothing was to run any longer in case people got bored. At one side of the stage was a blackboard with a light and written at the top was, 'Baby crying in chalet?' If, during the show, a baby *was* crying, a Redcoat would jump up on the stage, switch on the flashing light, and chalk the chalet number on the board. One of the plays was *Night Must Fall* by Emlyn Williams, in which the chief character is Danny, a hotel porter who is a murderer. There is a gripping climax to one of the scenes: Danny creeps up behind an old lady in a wheelchair and raises the cushion above her head to smother her; just as he is bringing it down there is a quick blackout – gasps from the audience. On one particular night, as Danny raised the cushion a Redcoat leapt up on to the stage, switched on the flashing light and wrote 'Chalet 56', leaving the poor actor holding the cushion illuminated in the blackout by the flashing light – it got one of the biggest laughs I've ever heard in a theatre.

The repertory company were the first group of professional actors

The Entertainments staff, Pwllheli, 1948. I'm on the back row, in the centre.

I'd ever met and, when they found out I was a drama student, they were very dismissive; I was just another young hopeful returning from the war to take the bread out of their mouths. They were at the very bottom of the ladder and most of them were extremely cynical. The one exception was the character actor of the company. He was probably in his mid-sixties and very much of the Old School. He first 'trod the boards' – as he called it – in 1905; he'd known how it felt to work in gaslight.

'Beautiful, dear boy,' he'd say. 'Things were never the same after the theatres converted to the electric light – the only snag, of course, was the damned hiss of the gas!' He was the most self-sufficient person I've ever met. 'This is a very nice little engagement,' he'd drone on. 'The governor always treats me very well; makes sure I have a chalet to myself. Mind you, I've worked for Mr Somerville for many years, seen him through thick and thin. My wife left me donkeys' years ago – sadly no issue, so I'm on my own. This season lasts seven months, and then there's pantomime. I always play Abanazer in *Aladdin*. My landlady is down in Brighton – looks after all my traps – and when the season's over I spend my time down there.' He leaned forward and whispered furtively, 'Don't tell the others, but the governor pays me eleven pounds a week and, with free food and board, I've managed to put quite a few bob away. Of course, I've always got my books.' He pointed to a shelf with about twenty beautifully bound volumes on it. 'So I'm all right,' he said, 'all right, old boy.'

I had to leave Butlin's early to start the new term at RADA and in a way I was sorry to go; it had been an amazing summer.

As we assembled for the start of the winter term, I looked around at the students who were filing into the theatre and my first impression was: why was everybody so surly and grim? We embarked on our various classes and productions. I always enjoyed my time at RADA, but I must confess I found my first term back rather heavy going after the light atmosphere of Butlin's.

Then I had a very unpleasant jolt: our make-up classes were, for some mysterious reason, taken by quite a well-known character actor called Percy Walsh. In those days we used to use sticks of greasepaint and, in order to economise, Percy suggested we bought a stick between two of us and cut it in half. During one of the classes a student said she'd paid one and six for a stick of make-up in a shop on Charing Cross Road.

'That's very expensive,' said Percy. 'Are they Jews?' There was a terrible pause and I felt a cold chill; I couldn't believe that anyone would make such an awful remark after the war we'd just been through.

Suddenly Warren Mitchell said, 'Mr Walsh, as a member of the Jewish faith I resent that.' I really can't remember what happened next, but I so admired Warren for speaking up when I'd been so cowardly – but I just didn't want any fuss or a scene. Of all the students during my term, Warren was the one who handled his career so skilfully, and always stuck to his principles. His kindness and generosity to my old friend Arthur English in the series *In Sickness and in Health*, when Arthur was so ill, is something I shall always remember. But Warren could also be a bit abrasive and awkward, and sometimes unintentionally funny. In the early days of our time at RADA we had lectures on theatre technique from Dame Irene Vanbrugh, which was really quite absurd – she was born in 1872!

I remember Warren piping up, 'Tell me, Miss Vanbrugh – what do you think of the Method?' (The American style of Method acting had just begun to filter through.)

She paused and said, 'What method is that, dear?' Warren tried to explain that it had been started up in America at the Lee Strasberg Studio in New York. 'I don't care for American actors, they're inclined to shout a lot. Are you an American, dear? I hope I haven't hurt your feelings.'

Warren gave up and sat down.

Alfred Hitchcock's daughter, Pat, was another member of our class. At first I thought, hello, she's only here because of her father's influence, it's the Old Boy Network, but as I got to know her I realised what a sweet, kind person she was. She developed amazingly as an actress, giving a touching performance in one of Hitchcock's great films, *Strangers*

Pat Hitchcock with Farley Granger, in Strangers on a Train.

on a Train. Hitch was planning a film set in London called *Stagefright*, starring Marlene Dietrich, Richard Todd and Jane Wyman. There were a few scenes set at RADA and he wanted the students played by real RADA students. I was absolutely livid that I wasn't picked to be in it – Lionel Jeffries and several of the other were chosen instead, but in the end I needn't have bothered, they were all filmed in long shot.

We had so many different tutors, but all of them seemed to work on the principle that everything we did was wrong. To be fair, I must have been a terrible actor at that time; I'd pull faces and think I was wonderful; everything I did was over the top. I thought I was brilliant at comedy and kept entering competitions at RADA, one of which was the Athene Seyler Trophy for Comedy. As usual, I wrote my own stuff, which was about the various types of flushing loos. In the audience sat the students and Athene Seyler. I entered, dressed as a plumber. My piece went something like this:

'Ladies and gentlemen, today I want to talk to you about water closets. Now, in my chosen occupation, I spend a lot of time fitting and mending WCs. I pride myself that if I'm shut in a lavatory blindfolded, I can tell at once – as soon as I pull and hear the flush – what particular type of WC it is. For instance, the Acme Thunderer has a flush like this—' then I'd impersonate the flush (whoosh, whoosh, whoosh). And so I'd go on with the Waterfall, (whoosh!), the Pyramid (whoosh!), the Cascade (whoosh, whoosh!).

Not a titter.

I ploughed on and then, at the end, I went and sat quietly in the audience. There was strange silence and the next pupil did her bit of comedy.

When everybody had finished, Miss Seyler gave her verdict: she went through everyone's efforts and, when she got to me, simply said, 'Mr Perry, I think, was a little too vulgar.'

A girl won the trophy. I could hardly believe my ears. Why wasn't it me? It was obvious that Miss Athene Seyler was senile!

There was a small radio studio at RADA, with a huge, old-fashioned microphone and walls hung with thick drapes. The lessons in Broadcasting were extraordinary. A man called Howard Rose took us for Shakespeare. He was a big name in radio and his productions from Broadcasting House were legendary. Well, I'd never heard of him. His methods of working were completely mad – he'd stop you before you got two words out. In his opinion everything you said, every single thing about you, was wrong. I went to two classes before I finally gave up. He was intoxicated with the power he had almost to destroy his students – well, he wouldn't destroy me!

The other teacher of broadcasting was Lionel Marsden, a charming man who'd been with the BBC since 1923, at Savoy Hill, and was chief announcer for many years. He had the most beautiful voice but – as was the custom at the time – he read the news with no expression whatsoever. To show any emotion was definitely out for to do so would mean that the announcer 'had opinions.' He gave us the leader from *The Times* to read. I drove him mad. 'You sound like an American announcer! Stop projecting, James!' he'd say. It was around this time that I started to rebel. In my long career I have done a lot of radio work over the years and I *always* project; it gives it that edge – that zing.

Joan Littlewood – my inspiration and mentor.

It took a long time really to make things work for myself. It was not until many years later, when I first joined Joan Littlewood's Theatre Workshop Company at Stratford East, that things started to jell. It was an actor named Bob Grant who first introduced me to Joan. She was looking for somebody to play the part of Bobby Kennedy in a show called *MacBird* loosely based on *Macbeth,* written by an American woman, Barbara Garson. It was all about the assassination of John F. Kennedy – this was before Bobby was killed and, when it really *did* happen, it made me feel very weird. To tell you the truth I hated the whole thing. I was not into deep political satire, especially American. Joan, it seemed to me, was so strange; I just couldn't get the hang of what she was on about and it must have been a subliminal process that made it sink in, not only during my time with her, but for many years afterwards. There was an actor in the company with me called Maxwell Shaw, who was a very snappy dresser and always well turned-out. We both loved clothes and we'd arrive at rehearsals looking as if we'd stepped out of a bandbox. One day Joan stopped us on the stairs backstage and lashed into us. 'Look at you!' she snapped. 'Call yourselves actors? You're just a couple of ponces! You should be running girls! I don't know why I even allow you in my theatre.'

She had an endearing term for me – she called me 'Fuck-Face'.

After a long, long time I really got to understand that the only thing she expected in a person's work was truth. She'd tantalise me by pulling a curtain aside so I could clearly see what everything was about, then she'd let it drop back and it was gone. There's no doubt that she was my mentor, as it was during my time with her that I started writing. Dear Joan, even after all these years I could never nail her down.

RADA – Class of '48.
Front row: Unknown, Lionel Jeffries, Eileen Walsh (who married Lionel), John Franklin-Robbins, Patricia Wilkie, Yevette Rees, Isobel Henderson.
Back row: Me, Teddy Thorpe, Harold Siddons, Louie Ramsey, Frank Murphy.

Back to RADA. I still loved Pam very much, but for some of the time had very little to do with her, especially during the long summer holidays when I was away at Butlin's. Her family lived at Moore Park, which was only half an hour on the train from Watford. They were extremely well off and lived in a large house. Her father and mother were both very kind and considerate towards me, but Pam and her sister Eileen had been hopelessly spoilt. On Sunday evenings I'd go over to the house and have dinner with them. They always had a large joint of meat, in spite of the fact that it was severely rationed, but her father was in the wholesale meat trade so it wasn't a problem. I can cast my mind back to sitting at their table on Sundays nights, looking at those two lovely girls. I was so confused – I think I loved them both.

So much potential talent surrounded me at RADA. This bred a strange atmosphere – 'hearts full of passion, jealousy and hate'. Some of us became friends, but our various ambitions always got in the way.

As well as the ones who became names there were others who remained in the profession as actors and managed to earn quite a good living – John Franklin Robbins, Peter Halliday who, to my mind, were just as talented as the others, but they never got the breaks; Brenda Cowling stayed the course, is still working today and has been happy doing what she'd always wanted to do: act. I used her quite a bit in various shows over the years, including the part of Mrs Lipton, the cook, in *You Rang, M'Lord?*. So many lovely girls: Yvette Rees, Isabel Henderson, Louie Ramsey and a beautiful blonde, Anne Howe, who married Peter Sellers. There were many others who never made it and just faded away, and some who had a short insect life and were quite in demand before they too faded away.

Brenda Cowling

Ronald Lewis – to me he seemed to have everything, so why did he take his own life?

I remember with affection my strange friendship with Ronald Lewis who subsequently became a big star in British films. He was inclined to be gloomy, but whenever I did anything serious he would fall about laughing. Once, as I was doing the *Henry V* speech, 'Once more unto the breach, dear friends . . .' I glanced into the wings and Ronnie was literally rolling on the floor, helpless with laughter.

Another time we were working on a new play by William Douglas-Home, *The Thistle and the Rose*. I was playing King James II of Scotland. It was a hot summer's afternoon and the rehearsal room was packed. The scene was a chapel, and I was praying as the bishop entered.

ME: What is't?

BISHOP (*played by Harold Siddons and his lisp*): Your Majethty, the Pope hath Exthcommunicated you.

ME: (*shrieking*): Oh, no! To be buried in unconsecrated ground. Oh, no, no, no! (*Drumming fists on floor.*)

The whole room, led by Ronnie, burst into laughter. I was furious! Afterwards Ronnie said, 'Don't you realise, Jimmy – you're a very funny man?'

Ronnie had everything, looks, a great voice and he was a fine actor yet at the height of his fame, he took his own life – why? And why did Nigel Green, Harold Siddons and Rachel Roberts – all at RADA with me – do the same?

In the summer of 1949 I returned to Butlin's. This time I had been promoted to camp producer. I wore a smart navy-blue blazer with regimental buttons and immaculate white slacks – for the ballroom in the evening, Morry had made me a brand-new dinner jacket and I felt a million

dollars. In the daytime I also wore a white shirt and white shorts, with immaculate shoes and socks. My salary was twelve pounds a week and I had a chalet to myself. I ran all the competitions and acted as feed and stooge to Gordon the Comic. He was got up as Mayor and the campers loved him. We never stopped. At lunchtime

Above: Prize giving at Pwllheli.

Below: Those lovely children.

Gordon would dress up as a waitress and carry a lot of cracked old china, then he'd pretend to trip and drop it, and it would smash into smithereens. This would be accompanied by a huge cheer and a cry of, 'Woah! Here she goes again!' I would follow with a broom and sweep up. Thinking back on it, all that china crockery could have been quite dangerous, but no one seemed to care. Gordon had two catchphrases: 'Do you

mind?' and 'We know!'. I never found out what they meant, but everyone laughed their heads off. Twice a week we had the star spot in the Redcoat Revue and – believe it or not – did the old 'Proposal' routine.

On Saturday evening, after the new batch of campers had settled in and had their evening meal, there'd be an early evening show in the theatre to introduce all the camp staff. I would compère and on would come the Redcoats and the entertainment staff – everybody – even the chief chalet maid. They'd come on and on until the stage was filled, and I constantly said to the audience, 'We're going to make sure that you, the campers, have the best holiday you've ever had in your lives! What are you going to have?' and they'd shout back, 'The best holiday we've ever had in our lives!'

I had to get the show over in half an hour, then there'd be half an hour before the next show, during which time we had to move 2000 people out of the theatre and another 2000 in – the whole two shows must not last longer than an hour and a half; strict instructions from Mr Butlin. Now, the ballroom was huge, with Eric Winston's band, and it was the focal point of the entire evening. In order to clear the bars at closing time the Redcoats would go round beating a large drum and singing – à la salvation Army – 'Come and Join Us!' All the drinkers would obediently follow in a huge line and end up perhaps 1000 strong; then they'd enter the ballroom, to be greeted with loud cheers as if they were a conquering army. Then it would start – everyone would join in with 'The Hokey-Cokey' and 'The Palais Glide'. Billy Butlin knew his stuff when it came to crowd control: the bar had been

Gloucester House marching into the future.

cleared, and everyone was happy.

The next morning it was the parades. The campers would be divided into four houses; they competed with each other and this kept everything in a constant state of hysteria. As they marched past the swimming pool Gordon, the Mayor, would take the salute, then they would wind their way on to the playing fields with each house holding their banners high. There was a boxing ring in the middle, and by the time they'd finished there'd be about 5000 or 6000 of them pressing round it. Gordon and I would then climb into the ring and lead them in a sing-song. Butlin's camps all had an amazing public address system, the very latest equipment, and to stand in the middle of 6000 people with complete control was quite extraordinary. Most of the songs had actions: 'I Saw The Old Homestead', 'Underneath the Spreading Chestnut Tree' etc. The crowd responded enthusiastically. 'Hi de hi!' would bring an enormous reaction of 'Ho de ho!'. One I always slipped in was 'Umpah, umpah!' and, without any prompting, back would come the huge roar, 'Stick it up your jumpah!'

Down the years, whenever I've told people about Butlin's their first

Happy campers! The cast of Hi-De-Hi!*.*

reaction is inclined to be a sneer, until I tell them that we'd been through a terrible war and all people wanted to do was to enjoy themselves, and I felt privileged to make them happy.

When David Croft and I decided to make a comedy series about a holiday camp, nearly everyone threw up their hands in horror. 'That old thing's been done so many times!' was the comment.

But all the others who'd done shows about holiday camps had got it the wrong way round: they were full of jokes about guards on the gates, barbed wire and escape tunnels. From the very start of working on the show our premise was: the campers had a wonderful time – which was the truth – the humour would come from the entertainments staff. We decided to set it in 1959 – the start of the rock 'n' roll era – because that was when holiday camps were really at the height of their popularity. It was before the start of cheap foreign package holidays. Now, we wanted to find a camp to film in that had old-fashioned chalet lines of the right period. We found some at Butlin's in Clacton and wrote to ask for permission to film there. Back came the reply that they wanted to see the script. We sent one. The next letter we got was from a firm of solicitors, pointing out that Butlin's had just spent over half a million pounds trying to get rid of the very image we were about to portray in *Hi-De-Hi!* and, if we went anywhere near them, they would take legal action. In the end we filmed at an old Warner holiday camp at Dovercourt near Harwich. It had just the right slightly frayed at the edges look. David knew holiday camps well as in the early days of his career he'd produced the revues there. And so we created our characters, all based on the entertainments staff we'd known at various camps.

To play the lead we needed someone who was going to be constantly embarrassed by everything that happened. I remember there had been a university professor with a drink problem at the camp where I worked. Our professor would not have this problem, but, instead, would take the job of entertainments manager to get away from university life, which was stifling him. We gathered our cast: Ruth Madoc, Jeff Holland, Leslie Dwyer, Felix Bowness. We had quite a job casting the camp comic and saw many known and

Left: Ruth Madoc –
'Hello, Campers!'
Middle: Leslie Dwyer –
''orrible kids.'
Right: Jeffrey Holland –
'Shall I wear my funny
policeman costume?'

Left: Felix Bowness – 'It's a
lie. I never pulled that race!'
Bottom middle: Diane
Holland and Barry Howard,
our ballroom champions.

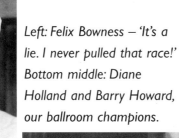

Above: Paul Shane –
'The first rule of
comedy…'

267

unknown actors, none of whom was really right. As time went by we were getting quite desperate and then one day I turned on the TV to *Coronation Street* and there, on the screen, was 'Ted Bovis' – he fitted the character to perfection. His name was Paul Shane. As David was away, I asked Paul to come up to see me in my flat in London

and I knew at once he was right for the part. As soon as David returned from holiday I arranged for him to meet Paul – he instantly agreed with me. Another last-minute piece of casting was the character of the university professor, Jeffrey Fairbrother. We tried so many actors and were almost in despair, then David found Simon Cadell. I read the part of his mother opposite him in a scene from the first episode and, before he'd said more than the first few lines, we knew he was the one.

Above: Simon Cadell – perfect casting.
Below: My friend, Su Pollard.

Su Pollard came into the show almost by accident: her agent, Richard Stone, kept pestering us to use her. I'd seen her several times in various shows and she'd been in a TV series called *The Comedians* but somehow she just couldn't find the right niche.

'You *must* have something for her in *Hi-De-Hi!?*' Richard kept

saying and there was, in fact, the small part of a chalet maid, which consisted of two and a half pages of dialogue. She came to see David and me at my flat in London, looking as if she'd been dressed by an Oxfam shop: odd stockings, odd earrings and rags in her hair. I couldn't resist it! I shouted, 'No clothes pegs today, thank you very much!' and shut the door in her face.

She knocked and shouted, 'I'm not a gypsy! It's me – Su!'

Both David and I thought she was really potty but there was something about her, so we cast her in the character of Peggy, the chalet maid. It was a very small part, but she was a sensation!

Where *Dad's Army* and *It Ain't Half Hot, Mum* took time to become popular, *Hi-De-Hi!* was an instant success – it was new and it was fresh. At the end of the first episode the university professor (Simon Cadell) decides to leave because he feels he is so out of place. I'd cast my mind back to the previous year at Butlin's. At the end of a week a couple gave me a half crown and thanked me for giving them such a great time, and added, 'You couldn't get a better job than this, young man.' And so, at the end of the first episode, Jeffrey is saying, 'I'm leaving. I just don't fit in here. I'm a square peg in a round hole.' And an elderly couple come to the door of his chalet, thank him for giving them such a great time and hand him half a crown. Geoffrey decides to stay – it was a very moving scene.

Then there were the minor fiddles the Redcoats used to make a bit of extra cash. One was 'The Birthday Scam'- a Redcoat would put a lot of birthday cards in his chalet and then invite the camp bigmouth in for a drink. He'd see the cards but they'd ask him not to mention it to the other campers and he'd reply, 'I'll be the judge of that.' And a few days later the campers would be queuing up with bottles of aftershave or chocolate.

In the *Hi-De-Hi!* version David and I used it for Ted Bovis (Paul Shane). Ted invites the camper in for a drink, takes out a bottle of whisky with just a small drop in the bottom and pours. The camper protests. 'No, no,' he says. 'You haven't got much.'

Ted says, 'Well, it's because we're so badly paid, but what can we do?'

Ted's wheezes were a great part of the show.

The camper notices the cards. 'Whose birthday is it?' he asks. Ted

269

goes into the routine.

Cut to a few days later. Ted's bed is covered with bottles of aftershave and booze and chocolates, and he explains the routine to a horrified Spike: 'You see, I've got a nice little arrangement with a bloke in the market.'

Ted's wheezes were a great part of the TV series and our heroes were always trying to think up a new one. They were all based on fact. When I was working at Butlin's I'd compère the 'Holiday Princess' competition dressed in a smart blue blazer and white flannels. It took place beside the pool and at the finish there'd be an argument with the Redcoats and they'd throw me into it. I'd protest, 'Oh no, don't, don't — you'll ruin my best clothes!'

'Throw the posh one in the pool!'

The campers showed no mercy and roared, 'Chuck 'im in the pool!' The Redcoats would then get hold of me and in I'd go.

What the campers didn't know was that about ten minutes earlier, during a lull in proceedings, I'd slip into a little room under the pool and pull on a pair of kitchen porter's trousers that had been well pressed, old canvas shoes that had been whitened and an old shirt. Then I'd slip my immaculate blazer back on and resume my introductions of the Holiday Princess contestants. When the Redcoats challenged me I'd shout, 'Do you want to fight?' and I'd take off my blazer, (which was then carefully removed, by another Redcoat, to a safe place), they'd grab me and in I'd go. The campers would go mad! They loved to see the 'Posh One' — as they called me — getting chucked in the pool.

Many years later as we were filming at Warner's camp, I saw a sad notice. It read: 'Do Not Throw Persons in the Pool. It Is Highly Dangerous.'

After doing shows that were restricted to men – old ones in *Dad's Army*, young ones in *It Ain't Half Hot, Mum*, it was a wonderful change to write something that featured plenty of attractive women, such as the part played by Ruth Madoc – the lovelorn Gladys Pugh, not only Chief Yellow Coat but Radio Maplin's announcer. Gladys resents the other Yellow Coats, Sylvia, Betty and April, and suspects they have designs on Geoffrey Fairbrother, the entertainments manager. Other characters included Mr Partridge, the children's entertainer who hates kids, and the snooty ballroom dancers, played by Diane Holland and Barry Howard, who are up to every racket in the book – giving private dancing lessons at five bob a time, and selling inferior quality dancing shoes to the campers. Then there was Spike (Jeffrey Holland), who gave up his job in a local government office to become a comedian, only to find himself being taught by Ted Bovis, who is a terrible comic – the campers love him and think he's brilliant but, if he works outside the camp, he dies on his feet. Fred, the riding instructor, is an ex-jockey who's lost his licence. Losers, every one of them.

Fred Pontin, the other holiday camp king, who lived well into his nineties, loved *Hi-De-Hi!* and once said to me, 'You know, Jim, I remember every one of those characters, they all existed.'

My last season at Butlin's was drawing to a close and, again, I had to leave early to start my final term at RADA. One night Dobbie, the entertainments manager, told me that the Great Man was coming down to the camp on one of his routine inspections and wanted to see me. I'd never met Billy Butlin before and couldn't imagine why he'd want to meet me. A couple of days later I arrived at the offices and waited. No one came anywhere near me and it all seemed very casual, then one of the glass doors opened and standing there was Sir Billy.

'I'll see you now, boy,' he said and in I went. The office was ridiculously small with piles of paper everywhere. Billy gestured to a

chair and I sat. He just about managed to squeeze himself behind the tiny desk and sat opposite me. 'Sorry about the mess,' he said, 'Everyone's so busy – or looking busy [he winked!] – that's because I've come down.'

I was stunned – so this quietly spoken, almost apologetic man was the great showman!

'Now, I haven't got a lot of time,' he went on in his strange accent (it seemed a mixture of west country and Canadian). 'We've been watching you – you've done well; you know how to get on with people; know how to mix; you've got the knack. How would

Billy Butlin – 'Throw in your lot with me, Jim…'

you like a permanent job? I'll pay you £20 per week and – of course – your keep, plus a company car, a nice little Morris Minor.' (Remember this was fifty years ago, when the average weekly wage was around £10.) I was so astonished all I managed to get out was, 'But I'm at RADA, I leave at the end of this year.'

'Then what you gonna do?'

'I really don't know,' I stammered.

'You want to marry, settle down and have a family, don't you?'

I nodded.

'Take it from me, boy, actors are ragged-arsed losers – I've met a few.' He stood up. 'Throw in your lot with me and you'll be set up for life. Think it over.' We shook hands and I left.

I walked down the chalet rows. Here was temptation! A steady income and, let's face it, I *liked* working at Butlin's and I could ask Pam to marry me. But what would happen to my career as a performer? This was the easy way out – NO. I would write Billy Butlin a very polite letter – after all, I didn't want to upset him (always the crawler!) – and decline the offer.

You Rang, M'Lord? was the last TV show David and I did. As I explained earlier, my grandfather had been a butler and my dad told me many stories about his life in service 'below stairs'. David's mum, Anne Croft, had been a famous musical comedy star in the Twenties and Thirties, so he was well versed in the behaviour of the Nobs

The cast of You Rang, M'Lord? *Clockwise from left: Brenda Cowling, Paul Shane, Bill Pertwee, Su Pollard, Jeff Holland, Suzy Brann, Michael Knowles, Donald Hewlett, Katie Rabett, Mavis Pugh, Perry Benson and Barbara New.*

'upstairs'. I don't think my friend Rosemary-Anne Sisson – who wrote many of the episodes of *Upstairs, Downstairs* – quite approved. But, as I explained, David and I wanted to show the nitty-gritty side of being in domestic service in the 1920s. We were both very proud of the series: wonderful sets and costumes, and a great cast gathered from all the different shows we'd made together over the years.

People I meet are so complimentary about *Dad's Army*; they seem to think that everything I touch turns to gold – *wrong!* Let me tell you about a few of my disasters – times when I've stood in the studio during a recording with my blood running cold as I try to *will* the audience to laugh and they don't. The humiliation of comedy writers when they realise that their stuff is just not working is terrible, when the actors, because they aren't getting the laughs, lose their confidence and start to go over the top as they become desperate. It never happened to me with anything I did with David Croft – we seemed to go from one success to another – but when I'm on my own, things are not so easy. The first show I ever wrote solo was a comparative success. It was called *The Gnomes of Dulwich*, starring Terry Scott and Hugh Lloyd, and was the first ever sitcom made in colour. It was set in a front garden where Terry and Hugh were the gnomes who sat round the pool. It was a sort of satire on human behaviour, as viewed by two stone garden ornaments. The producer/director was Sidney Lottersby, it went out on BBC2 and got very good reviews. Well, after that I was very cocky but, just to teach me a lesson, that thing came round the corner once again and hit me in the lower parts.

In 1969 ATV were looking for a vehicle for Peggy Mount. They wanted her to star opposite Hugh Lloyd in a domestic comedy – so I got to work. The title was (I hardly dare to say it, but I must be brave) *Lollipop Loves Mr Mole*. It also starred Rex Garner and Pat

Coombs. Now, Peggy had made her name in a comedy called *Sailor Beware!* in which she played a battleaxe. It was a part that suited her down to the ground and she was wonderful in it, with a voice like a foghorn. The trouble came when, in the first week of rehearsal for *Lollipop*, she was playing the part in a very quiet way. I'd written it for an aggressive, dominant woman with a heart of gold, which made a wonderful contrast to the meek and mild Hugh Lloyd. When I tackled Peggy about it she said, 'Oh, I don't want to play aggressive, shouting women any more.'

What could I say? The whole premise of the series was shattered. We made six episodes, then Bill Ward, head of ATV at the time, asked me to go and see him.

He came straight out with it: 'I'm taking up your option for another series, Jim.'

'But it's *rubbish*,' I protested. 'It doesn't work!'

'I'll be the judge of that. It's getting sixteen million,' was Bill's answer. 'But I'm going to cut that arty-farty signature tune you wrote and put in something jazzy.'

That was my last, and only, attempt at domestic comedy. None of my series ever takes place in a house – with the possible exception of *You Rang, M'Lord?*, but that takes place in a mansion!

I got a call from Thames TV who'd bought an idea from a head waiter at the Royal Lancaster Hotel. They wanted to call it 'Room Service' and would I write the scripts? I broke every rule in my book – it was the first time I'd written something that was not my own creation. What did I know about hotels? I'd no interest in the subject whatsoever, so I deserved everything I got. I went to work for a few weeks at the Royal Lancaster as a room service waiter to get experience; I hated it and I didn't much care for the waiters either. I realised I'd made a dreadful mistake; for the first (and very last) time

A Stupid Boy

I'd done a series just for the money. Result? Disaster. I was so ashamed that when we were in the studio recording the show, I used to hide behind the cameras.

It was the custom at RADA for the senior students who were in their last term – that was us – to have a rather informal chat from the Principal, Sir Kenneth Barnes. 'Well, ladies and gentlemen,' he said. 'I hope you're well refreshed from your summer break.' Then he asked various students what they had been doing in the break to improve their study of the theatre.

When he said, 'And what did you do, James?' I came back quickly with, 'Working at Butlin's holiday camp, Sir Kenneth.'

There was a pause.

'I beg your pardon?' he said. 'What did you do there?'

'Well, I organised the competitions and various shows like the campers' concert and the Redcoat variety shows.'

I could feel the sneers of my fellow students swirling round me. After another pause Sir Kenneth's face broke into a broad smile of approval: 'That's very good, James; working in the rarefied atmosphere of the

On the roof at RADA, final term.
Back row: Isobel Henderson, Unknown, Frank Murphy, Peter Halliday, Pat Hitchcock, Me.
Front row: Louie Ramsey, Patricia Wilkie.

276

theatre, one must maintain contact with the outside world – the man in the street as 'twere!'

I looked round at the expressions on my fellow students' faces and thought, 'You're only jealous – Billy Butlin didn't offer *you* a job at a thousand pounds a year with a Morris Minor car!' Then I realised that in no way was I anything like them.

There was a very attractive young girl among the new intake of students. She was rather like a sophisticated schoolgirl and she'd sit in the corner of the canteen with her cronies, turn her back on the room, take out her compact mirror and start to powder her nose, at the same time casing the joint for any man she'd like to get acquainted with. Her name was Joan Collins.

I was having dinner with Pamela and her family one Sunday evening – it was to turn out to be the last. Afterwards we sat down to watch television – in 1949 very few people had a set and there was only one station: BBC.

Pamela's father nodded to me urgently and I followed him into another room. 'I haven't got much time,' he said. 'I know you're very fond of my Pam and I should like to have you as a son-in-law, but under no circumstances would I consent to her marrying an actor. But if you'd come into the meat business with me I'd be very happy.'

I could hardly believe my ears – I was simply not psychologically adjusted to this. Pam walked with me to the station; I didn't mention what her father had said, as I'd made up my mind that, if I was going to follow my star, I would have to make a lot of sacrifices. I kissed Pam goodbye and then got on the train to Watford. (It was, of course, the last scene of *Brief Encounter*.) I never saw her again.

Never one to waste good material, David and I used this as a plot for an episode of *Hi-De-Hi!* – Spike falls for a girl, whose father is a wealthy sausage manufacturer. He wants Spike to come into his business, but Spike tells Ted he cannot see the girl again, he must fulfil his ambition to become a comedian. The title was 'Sausages or Limelight?'.

Coming up to the end of the last term, it was decided that we would stage a revue. Of course I was right in there from the start. Unfortunately, a pushy American student called Al Herwitz got in first and instantly took charge. At that time there were quite a few Americans at RADA and they were all great; full of enthusiasm and fun. Like us, they were ex-servicemen and women who were on a US government grant. (True, they *did* think they'd won the war on their own, but we'll let that pass.) Al, however, was a different kettle of fish; he knew all about show business and he was going to teach us Limeys how it was done. After various altercations with him we reached a compromise – I'd do four spots on my own. When I told him what they were, his reaction was, 'You're not going to do that old-fashioned, corny stuff? OK – it's your funeral.'

The bubbly Joan Sims.

During the – rather heated – rehearsal period I picked up with a girl whose name was Joan Sims and asked her if she'd work with me, and she was a delight. I'd do my scoutmaster with Joan 'feeding' me, a sergeant-major, a duet with Joan ('Give Me the Moonlight' – long before it became Frankie Vaughan's signature tune) and, of course, my pièce de résistance; 'The Hunchback of Notre Dame'. All tried and true stuff I'd worked for years. We did the show and Joan and I wiped the floor with them. We were the hit. All the rest of the cast paled into insignificance, like complete amateurs, and Al learned that, as regards show business, we Brits could come up with the goods just as much as the Yanks.

After we'd finished the show I did not see Joan again for fifty years and then I met her at a party given by Ronnie Barker just a year before she died. She was no longer the bubbly girl I'd known so long ago and time had not been kind to her. Sadly she hardly recognised me.

On the last day of term we had our graduation ceremony and we were presented with a diploma. Later, we celebrated at the Old Vienna at Lyons Corner House in Tottenham Court Road: sausages, sauerkraut, mashed potatoes and a tankard of beer, plus a camp gypsy orchestra, all for three bob a head – not bad.

What I didn't know – until I spoke to Lionel Jeffries on the phone recently – was that he'd said to one of the tutors, 'Will this Diploma help me get a job?'

'I'm afraid not,' was the reply.

One picture has always stayed with me: after our little celebration, as we all stood on the platform of Tottenham Court Road underground station, Lionel held up his diploma and said, 'This is

useless!' Then he tore it into pieces and threw it on the line.

As the lights of the approaching train picked up the swirling fragments of paper, I thought, 'What will happen to us all?'

The date was December 1949.

Well, I never did become a famous film star, or a great comedian, but I like to think I've made people laugh and reminded them of the time when this dear country of ours stood alone against the most evil regime the world has ever seen.

Yes – we stood alone and were not found wanting.

INDEX

Y

Z